Making Threats

Making Threats

Biofears and Environmental Anxieties

Edited by
Betsy Hartmann,
Banu Subramaniam, and Charles Zerner

ROWMAN & LITTLEFIELD PUBLISHERS, INC.
Lanham • Boulder • New York • Toronto • Oxford

ROWMAN & LITTLEFIELD PUBLISHERS, INC.

Published in the United States of America   *cat*
by Rowman & Littlefield Publishers, Inc.
A wholly owned subsidiary of The Rowman & Littlefield Publishing Group, Inc.
4501 Forbes Boulevard, Suite 200, Lanham, Maryland 20706
www.rowmanlittlefield.com

PO Box 317
Oxford
OX2 9RU, UK

British Library Cataloguing in Publication Information Available

Library of Congress Cataloging-in-Publication Data

Making threats : biofears and environmental anxieties / edited by Betsy Hartmann,
Banu Subramaniam, Charles Zerner.
    p. cm.
  Includes bibliographical references and index.
  ISBN 0-7425-4906-2 (cloth : alk. paper) — ISBN 0-7425-4907-0 (pbk. : alk. paper)
  1. Environmental health—Psychological aspects. 2. Bioterrorism—Psychological
aspects. 3. Health risk assessment. I. Hartmann, Betsy. II. Subramaniam, Banu,
1966– III. Zerner, Charles.
  RA566.M25 2005
  363.34'97—dc22   2005011207

Printed in the United States of America

♾™ The paper used in this publication meets the minimum requirements of
American National Standard for Information Sciences—Permanence of Paper for
Printed Library Materials, ANSI/NISO Z39.48-1992.

Contents

Preface

In March 2002, six months after the events of September 11, the three of us came together to lead a faculty seminar sponsored by the Hampshire College Global Migrations Program entitled "Imaging Immigration: From Biological Invasions to National Security Threats." Our goal was to explore negative images and narratives of migration, particularly those drawing on environmental and biological fears, in the contemporary United States where the "war on terror" was targeting immigrants as national security threats.

On a snowy March morning, we tramped down a country road surrounded by woodlands and farms. Although we came to the subject from different disciplinary perspectives—Betsy from population studies, Banu from biology and women's studies, and Charles from environmental studies—we discovered that our recent work shared much in common. Betsy was looking at how fears of population pressure and migration were central to the development of the environmental security field, Banu at the close parallels between representations of biological invasions of nonnative plant and animal species and anti-immigrant rhetoric, and Charles at the way imagery and narratives of viruses such as Ebola reinforce prejudice against Africans in particular and migrants in general. While each topic had a different history and etiology, we were struck by the commonalities between them and the synergy of our analytical approaches.

Moreover, we felt that in the climate of fear generated by the September 11 attacks and their aftermath, there was a pressing need for more research on the complex ways that threats to local, national, and international security are constructed. In developing this anthology, we chose to focus on environmental and biological fears not only because of our prior work but because they play such an important role both in shaping (and often narrowing) the worldview of Americans—from the proverbial man or woman on the street to the high-level policymaker—and, more significantly, in naturalizing racial and ethnic prejudices.

We have worked hard to make this volume jargon-free and accessible to nonacademic as well as academic audiences. The primary audience is students at both the undergraduate and the graduate level. In fact, two of us (Betsy and Charles) taught much of this material in our undergraduate courses at Hampshire College and Sarah Lawrence College, respectively, during spring 2004, with great responses. The book works well in a range of disciplines, including environmental studies, political science, sociology, peace and security studies, and cultural studies. Another key audience is scholars who are concerned with the themes of the book and those who are working on the development of new theoretical approaches to the study of fear and threat that cross disciplinary boundaries. The book will also be of interest to environmental, peace, and social justice activists, as well as policymakers in the public health, environment, and security fields.

The book is designed to make readers—students, scholars, activists, and policymakers—think critically about how fears are propagated and how threats are constructed in everyday life, as well as in public policy. Although it focuses on environmental and biological discourses, it offers tools of analysis that can be applied to a range of related issues. It is intended to spark controversy and creative thinking. Just the process of pulling this volume together has pushed our own intellectual boundaries. We have learned much from each other and the other authors in this volume. We view the book as the beginning of a much longer intellectual and political project of understanding and responding to the dangerous fears that surround us.

Acknowledgments

We are grateful to the many people who have helped us in our journey from conceiving this volume to completing it. We could not have done it without them.

At Hampshire College we would like to thank the Global Migrations Program, for first bringing us together, and the Population and Development Program and the Civil Liberties and Public Policy Program, for their key financial and moral support. At Sarah Lawrence College our thanks to Dean Barbara Kaplan and the Advisory Committee on Appointments for awarding a Bogart grant supporting research to Charles Zerner and for its generous contribution for preparation of a scholarly index. Claire Campbell offered intelligence and wit in preparation of the manuscript for publication. At UMass, thanks to Smita Ramnarain for her efficient and careful work in preparing the manuscript for publication. We would like to thank Susan Yard Harris for her painstaking editorial work on the first draft of the manuscript. At Rowman and Littlefield, acquisitions editor Brian Romer, production editor Lynn Weber, and editorial assistant Sonya Kolba have shepherded the book along with great patience, enthusiasm, and efficiency. We are also grateful to the anonymous reviewers who gave us many good suggestions on how to improve the book. It has been a real pleasure working with all the contributors. We have learned so much from each of them and appreciate their commitment to the volume and their keen insights into the contemporary production of fear and threat. Finally, we would like to thank Jim Boyce and Toby Volkman for their support, guidance, and good humor throughout the process of producing this book.

Chapter 2: An earlier version of this chapter was published as "The Militarization of Inner Space," *Critical Sociology* 30, no. 2 (2004): 451–81.

Chapter 6: An earlier version of this chapter was published in the journal *Meridians: feminism, race, transnationalism*, vol 2, no. 1 (Bloomington: Indiana University Press, 2001): 26–40.

Chapter 7: An earlier version of this chapter, containing more extensive notes, was published as "The Viral Forest in Motion: Ebola, Africa, and Emerging Cartographies of Environmental Danger," in *In Search of the Rainforest* (Durham, N.C.: Duke University Press, 2003). This chapter is published with permission of Duke University Press.

Cowardly Lion: I do believe in spooks. I do believe in spooks. I do! I do! I do! I do believe in spooks. I do believe in spooks. I do! I do! I do! I do!
Wicked Witch of the West: You'll believe in more than that before I'm finished with you.

Wizard of Oz

1

Introduction

Making Threats: Biofears and Environmental Anxieties

Betsy Hartmann, Banu Subramaniam, Charles Zerner

We live in times of proliferating fears. The daily updates on the ongoing "war on terrorism" invoke, provoke, and amplify fear and anxiety as if they were necessary and important aspects of reality in the twenty-first century. "Fear Is Everywhere," a bumper sticker warns. "Scary Ads Campaign to a Grim New Level," declares the *New York Times*, referring to the use of fear in the presidential campaigns of 2004.[1] Indeed, we are told to be alert—to people, plants, animals, things, sky, ground, air, and water—always vigilant to the possibilities of attack inside the house and out, at work and at play.

Narratives and images that invoke these anxieties abound in discussions about the environment: in media portrayals of certain deadly viruses and bacteria or lethal germs released into the air, water, or food supplies; in concerns about teeming Third World populations overrunning the United States; in images of exotic and alien species invasions that threaten to take over and destroy native and natural habitats; and in worries about imminent scarcity of oil, food, and water and soaring prices. What is at stake, we are told, is nothing short of "our way of life."

This volume addresses how such environmental and biological fears are implicated in the identification and construction of threats to individual, national, and global security. Fear begets threat, and threat begets fear. This synergy is all the more stark in the contemporary United States, where the population, still terrorized by the events of September 11, is paying with money and lives for a "war on terror" in Iraq and elsewhere, while public culture and discourse are increasingly militarized.

Today, even what before would have been a routine story about the chicken flu is painted in the lurid colors of imminent threat. According to the *New York Times*,

> These are fearful days in the birthplace of the American chicken industry. . . . Like a medieval plague that appears without warning and spreads with speed, an avian flu has infected chicken farms near here, threatening to cut a deadly swath through the most valuable agricultural industry in Delaware and Maryland.[2]

Despite the fact that the influenza strain that infected the flock "is not a danger to humans, and is not even particularly deadly for chickens," the farms were placed in quarantine, and sixty-three thousand chickens were killed in a preemptive measure. The reporter continues to work on our frayed nerve ends by making links to September 11 and by describing the high-tech, sci-fi garb of the health workers:

> These days, farmers wait by their televisions and radios each day for reports on whether new outbreaks have been found. "It's kind of jittery, like right after 9/11," said a man named Johnny at a farm equipment store in town. . . . Adding to the surreal quality of the quarantine, health officials in white biohazard suits have arrived in government-issue vans, stopping to draw blood from sample chicken carcasses that farmers leave in roadside containers. "It's pretty weird," said Louise Messick, 68, who runs a chicken farm with her husband, Bill, 69, half a mile from the original outbreak. "Everyone is scared right now."[3]

We developed this collection out of concern for the consequences of this escalating rhetoric of fear and threat in our supersaturated news world. We are not alone in this endeavor—fear, in fact, is a growing area of study. This volume is an attempt to begin a systematic examination of how environmental and biological fears in particular are produced and deployed. There is no one neat approach to the study of fear and threat, nor does this volume attempt to present all possible approaches. Rather, it shows how different disciplinary perspectives and theoretical insights can help illuminate how environmental and biological fears are produced and how threats to security are constructed. The contributors to this volume come from a variety of disciplines, including environmental studies, political science, international security, biology, sociology, and anthropology. What they share in common is the view that fears should be seriously interrogated and critically examined in order to avoid unnecessary panic and alarm; the scapegoating of certain populations and nations as the "enemy Other"; and the formulation of social, environmental, health, and national security policies on the basis of false or misleading premises. At a time of heightened anxiety and war, the contributors call for engaged reflection. The different analytical approaches they present are tools that the reader can use and apply to fear mongering and threat making in a variety of contexts—past, present, and future.

Our decision as editors to focus on environmental and biological fears emerges not only from our work in this area but from the belief that these fears play a particularly powerful role in obscuring and naturalizing social, economic, and political processes and attendant policy choices. If, for example, one believes that "overpopulation" is the driving force behind poverty, environmental degradation, and political instability in the Third World, one is much less likely to look at the role of social and economic inequalities, undemocratic governance, and foreign interventions in generating these negative outcomes. Apocalyptic predictions of environmental collapse, so prevalent in American environmentalism, also predispose the public and policymakers to view the world as a dangerous place, and the country in need of protection from imminent threat (see Matthew, this volume).

Engaging critically with fear does not mean that we deny the existence of empirically verifiable threats—whether environmental, biological, political, social, cultural, or economic. We argue, however, that fears are historically contingent. For example, the "Communist" is no longer a significant figure of fear; indeed, red has shifted from being the color of dangerously radical areas of the globe to the color of the states that went for Bush in the 2004 presidential elections. Fears are the products of particular historical intersections and political, cultural, and technological conjunctures. It would be impossible to write one overarching history of fear. Rather, the chapters in this volume focus on the different histories of selected fears primarily in the United States, though in many cases there are important overlaps between the ideologies and imageries they draw on and the institutions that propagate them.

In revealing these histories, the authors show us how fears are literally and literarily produced. When Dorothy, the protagonist of Frank Baum's *The Wizard of Oz*, steps into the room where the Wizard stages his performances, she beholds

> an enormous Head, without body to support it or any arms or legs whatever. There was no hair upon this head, but it had eyes and nose and mouth, and was bigger than the head of the biggest giant. As Dorothy gazed upon this in wonder and fear the eyes turned slowly and looked at her sharply and steadily. Then the mouth moved, and Dorothy heard a voice say: "I am Oz, the Great and Terrible."[4]

It is only at the end of her many journeys to fulfill her promises to the Wizard that Dorothy comes to understand the tawdry fictions—papier-mâché constructions—that were used to produce the Wizard's fear-inducing spectacle.

It would be salutary indeed if the relationship between the fears and threats examined in this volume was one of simple fabrication, of production in a material as well as a sociopsychological sense. If only we, like Dorothy, could step behind each "curtain"—that is, each of the environmental and biological fears treated in this volume—and reveal the machinery of illusion.

As a metaphor for the McCarthy-era scaremongering of the 1950s, Baum's imagery and stage setting for the Wizard's social illusions are apposite.

But the questions posed by the environmental and biological fears analyzed in this volume are not as clearly either/or, yes/no, or reality/illusion. The terrain is much more difficult to discern; the boundaries between fabrication and empirical realities are ambiguous. In the case of Ebola, for instance, it is clear that the virus causes a miserable, quick, and bloody death (see Zerner, this volume). It is also the case, however, that the chances of Ebola actually causing an epidemic of significant proportions in the United States or Northern Europe are miniscule. The more interesting questions center on how Richard Preston, as the author of the best-selling *The Hot Zone*, was able to produce a "nonfiction" novel that terrified and thrilled audiences despite its fictional basis. What historical templates and attitudes about Africa, race, and epidemics formed the cultural capital on which Preston was able to fashion a terror-saturated fable? How was environmental and biological fear of a specific virus produced?

All fears and threats are, in some sense, "produced." But if we are not talking strictly about whether a given fear or threat is illusory or real, what can it mean to say some are "more produced" than others?

We argue that many of the fears and threats described in these pages are productions in two senses. They are productions in that they are made, literally produced, in the sense of fabrication. And they are productions in the sense of theatrical productions: designed and executed spectacles, meant for public consumption and with intended—as well as unintended—effects. Fear can sometimes get out of hand, as in Orson Welles's famous broadcast about the invasion of aliens that generated widespread public panic.[5] One of the major tasks for the writers of these chapters and the readers of this volume is to figure out what kinds of techniques have been deployed, and what forms of making—joining, image making, scripts, lighting—have been used, to fashion fear and threat. What is the structure of the scaffolding, the stage setting, the narrative techniques, and the dramaturgy that make a particular environmental or biological concern so fearsome that it becomes a security threat?

The following three sections describe some of the key conceptual lenses that we have found useful in addressing these questions.

FOLLOW THE YELLOW BRICK ROAD: LITERARY, RHETORICAL, AND PERFORMATIVE LENSES

Fortunately, the past decade of scholarship within environmental history and environmental studies—including rhetoric, performance studies, and literary interpretation—provides an intellectual legacy on which we can rely, in part, in accounting for these fear-provoking productions. Within the field of environmental studies, William Cronon opened a window for interpretation by establishing the theoretical groundwork for understanding environmental issues with a narrative framework. It was Cronon's elegant theorization of competing causal narratives about the historical origins of the Dust Bowl that brought narrative theory into the world of "real" environmental problems. Cronon's reflections on the role of narrative in relation to the causal analysis of the Dust Bowl are equally relevant to the study of narratives of environmental fear:

> By writing stories about environmental change, we divide the causal relationships of an ecosystem with a rhetorical razor that defines included and excluded, relevant and irrelevant, empowered and disempowered. In the act of separating story from non-story, we wield the most powerful yet dangerous tool of the narrative form. It is a commonplace of modern literary theory that the very authority with which narrative presents its vision of reality is achieved by obscuring large portions of that reality. Whatever its overt purpose, it cannot avoid a covert exercise of power: it inevitably sanctions some voices while silencing others.[6]

The work of George Lakoff and Mark Johnson, beginning with the publication of *Metaphors We Live By*,[7] as well as a voluminous literature on the uses, effects, and strategies for deploying metaphor as an instrument through which we think,[8] created a theoretical foundation for beginning to consider how we make sense of "the environment" and "environmental problems." Susan Sontag's essays, including *Illness as Metaphor* and *AIDS and Its Metaphors*, are provocative, groundbreaking explanations of the ways in which diseases are freighted with historically specific metaphorical associations that can terrify, transfix, or repel.[9]

More recently, in *In Search of the Rainforest*, Candace Slater and her colleagues have added three terms to the lexicon of critical environmental studies, "icon," "bio-script," and "spectacle," which offer us new lenses through which to examine the construction, narration, and communicative strategies associated with specific biofears and environmental anxieties. For Slater and her colleagues, icons are "vivid simplifications that stand in for a far more complex set of places and people, and the ways they interact."[10] The figure of alien invaders in native ecologies in Subramaniam's chapter, the fulminating Ebola virus in Zerner's chapter, and the "youth bulge" in Hartmann and Hendrixson's chapter are examples of governing images or icons of environmental fear or threat, around which a penumbra of meanings, some contradictory, are associated. A *bio-script*, kin to what Cronon would call an environmental narrative, is a generalized scenario that incorporates an environmental icon in a recognizable storyline that has a particular trajectory, actors, a temporal sequence, and consequences. If environmental icons are easily recognizable configurations, environmental spectacles are events "staged by particular actors for a designated audience." As Slater observes, "the dramas we describe often have serious, often directly material effects." The staging of an America in imminent danger of nuclear attack (as in Orr's chapter, this volume)—or the portrayal of American cities in a situation of imminent danger due to the probability of another anthrax event but one infinitely more lethal and widespread (as in Lipschutz and Turcotte's chapter)—can be lethal in themselves, as the possibility of public panic lies in the shadow of such fear-saturated environmental spectacles. What the spectacle means, and what its psychological and material consequences are, is largely determined by the actors who stage it and, literally, by the location where it is staged. Thus, Ebola was staged in the Turning Point advertisements (see chapter 7) as a terrifying stand-in for the purported horrors of uncontrolled genetic engineering. In the hands of other producers, Ebola is a marker of America's vulnerable national security. Ebola, in the hands of other storytellers, has become a stand-in for a dangerous world of "emerging infectious diseases."

Intensified interest in the constitutive functions of rhetoric in literary and cultural studies, as well as in the arena of environmental politics, resistance, and policy debates, offers a fourth source of insight into the production of fear. The work of Stanley Fish offers creative avenues for interpreting the production of environmental fear, on two points: one, on the layered, intersecting relationships between representations and the realities they represent; and, two, on the investigations of "image politics," an examination of the rhetorical strategies of environmental resistance movements and the private-sector and state "framing" of the meanings of these actions.[11] Kevin DeLuca, in *Image Politics: The New Rhetoric of Environmental Activism*, shows how the strategic framing of a film showing the conflict between an antiwhaling Greenpeace crew seated within an inflatable, motorized raft on the one hand and an enormous Russian whaling vessel equipped with an automatic harpoon gun on the other was made to seem like a battle between David (Greenpeace) and Goliath (the Russian crew/gun/trawler).

If attention to metaphor, imagery, and narrative constitutes some of the "windows" that the authors in this volume use to understand the production of biofears and environmental anxieties, there is a further dimension—performance—that has a disciplinary lineage. It is in performance of environmental threats that the work on imagery, narrative, and discourse meet and merge with the spectacle. In Michael Lewis's volume *Inventing Global Ecology: Tracking the Biodiversity Ideal in India, 1947–1997*, we see how a group of highly respected conservation biologists who called themselves the "rainforest mafia" intentionally produced and publicized the idea of a global crisis in biodiversity conservation.[12] Environmental threats are not often produced in the isolated garret of the romantic artist: they are fashioned collectively and are often deployed, with a variety of intentions, to affect public consciousness and public policy. How are they "broadcast" or, indeed, performed? for whom? and in what arenas—whether public spaces including cities, streets, rooftops, or the skies; the print media; or on the ever-ramifying networked televisual sphere in which computers, cell phones, and ubiquitously placed screens confront us?

The work of Richard Schechner and Diana Taylor (performance studies), and Susan Foster (dance/choreographic theory) and Baz Kershaw (theater) forms a tacit yet fertile theoretical backdrop for several of the chapters in this volume.[13] The state-designed and state-enacted mass "performances" of atomic attack, mobilized and staged by the millions in the 1950s and 1960s, for example, constitute some of the more astonishing performative dimensions of threat creation (see Orr, this volume). Not only do state-sponsored mass performances of "threat responses" function as psychological and material preparations for the possibility of an event, but they also normalize, modulate, stimulate, and yet contain fear of these possibilities. The performances of George W. Bush, in blue jeans with shirt sleeves rolled up, feet planted in the soggy ground of a Florida bog, accompanied by the headline "Digging Up Alien Species," was but another performance of environmental threat and its interdiction.

None of these disciplinary optics on the production of environmental threats, fears, and anxieties, however, will offer us the revelation that comes to Dorothy as she steps behind the Wizard's screen. When Dorothy and her companions fulfilled their promises to the Wizard, including dissolving the Wicked Witch of the West into a puddle of dark water, the Wizard refused to fulfill his promises to them. As Toto tipped over a screen that stood in a corner,

> it fell with a crash. . . . They looked that way, and the next moment all of them were filled with wonder. For they saw, standing in just the spot the screen had hidden, a little, old man, with a bald head and a wrinkled face, who seemed as much surprised as they were. The Tin Woodman, raising his axe, rushed toward the little man and cried out, "Who are you?" "I am Oz, the Great and Terrible," said the little man, in a trembling voice, "but don't strike me—please don't!—and I'll do anything you want me to."[14]

As if they were talking about the plethora of environmental fears that are part of our quotidian landscape, the revelatory conversation continues:

> "I thought Oz was a great Head," said Dorothy. . . .
> "And I thought Oz was a terrible Beast," said the Tin Woodman.
> "And I thought Oz was a Ball of Fire," exclaimed the Lion.
> "No; you are all wrong," said the little man, meekly. I have been making believe. . . . I am a humbug."[15]

In the cases of environmental fear analyzed in this volume, boundaries between metaphorical exaggeration and empirical realities are not so easily discernable. Ebola is a real virus, and many hundreds of African people have died from it, enduring awful suffering. But Ebola does not pose much of a threat as a "traveling" virus, because it kills too quickly, unlike the AIDS virus, and therefore cannot infect many people. Nonnative species (if we accept the idea of coherently formed and bounded native ecologies) also exist and are part and parcel of ecological change in many areas of the globe. After all, as Banu Subramaniam asks, who is a "native"? Who is "native" in most discourses of plants, animals, and indeed people is the acceptance of an arbitrary date (although not always politically innocent) after which species or peoples are deemed "alien."

The kinds of insights offered by literary, rhetorical, and performative "lenses," however, permit us to ask questions beyond "how is the image constructed or performed?" We should ask, following Paul Farmer's lead, "Why are we paying so much attention to Ebola, when there is an existing epidemic of tuberculosis among our urban poor?" Farmer quotes a colleague:

> "Amidst a flood of information," complains one of the chief chroniclers of disease emergence, "analysis and context are evaporating. . . . Outbreaks of flesh-eating bacteria may command headlines, but local failures to fully vaccinate preschool children garner little attention unless there is an epidemic."[16]

Why, we might ask, are we paying more attention to Asian fish "invaders" rather than the attempts to reinvigorate our ailing and dangerous nuclear energy industry or the imminent and increasingly apparent effects of global warming? Attention to the imagery, rhetoric, narratives, and staging of specific environmental issues may open a critical public space in which a variety of environmental priorities and policies are subjected to a heightened degree of scrutiny.

The rhetoric of environmental apocalypse did not begin with the events of September 11. It follows a long and sometimes brilliant trajectory. Rachel Carson, whose uncanny bio-script involving invisible threats destroying the biological fabric of daily life provoked a reality-based revolution in public consciousness involving deep anxieties, was a master environmental rhetorician. According to recent scholarship, Carson consciously described the attributes of chemical poisons in ways that resonated with widespread fears of nuclear radiation, the paradigmatic environmental threat of the 1950s whose silent, invisible, and deadly "rays" could penetrate through walls and bodies, making its insidious mutagenic mischief without our sensing its destructive capacities.[17] Carson's metaphorical implications, however, were thoroughly grounded in empirical realities.

The approaches and cases in this volume do not provide an empirical litmus test in which the truth or falsity of a particular case will be indicated by a scrap of paper turning red or blue. More than three decades of science studies have shown us that a crude, empiricist "test" that can yank the cloak of rhetorical illusion cleanly from the "facts" is a chimera. We turn to this in our next section.

THE TIN MAN OR THE SCARECROW? NATURE/CULTURE, SCIENCE/SOCIETY

Binaries are common to Western philosophical, social, and political thought, including environmental thought.[18] Binaries are terms that are considered opposites and that present two separate and often mutually exclusive categories—for example, man/woman, nature/culture, nature/nurture, science/society. A binary presents two choices with nothing in between. As Jacques Derrida argues, in a binary, a category is constructed only by an absence—that is, women are women because they are not men. Derrida challenges the idea that identity and truth need to be represented in oppositional terms.[19] Feminists further challenge the implicit hierarchies in binaries, where, for example, man is seen as being superior to woman, and they call for a plurality of choices, instead of just two. Returning to the world of Oz, we have the Tin Man, who is all brains and no heart, and the Scarecrow, who is all heart and no brains.

The authors in this volume highlight how two particular binaries—natural/cultural and science/society—are particularly important in framing debates on the environment, often with profound consequences. First, the natural/cultural binary presents ideological frameworks on how we think about "nature" that are deeply problematic. In one narrative, "nature" is presented as a realm that is pure/virginal and untouched by humans. In this antimodernist narrative, human beings are argued to have destroyed nature and "nature" must be protected by keeping humans out, and the "natural" protected by keeping the "cultural" away. In an ideologically different narrative, "nature" is presented as the realm that is available for humans to exploit for human survival, growth, and pleasure. Both these narratives underpin the representations of nature in this volume.

But both these narratives presuppose the discrete realms of "nature" and "culture." It is this theorizing of nature/culture as binary opposites that many authors in our volume challenge and urge us to revisit. William Cronon lucidly argues that "nature," "natural," and "wilderness" should be understood as being historically contingent.[20]

> The more one knows of its peculiar history, the more one realizes that wilderness is not quite what it seems. Far from being the one place on earth that stands

apart from humanity, it is quite profoundly a human creation—indeed, the creation of very particular human cultures at very particular moments in human history.[21]

As he argues, as late as the eighteenth century, wilderness evoked images of deserted, savage, desolate, and barren land—unknown dark places. By the end of the nineteenth century, this conception had changed: "Wilderness had once been the antithesis of all that was orderly and good—it had been the darkness, one might say, on the far side of the garden wall—and yet now it was frequently likened to Eden herself."[22] By the end of the eighteenth century, the doctrine of the sublime entered nature. And today, in the beginning of the twenty-first century, when we travel far in search of "nature," SUVs advertise their vehicles as being so quiet as not to disturb "nature." Thus happily ensconced in our gas-guzzling vehicles, we can "find" the nature we came in search of (a practice that yet others argue is destroying the very nature we "found").

A profound irony that we can discern in many of these chapters is the ease with which we have maintained our robust distinctions of the natural and the cultural. Scholars of the social (especially feminist) studies of science have spent the last many decades demonstrating how inextricably the worlds of nature and culture are connected. Bruno Latour argues that we can understand this distinction of the worlds of nature and culture by paying attention to narratives of "how we became modern." He argues that contrary to our narratives, a historical analysis demonstrates that "we have never been modern." Latour suggests that we have two simultaneous processes that are ongoing.[23] First is the work of "purification," where we create two pure and distinct realms: one of "nonhuman/nature" and one of "human/culture." These realms are codified in the analytic frameworks that we use and that span the academy and are presupposed in academic disciplinarity itself. Note how the university is organized into the humanities, social sciences, and the natural sciences—the natural world is relegated to the natural sciences while humans and cultures are relegated to the social sciences and humanities. However, he argues that while we have "purified" the world into these allegedly distinct and binary zones, hybrids proliferate. Through a process he calls "translation," natures and cultures mix, and we see hybrids of the natural and cultural everywhere around us. Human beings profoundly shape the ozone level above, the landscapes below, and the mobility and extinction of species. Conversely, the "natural" shapes human societies and needs. Such, according to Latour, is the paradox of the moderns—"the more we forbid ourselves to conceive hybrids, the more possible their interbreeding becomes."[24]

Our task then is to understand the natural and the cultural as being deeply and inextricably interconnected. Indeed, as Cronon suggests, our very understanding of these terms is a product of our natural, historical, and cultural times. The nature/culture binary also shapes our understanding of the sciences (see Gusterson, this volume). Another binary of the science/ humanities shapes the ideological and political import of choices, such as genetically modified food. Science by virtue of this binary is presented as the objective/value-free/neutral zone of inquiry, while the humanities are re-garded as subjective/value-laden/political zones. What should we choose? The Tin Man, who is all brains and no heart, or the Scarecrow, who is all heart and no brains?

What the authors in this volume, and what the scholars in the social stud-ies of science, suggest is that we choose neither and refuse the binary that forces us into artificial, unnecessary choices. Scholars, especially feminist scholars, offer us many ways in which to extricate ourselves from these false binaries and into worlds of plurality, filled with choices. We can do this by tracing hybrids,[25] Haraway's "situated knowledges"[26] or "naturecultures,"[27] Harding's "strong objectivity,"[28] Longino's "science as social knowledge,"[29] or Latour's "circulating references"[30] or actor-network theory.[31] These frame-works move us beyond the binaries of science/society, nature/culture, good/bad, war/peace, fear/calm to challenge the monolithic discourses of fear and allow us to reframe environmental issues and debates. More than ever, these are times when we cannot have to choose between the mind and the heart, nature and culture, science and society, the Tin Man and the Scare-crow. We need them all.

ALERT STATUS GREEN: CONSTRUCTING SECURITY THREATS

While the conceptual approaches in the previous two sections shed light on how biofears and environmental anxieties are produced, understanding how they are translated into contemporary security threats requires looking criti-cally at the field of security itself, especially the broadening of security that occurred with the end of the Cold War. In what Emma Rothschild calls a geometry of "dizzying complexity," the concept of security was extended in the 1990s downward from nations to groups and individuals, upward to the international system and biosphere, and horizontally to include not just mil-itary but "political, economic, social, environmental, or 'human' security."[32]

While at first the extension of security appeared to be a progressive exercise, challenging narrow notions of Cold War military superiority and superpower ri-valry, it had the unfortunate effect of increasing the range and number of sup-posed threats to the United States and the West. In the environmental security field, which came to occupy pride of place in the new conceptions of security, scholars and practitioners mainly focused on "environmental conflict" induced by demographic pressures (see Hartmann and Hendrixson, this volume) and infectious diseases in the Third World as sources of imminent danger.[33] Both, in turn, were embodied in images of the violent or diseased Third World poor.

Biofears and environmental anxieties were thus writ large on the national security screen, as well as in more popular venues. In *Top Guns and Toxic Whales*, a companion book for a television documentary on environment and security, Gwyn Prins and Robbie Stamp present a positive vision of a new, high-tech war room called Cassandra, where military planners monitor threats to the global environment just as they would enemy aircraft. At the center of the war room is the "Population Screen," since population heads the list of environmental threats. In an accompanying picture, a board flashes "Alert Status Green" over a map of Egypt, with the word *population* written over it.[34]

The extension of security into such domains captured the eye of many critical security scholars, generating considerable intellectual debate about how and by whom security threats are constructed and with what results.[35] As Ronnie Lipschutz notes, defining security is often a competitive process: "There are not only struggles over security among *nations*, but also struggles over security among *notions*. Winning the right to define security provides not just access to resources but also the *authority* to articulate new definitions and discourses of security."[36]

Buzan, Waever, and de Wilde developed the conceptual framework of "securitization" to elaborate the ways in which a particular issue or threat becomes an actual object of security policy. They start from the basic premise that security is a self-referential practice; it is not necessarily because something is an actual existential threat that it gets securitized. First, there needs to be a compelling argument (a "securitizing" move) for why a particular issue is a serious threat requiring emergency measures. For the agent, "the task is not to assess some objective threats that 'really' endanger some object to be defended or secured; rather it is to understand the processes of constructing a shared understanding of what is to be considered and collectively responded to as a threat."[37]

Securitization, the authors stress, is generally not a positive phenomenon, since it represents the failure to deal with issues as normal politics and tends to reinforce state and elite power. During the Cold War the most progressive and transformative strategy was to minimize high-stakes security and return contested issues to the political realm, unlike the strategy of today, where the trend is to broaden or maximize the security agenda. Desecuritizing issues that have been securitized may, in fact, be a worthy goal.[38]

How does one go about "desecuritizing" security threats? As the chapters in this anthology illustrate, a critical eye is needed on many different levels. On the level of language, the literary and rhetorical lenses described in the preceding can help identify why certain images and narratives garner public attention while others do not. Critical discourse analysis is also useful in understanding the ongoing construction of the enemy "Other," so essential for the pursuit of both domestic repression and imperialist foreign policy.[39] One of the ways this construction occurs is through the persistence of core negative stereotypes and myths often drawn from the colonial imagination. Karim H. Karim defines *topos* (plural *topoi*) as the primary stereotype or reservoir of core ideas and images that functions "as the referential basis of interpretation and is essential in making a textual account seem coherent within a particular culture's norms."[40] Reinforcing *topoi* are "hegemonic myths," those "fundamental propositions or assumptions that are unquestionable within the context of a particular discourse."[41] These clusters of core ideas, images, stereotypes, and myths often serve to naturalize discourses of exclusion, making them seem commonsense and apolitical. They also serve as a common thread connecting the racialized past to a racialized present and future.

The salience of old *topoi* and myths, recapitulated and reconstituted into new articulations of national and global security, add a certain déjà vu quality to contemporary threat representation. With the disappearance of the Soviet Union as Enemy Number One, the race card in particular came to trump all, as the heart of darkness returned to the Third World in "a continuing complicity with colonial representations."[42] Race also forms a critical link between external and internal threats, with the jungle of the black urban ghetto serving as the Third World within the First.

Most of all, it is the dark-skinned immigrant—whether so-called environmental refugee or economic migrant—who is the lightning rod for malaise and fear. As Liisa Malkki notes, refugees have long been perceived as "an objectified, undifferentiated mass that is meaningful primarily as an aberration of categories and an object of 'therapeutic interventions'"; what is "natural" is sendentarism, and displacement is pathological.[43] While refugees are aberrations, immigrants are dangerous. Throughout U.S. history, successive waves of immigrants have been perceived as threats to both the cultural identity and the security of the nation. Now as the "war on terror" shifts the heart of darkness to the Middle East, it is the Muslim immigrant who is the main object of concern (and state repression).

Meanwhile, fear of the Muslim "Other" is further reinforced by what Mahmood Mamdani calls "culture talk," sweeping generalizations about Islamic "traditional" culture based in large part on old colonial stereotypes. "By equating political tendencies with entire communities defined in nonhistorical terms, such explanations encourage collective discipline and punishment—a practice characteristic of colonial encounters," he writes. Terrorists are equated with Muslims, justifying punitive wars against entire countries, such as Iraq and Afghanistan.[44]

It would be simplistic to suggest that these negative stereotypes, images, and myths persist just because they are deeply ingrained in the collective cultural psyche. In the security field, as elsewhere in the policy arena, language and framing matter but cannot be separated from the material interests—political and economic—that privilege one way of understanding the world over another. In the political economy of danger, money talks and power speaks its versions of the truth.[45] As Foucault notes in his discussion of the political economy of truth, if one wants to change the world, one must change "the political, economic, institutional regime of the production of truth."[46]

Thus, one needs to look closely at the identities and intentionality of specific actors and institutions in the construction of threats. This includes not only agencies of the government but private institutions as well. In the United States, private foundations serve as a major link in the chain joining corporate, academic, and public-policy interests in the production of knowledge. The Ford and Rockefeller foundations were instrumental in making neo-Malthusian fears of overpopulation a central focus of demographic science and foreign policy during the Cold War.[47] In the post–Cold War period, private foundations were critical in promoting environmental conflict as a key national security threat (Hartmann and Hendrixson, this volume).

In her study of the Rockefeller Foundation and the rise of molecular biology, Lily Kay calls attention to the "negative space" outside the prevailing knowledge consensus where those with less-fashionable views receive less support, while the massive resources available to the chosen fields accelerate their pace and create "a sense of rapid progress and public excitement," which in turn reinforces the authority of their knowledge claims.[48] In other words, it is important to look at not only what is funded but what is not—and why. Why, for example, in the field of environmental security, did models of environmental conflict in the Third World receive disproportionately more resources and attention than did threats to the global environment and human health posed by industrial pollution and the automobile?

The media is another key institution involved in the construction of threats. In his book *Creating Fear: News and the Construction of Crisis*, David Altheide argues that in order to sell news as entertainment, the mass media has developed "a highly rationalized problem frame that generates reports about fear." A secular alternative to the morality play, the problem frame unambiguously identifies specific dangers and threats, often exaggerating the number of people they affect, and presents mechanisms for fixing the problem, which usually involve government intervention. "Fear is more visible and routine in public discourse than it was a decade ago," Altheide argues. "Indeed, one of the few things Americans seem to share is the popular culture that celebrates danger and fear as entertainment organized with canned format delivered through an expansive and invasive information technology."[49]

Altheide analyzes the prominent role the military has come to play in the news and entertainment industry, giving rise in the post–Cold War period to what he calls "the military-media complex."[50] This close partnership has evolved through the expanding use of satellites for both military and communication purposes, changes in the technology of warfare that include target-based cameras that produce dramatic visuals (as in the Gulf War), the use of retired military officers as news commentators, and the defense industry's interest in sustaining a climate of fear through reportage on the wars against crime, drugs, gangs, and illegal immigration. Now, there is the added feature of journalists being "embedded" in the military in Afghanistan and Iraq. The militarization of the media is clearly a powerful institutional force—political, economic, cultural—in the construction and proliferation of threats.

Other conceptual approaches to analyzing the production of fear and the construction of threat can be found throughout this volume, which we hope will spark further interdisciplinary work and dialogue. Fear and threat are complex phenomena, and to understand them requires the development of the kind of hybrid knowledges that transgress narrow academic binaries and boundaries. If we may use a metaphor from nature, cross-fertilization is encouraged.

STRUCTURE OF THE BOOK

Making Threats is organized into five parts—Security, Scarcity, Purity, Circulation, and Terror—key conceptual motifs in the production of biofears and environmental anxieties and the propagation of threats. These are not discrete motifs; rather, they interact and articulate with each other and often draw on a common currency of metaphors, narratives, and tropes. Each part contains one or two chapters and a shorter, reflection piece designed to inspire further discussion and debate.

The contributions in part I, Security, focus on the representation and construction of threats and the roles played by powerful institutions of the government, market, and media. Ronnie Lipschutz and Heather Turcotte's "Duct Tape or Plastic? The Political Economy of Threats and the Production of Fear" explores how fear is produced through a political economy of threats and literally and figuratively sold to the American public. The authors propose that only through a careful examination of the ways that language, social relations, and material things are combined into a finished package of danger can the production of fear be understood, not as warning, but as the creation of terrified and terrorized populations seeking protection from the very state that produces those fears. They illustrate their arguments through an analysis of the "code orange" terror alert called by the Bush administration in February 2003.

In "Making Civilian-Soldiers: The Militarization of Inner Space," Jackie Orr considers the contemporary militarization of U.S. civilian psychology within the historical context of World War II and Cold War efforts to target the psychic and emotional life of U.S. civilians as a necessary battlefield. The militarization of civilian psychology—that is, the psychological organization of civil society for the production of violence—becomes historically visible as an administrative and administered imperative of U.S. domestic policy. This visibility is particularly important in interrogating and intervening in the complex politics and cultures of terror today.

In his reflection piece "Consuming National Security," Paul A. Passavant argues that the post-Fordist, neoliberal state governs in large measure through consumption and that governing subjects as consumers means inserting them into "networks of surveillance that can vastly expand state power." This kind of power is not only repressive. Through the pleasures of purchasing, consumers are implicated in "an aesthetics of consent" for state policies. Passavant notes how many of the same technologies that make consumers feel safe when shopping (e.g., surveillance cameras and private security guards), and make shopping easier (e.g., computer tracking systems), are also tools of political surveillance.

The authors in part II, Scarcity, illustrate how literary, rhetorical, and performative lenses can be employed to understand the generation and persistence of fears of scarcity—in particular, Malthusian narratives of overpopulation that for over two centuries have exercised so much influence on economic, political, and environmental thought in the West. In "Malthusianism and the Terror of Scarcity," Larry Lohmann analyzes the relationship between "daylight" Malthusianism—the quasi-logarithmic relationship between food and population growth that underpins two centuries of thinking about private property, government policy, development, and biology—and the darker, "Us vs. Them" Malthusian terror narrative, in which the overbreeding poor threaten civilization and planetary survival. Malthusian arithmetic/logic not only helps construct a "Them" easier to scapegoat but provides the necessary sense of tragic destiny to raise the terror narrative to the level of biblical parable.

In his reflection piece "Scarcity, Modernity, Terror," Michael Watts explores three narratives of scarcity—population growth as a driving force of resource scarcity and conflict (Malthusian scarcity), the "crisis" of oil scarcity (the artificial scarcity of rents), and the never-to-be-satisfied, always escalating consumer demand (the social world of scarcity)—and he examines how they are intertwined threads central to the discourse and practices of liberal governmentality.

In part III, Purity, the authors explore the consequences of the problematic nature/culture binary, and the related rhetoric of purity and pollution, in the construction of threats to the body and the environment. In "Decoding the Debate on 'Frankenfood,'" Hugh Gusterson analyzes how opponents of genetically modified foods often employ narratives of an idealized, pure nature threatened by a homogenized evil science in order to build public support, reinforcing unhelpful stereotypes and stymieing serious consideration of real risks.

In "The Aliens Have Landed! Reflections on the Rhetoric of Biological Invasions," Banu Subramaniam examines the contemporary discourse on biological invasion and traces the interconnections between scientific theories and rhetoric about nature with changing cultural and political conceptions of human immigration and foreigners. She follows the traffic between the worlds of nature and culture and suggests that this reflects a pervasive nativism, a nativism that blames the alien and the foreign for the changing U.S. landscape.

In his piece "Impure Biology: The Deadly Synergy of Racialization and Geneticization," Alan Goodman reflects on the salience of our obsession with "purity." He suggests that "race" and the history of race are key to understanding our quest for a "pure" nature and our fears of mixtures, hybrids, and miscegenation. He summarizes the literature in the biological sciences that have for decades critiqued the simplistic idea of "race" but argues that race is ever present in public and scientific discourse and rhetoric. He warns that with the increased focus on "genetics" of difference, we must pay attention to the growing links between racialization and geneticization.

Part IV, Circulation, builds on the previous discussion to explore the powerful contradictions and connections between the rhetorics and politics of purity/nativism and the expansion of global capitalist ideology, markets, and institutions. In "Emerging Cartographies of Environmental Danger: Africa, Ebola, and AIDS," Charles Zerner examines the production of environmental imagery and rhetorics and their links to racist geographies of African culture and environment in policy discussions, fiction, nonfiction, and film. Zerner analyzes the ways in which the Ebola virus is configured as a "terror"; the historic layering of imagery about Africa, women, and viruses; as well as the trajectories of dissemination—nationally and globally.

In her reflection "Feeling Invasion," Emily Martin describes an essential emotional contradiction of capitalism: at the same time that many of its activities deaden and flatten feeling or cause anxiety, it depends on consumer confidence and enthusiasm as well as manic market exuberance to function. In the wake of September 11, many Wall Street traders and financiers exhibited a "hyper-energized fearlessness" while government leaders were simultaneously encouraging states of anxiety. This contradiction is worth watching, she notes; we should not assume that fear is the only emotion to rise in the present moment.

Part V, Terror, analyzes the rhetorical strategies of state and nonstate actors in the construction of national security threats and their relation to the production of violence. Rhetoric not only matters; it can have potentially lethal consequences.

In "Inventing Bioterrorism: The Political Construction of Civilian Risk," Jeanne Guillemin describes how outbreaks of life-threatening infectious diseases and the dangers of biological weapons are conventionally dichotomized into categories of "natural" and "intentional" epidemics. Yet both have common structural causes, which she terms "embedded terrorism." New U.S. government programs to counter potential bioterrorism attacks by foreign aggressors demonstrate the "fright value" of epidemic disease for producing fear and expanding target populations on the basis of imagined, politically driven simulations of national devastation—which, in their apocalyptic vision, strip the present of social meaning.

In "Pernicious Peasants and Angry Young Men: The Strategic Demography of Threats," Betsy Hartmann and Anne Hendrixson explore the framing of national security threats in demographic terms. They examine two narratives vital to today's strategic demography: the "degradation narrative," the belief that population pressures in rural areas precipitate environmental degradation, migration, and violent conflict; and the "youth bulge," the presence of a large male youth cohort in countries of the global South, which ostensibly predisposes them to political unrest and violence. In the current "war on terror," the "youth bulge" is used to build and sustain anti-Islamic prejudice. It also reinforces sharp gender binaries and the criminalization of young black men.

In "Bioterrorism and National Security: Peripheral Threats, Core Vulnerabilities," Richard A. Matthew writes about how the perennial alarmism of a large wing of the environmental movement has helped convince the public and policymakers that the world is a frightening and dangerous place. He explores how this perception can enable problematic national security policies that do not accurately assess actual risk, taking as an example the current Bush administration's "war on terror" and doctrine of preemption.

There is no reason to assume that the forms and representations of fear analyzed in this volume will be with us forever or even into the foreseeable future. The objects of fear change over time. In the United States, the bald eagle—the national emblem—was once feared and despised, depicted as an evil baby-snatcher and butchered with abandon. Then, as the eagle faced extinction, heroic efforts were launched to save it, and now it is the icon of American survival, freedom, and imperial power.

By locating the production of environmental fears in specific sites; by identifying, in many cases, the actors and institutions staging these fears; by analyzing the dramaturgy, discourse, and imagery used in creating fearsome environmental "spectaculars"; in short, by giving fears histories, the authors in this volume contribute to scholarship on the environment and security that engages with some of the more potent and disturbing political and cultural aspects of the contemporary scene. If we cannot step behind the curtain like Dorothy and immediately see the ways in which the spectacle of biofears and environmental anxieties has been organized and operated, detecting at a glance the banal stagecraft underlying a fearsome illusion, then perhaps, at the very least, we can be more discerning viewers. Perhaps, in viewing these productions of fear and constructions of threat, we can make less-fevered judgments about the decisions, policies, and practices that seem to issue so naturally from them.

NOTES

1. Jim Rutenberg, "Scary Ads Campaign to a Grim New Level," *New York Times*, October 17, 2004, 1(1).

2. James Dao, "Bird Flu Outbreak Has Farmers Jittery," *New York Times*, February 16, 2004, www.nytimes.com/2004/02/16/national/16CHIC.html (accessed February 16, 2004).

3. Dao, "Bird Flu Outbreak."

4. Frank Baum, *The Wonderful Wizard of Oz* (New York: Harper Collins, 1987 [1899]), 149.

5. Hadley Cantril, *The Invasion from Mars: A Study in the Psychology of Panic* (Princeton, N.J.: Princeton University Press, 1966).

6. William Cronon, "A Place for Stories: Nature, History, and Narrative," *Journal of American History* 78, no. 4 (March 1992): 1349–50.

7. George Lakoff and Mark Johnson, *Metaphors We Live By* (Chicago: University of Chicago Press, 1980).

8. These include Max Black, *Models and Metaphors* (Ithaca, N.Y.: Cornell University Press, 1962). See also Sheldon Sacks, *On Metaphor* (Chicago: University of Chicago Press, 1979); and Andrew Ortony, *Metaphor and Thought* (Cambridge: Cambridge University Press, 1979).

9. Susan Sontag, *"Illness as Metaphor" and "AIDS and Its Metaphors"* (New York: Doubleday, 1990).

10. Candace Slater, "In Search of the Rain Forest," in *In Search of the Rain Forest*, ed. Candace Slater (Durham, N.C.: Duke University Press, 2003), 8.

11. We understand rhetoric as being embedded in, and inseparable from, all accounts of the world, following Stanley Fish, "Rhetoric," in *The Stanley Fish Reader*, ed. H. Aram Vesser (Malden, Mass.: Blackwell, 1999), 114–42. See also Richard Rorty, who asserts, "There . . . are two ways of thinking about various things. . . . The first . . . thinks of truth as a vertical relationship between representations and what is represented. The second . . . thinks of truth horizontally—as the culminating reinterpretation of our predecessors' reinterpretation of their predecessors' reinterpretation. . . . It is the difference between regarding truth, goodness, and beauty as eternal objects which we try to locate and reveal, and regarding them as artifacts whose fundamental design we often have to alter." Rorty, *The Consequences of Pragmatism* (Minneapolis: University of Minnesota Press, 1982), 92.

12. Michael L. Lewis, *Inventing Global Ecology: Tracking the Biodiversity Ideal in India, 1947–1997* (Athens: Ohio University Press, 2004).

13. On performance theory, see Richard Schechner, *Environmental Theater* (New York: Hawthorn Books, 1973); Schechner, *Future of Ritual: Writings on*

Culture and Performance (New York: Routledge, 1993); Schechner, *Performance Studies: An Introduction* (New York: Routledge, 2002); Schechner, *Performative Circumstances: From the Avant Garde to Ramlila* (Calcutta, India: Seagull Books, 1983); Schechner, *Ritual, Play, and Performance: Readings in the Social Sciences/Theatre* (New York: Seabury Press, 1976); Schechner, *Theatres, Spaces, Environments: Eighteen Projects* (New York: Drama Book Specialists, 1975); Diana Taylor, *The Archive and the Repertoire: Performing Cultural Memory in the Americas* (Durham, N.C.: Duke University Press, 2003); Diana Taylor, *Disappearing Acts: Spectacles of Gender and Nationalism in Argentina's "Dirty War"* (Durham, N.C.: Duke University Press, 1997); Susan Leigh Foster, "Choreographies of Protest," *Theatre Journal* 55, no. 3 (October 2003): 395–412; Baz Kerhsaw, "Fighting in the Streets: Dramaturgies of Popular Protest, 1968–1989," *New Theatre Quarterly* 13, no. 51 (August 1997): 255–76.

14. Baum, *Wonderful Wizard of Oz*, 216.

15. Baum, *Wonderful Wizard of Oz*, 216.

16. Paul Farmer, *Infections and Inequalities: The Modern Plagues* (Berkeley: University of California Press, 1999), 53.

17. Ralph Lutts, "Chemical Fallout: Rachel Carson's *Silent Spring*, Radioactive Fallout, and the Environmental Movement," *Environmental Review* 9, no. 3 (Fall 1985): 211–25.

18. Maggie Humm, *The Dictionary of Feminist Theory* (Columbus: Ohio State University Press, 1999).

19. Jacques Derrida, *Of Grammatology* (Baltimore: Johns Hopkins University Press, 1974).

20. William Cronon, "The Trouble with Wilderness," in *Uncommon Ground: Rethinking the Human Place in Nature*, ed. William Cronon (New York: Norton, 1996), 69.

21. Cronon, "Trouble with Wilderness," 69.

22. Cronon, "Trouble with Wilderness," 71.

23. Bruno Latour, *We Have Never Been Modern* (Cambridge, Mass.: Harvard University Press, 1993).

24. Latour, *We Have Never Been Modern*, 12.

25. Donna Haraway, *Modest_Witness@Second_Millennium.FemaleMan_Meets_OncoMouse: Feminism and Technoscience* (New York: Routledge, 1996); and Latour, *We Have Never Been Modern*.

26. Donna Haraway, *Simians, Cyborgs, and Women: The Reinvention of Nature* (New York: Routledge, 1991).

27. Thyrza Nichols Goodeve, *How like a Leaf: An Interview with Donna Haraway* (New York: Routledge: 1999).

28. Sandra Harding, *Whose Science? Whose Knowledge?* (Ithaca, N.Y.: Cornell University Press, 1991).

29. Helen Longino, *Science as Social Knowledge* (Princeton, N.J.: Princeton University Press, 1990).

30. Bruno Latour, "Circulating References: Sampling the Soil in the Amazon Forest," in *Pandora's Hope: Essays on the Reality of Science Studies* (Cambridge, Mass.: Harvard University Press, 1999).

31. See, for example, Latour, *We Have Never Been Modern*; and Bruno Latour, *Science in Action: How to Follow Scientists and Engineers through Society* (Cambridge, Mass.: Harvard University Press, 1987).

32. Emma Rothschild, "What Is Security?" *Daedalus* 124, no. 3 (Summer 1995): 53–98.

33. See, for example, U.S. National Intelligence Council, "National Intelligence Estimate: The Global Infectious Disease Threat and Its Implications for the United States," excerpted in *Environmental Change and Security Project Report*, no. 6 (Summer 2000): 33–65.

34. Gwyn Prins and Robbie Stamp, *Top Guns and Toxic Whales: The Environment and Global Security* (London: Earthscan, 1991), 38–39.

35. See, for example, Simon Dalby, *Environmental Security* (Minneapolis: University of Minnesota Press, 2002).

36. Ronnie D. Lipschutz, ed., *On Security* (New York: Columbia University Press, 1995), 8.

37. Barry Buzan, Ole Waever, and Jaap de Wilde, *Security: A New Framework for Analysis* (Boulder, Colo.: Lynne Rienner, 1998), 26.

38. Ole Waever, "Securitization and Desecuritization," in Lipschutz, *On Security*, 46–86.

39. See Stephen Harold Riggins, ed., *The Language and Politics of Exclusion: Others in Discourse* (London: Sage, 1997); also see David Campbell, *Writing Security: United States Foreign Policy and the Politics of Identity* (Minneapolis: University of Minnesota Press, 1998).

40. Karim H. Karim, "The Historical Resilience of Primary Stereotypes: Core Images of the Muslim Other," in Riggins, *Language and Politics of Exclusion*, 153.

41. Michael Thompson and Steve Rayner, "Cultural Discourses," in *Human Choice and Climate Change*, vol. 1, *The Societal Framework*, ed. Steve Rayner and Elizabeth L. Mallone (Columbus, Ohio: Battelle Press, 1998), 289.

42. Roxanne Lynn Doty, *Imperial Encounters: The Politics of Representation in North-South Relations* (Minneapolis: University of Minnesota Press, 1996), 170.

43. Liisa H. Malkki, "National Geographic: The Rooting of Peoples and the Territorialization of National Identity among Scholars and Refugees," in *Culture, Power, Place: Explorations in Critical Anthropology*, ed. Akhil Gupta and James Ferguson (Durham, N.C.: Duke University Press), 65. Malkki also explores how these views of refugees are often reinforced through botanical metaphors as part of the process of naturalization.

44. Mahmood Mamdani, "Good Muslim, Bad Muslim: A Political Perspective on Culture and Terrorism," *American Anthropologist* 104, no. 3 (September 2002): 766–75.

45. See Ronnie D. Lipschutz, "Terror in the Suites: Narratives of Fear and the Political Economy of Danger" (paper presented at the International Studies Association annual convention, Washington, D.C., February 1999), 1–21.

46. Michel Foucault, *Power/Knowledge: Selected Interviews and Other Writings, 1972–1977* (London: Harvester Wheatsheaf, 1980), 133.

47. See, for example, John Sharpless, "Population Science, Private Foundations, and Development Aid: The Transformation of Demographic Knowledge in the United

States, 1945–65," in *International Development and Social Sciences: Essays on the History and Politics of Knowledge*, ed. Frederick Cooper and Randall Packard (Berkeley: University of California Press, 1997).

48. Lily E. Kay, *The Molecular Vision of Life: Caltech, the Rockefeller Foundation, and the Rise of the New Biology* (New York: Oxford University Press, 1993), 281.

49. David L. Altheide, *Creating Fear: News and the Construction of Crisis* (New York: Aldine de Gruyter, 2002), 84, 89.

50. Altheide, *Creating Fear*, 126.

I

SECURITY

2

Duct Tape or Plastic?
The Political Economy of
Threats and the Production of Fear

Ronnie D. Lipschutz and Heather Turcotte

According to the FBI, there is only one instance in which a terrorist group operating in the United States actually employed a chemical or biological agent. This incident took place in September 1984. The perpetrators were members of the Rajneeshee, a religious cult that established a large community in Wasco County, a rural area east of Portland, Oregon. The Rajneeshees used *salmonella typhimurium*, which causes salmonellosis or food poisoning, to contaminate restaurant salad bars. An estimated 751 people became ill because of that attack, including about 45 who were hospitalized. There were no fatalities. This is the only bioterrorism incident in which human illness has been verified.

—W. Seth Carus, *Bioterrorism and Biocrimes*

We estimate that foodborne diseases cause approximately 76 million illnesses, 325,000 hospitalizations, and 5,000 deaths in the United States each year.

—Paul S. Mead and colleagues,
"Food-Related Illness and Death in the United States"

When the followers of Bhagwan Shree Rajneesh (the Rajneeshee) attempted to take over the small Oregon town of Antelope in 1984, trying to turn it into a political outpost for their activities, most Americans thought it just another bizarre activity of a religious group already well known for its eccentricities.[1] No one used the terms *terrorist* or *biological terrorism* to describe the Rajneeshees' efforts to contaminate the salad bars of Wasco County. Indeed, not until the 1990s did the case enter the pantheon listed by W. Seth Carus in his book *Bioterrorism and Biocrimes—the Illicit Use of Biological Agents in the*

20th Century.[2] Two other authors thought the incident merited an entire chapter in their scholarly works,[3] as did Judith Miller and her colleagues at the *New York Times*, in their book published in 2001, *Germs: Biological Weapons and America's Secret War*.[4] By 2003, fear of biological attacks had become so engrained in the public mind that hardware stores had trouble keeping duct tape and plastic sheeting in stock whenever the federal government raised the terrorism alert level to orange. Aside from the anthrax-laden letters delivered to various recipients in 2001, however, no actual incidents of biological terrorism were recorded within the United States between 1990 and 2003,[5] even as hundreds of car, truck, plane, boat, and suicide bombings resulted in more than four thousand fatalities around the world. Why, then, has there been so much focus on the release of biological agents?[6]

In this chapter, we argue that this paradox grows out of the political economy of terrorism/counterterrorism (T/CT): the need to "produce" threats in order to "reproduce" the discourse of T/CT. We use the term *political economy* not to suggest that the defense sector needs threats in order to stay in business but, rather, to describe a nexus of politics, markets, and power, with a history, ideology, and material manifestations.[7] Counterterrorism is more than a response to acts of terrorism; it is an autonomous arena of supply that requires a demand to survive and succeed. But the demand for counterterrorism and the protection it ostensibly provides are not automatic; they must be created and sustained. The division of labor within the counterterrorist arena means that, like toothpaste, cereal, and SUVs, different products require different sales strategies.[8]

Note that we do not claim here that there are no dangers, risks, or threats from those who might wish us ill and act on their desires—the events of September 11, 2001, demonstrate that acts of terrorism are real. We do propose, however, that a careful examination of the ways that language, social relations, and material objects are combined into a finished package of danger will help us understand that the state produces fear not merely to warn but also to produce terrified and terrorized populations, who then seek its protection.

We begin the chapter with a general discussion of the relationship between political economy and "discourse." As we use the term here, a *discourse* is a set of beliefs, practices, and material manifestations. Counterterrorism and its counterpart, terrorism, constitute such a discourse. The ostensible objective of T/CT is the protection of the public through the prevention of terrorist incidents. But, because the number of actual terrorist incidents within the United States has been rather small, and those occurring outside of the country are generally regarded as being rather distant, counterterrorism must find ways to sustain the discourse. It is at this point that political economy appears.

The matter of risk looms large in this discussion: just how great is the threat? This question is addressed in the second part of this chapter. Commentators opine that a bioterrorist attack is "virtually certain." What they cannot specify is what, when, where, why, and how. The problem here is that risk estimates rely on a statistical sample composed of some large number of similar, if not identical, incidents to specify the "what." Vulnerability looms large in this equation—some experience higher levels of risk than others because of a number of differing social and technological factors—but the discourse of counterterrorism makes no such distinctions.

In the third part of the chapter, we examine how this political economy operates, both historically and materially. Just prior to the launching of war on Iraq, the Department of Homeland Security raised the national terrorist threat level from yellow to orange, based on unconfirmed intelligence reports that several shadowy figures might have entered, or might enter, the United States. After several weeks, the threat level was lowered back to yellow, although, in the interim, the hysteria generated by these announcements was palpable, as secretary of homeland security Tom Ridge suggested that the public protect itself by purchasing certain widely available household goods—to wit, plastic sheeting and duct tape. The alert was something of a fiasco, but it had its intended effect: creation of demand for state protection against weapons of mass destruction in the hands of Saddam Hussein and others of his ilk. A great deal of money changed hands, and trading in counterterrorist stock was bullish.

In the final part of the chapter, we propose that one can understand the political economy of threats and the production of fear manifest in the discourse of T/CT only by considering that the latter is embedded within capitalism. Like corporations, discourses must grow if they are to survive and succeed, and that means the creation of demand. In aggregate, the counterterrorist "business" surely involves expenditure of more than $100 billion each year (terrorists, by contrast, could not be spending more than a few tens of millions per year) and offers both great opportunity and profit for those who are able to get a cut of the action. So long as fears can be stoked, there is no need for actual attacks, since no one can know how many were "deterred" by the T/CT business and all of its activities.

THE POLITICAL ECONOMY OF DISCOURSE AND THE DISCOURSE OF POLITICAL ECONOMY

What is a *discourse*? Although the term is generally understood as having to do with language alone, under the influence of Michel Foucault's writings, discourse has come to mean a set of interlinked statements whose "truth" is confirmed by those statements and the accompanying "substructure." In

Discipline and Punish, Foucault, speaking of what he calls "generalized punishment," writes that a "discourse provide[s], in effect, by means of the theory of interests, representations, and signs, by the series and geneses that it reconstitute[s], a sort of power over men."[9] According to Stuart Hall,

> A discourse is a group of statements which provide a language for talking about—i.e., a way of representing—a particular kind of knowledge about a topic. When statements about a topic are made within a particular discourse, the discourse makes it possible to construct the topic in a certain way. It also limits the other ways in which the topic can be constructed. A discourse does not consist of one statement but of several statements working together to form what Michel Foucault calls a "discursive formation." The statements fit together because any one statement implies a relation to all the others.[10]

Finally, in a rather different vein, Karen Litfin has written,

> As determinants of what can and cannot be thought, discourses delimit the range of policy options, thereby functioning as precursors to policy options. . . . The supreme power is the power to delineate the boundaries of thought—an attribute not so much of specific agents as it is of discursive practices.[11]

Here, Litfin describes a "hegemonic" discourse, one not only accepted as a self-validating truth but generally believed by all classes and groups to represent a society's shared interests.[12]

To be regarded as broadly valid, a discourse must be more than simply a self-referential set of interlocking statements; it must also be confirmed repeatedly by material outcomes for which it can claim responsibility (of course, the discourse does not "speak" for itself but is articulated through "speech acts" by "spokespersons"[13]). The beliefs articulated in a discourse are both ontological and methodological: they make statements about the nature of reality and offer means of shaping that reality. These means, or practices, serve to create and maintain the material results of those practices. When a discourse is dominant, or hegemonic, it is a closed system—there are no points at which contrary data or truths can intervene to invalidate it (see figure 2.1).

One might object to this schema. After all, if the beliefs and practices associated with a discourse actually lead to the specified material outcomes, does that not "prove" that the propositions offered by the discourse are "true" and accurately describe reality? And, contrarily, if the outcomes are different from what was predicted, does this not disconfirm the discourse's propositions? These questions confuse things on two counts. First, simple causality cannot account for social processes, which are always complex and overdetermined. Moreover, different beliefs and practices can lead to identical outcomes, while different outcomes can be the result of identical beliefs

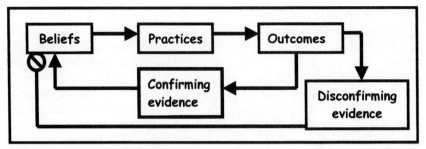

Figure 2.1.   The structure of a discourse

and practices.[14] Second, because discourse is impervious to contrary evidence
—it does not succumb to changing evidence, as does science in Kuhn's "paradigm shift"[15]—it cannot be disproved. It is always possible to interpret data
in such a way as to confirm the propositions. As we shall see, the matter of
concern in this chapter—bioterrorism—is made more complicated by the absence of the outcomes specified by the discourse, in addition to misspecifi-
cations internal to the discourse. This is not a new problem: public support
for civil defense during the Cold War was repeatedly undermined by the absence of evidence that it was possible to survive a nuclear attack.[16] This did
not prevent the purveyors of the discourse from repeatedly offering civil defense as a "solution" to the nuclear dilemma.

Because a discourse includes elements of materiality, it is also closely
linked to political economy. Foucault tended to shy away from discussions of
political economy, although a close reading of *Discipline and Punish*, for example, makes clear that the "carceral" system was very much bound up with
an "economy of power" and an "apparatus of production."[17] These concepts
relate, of course, to the production of normalized and disciplined society that,
in Marxist terms, has to do with both relations of production and social relations or, in other words, order. Mitchell Dean, in his analysis of neoliberal
governmentality, makes clear how freedom, discipline, and order are all implicated with the market in modern capitalist societies. As he puts it,

> Neo-liberalism ceases to be a government of society in that it no longer con-
> ceives its task in terms of a division between state and society or of a public sec-
> tor opposed to a private one. The ideal here is to bridge these older divisions so
> that the structures and values of the market are folded back onto what were for-
> merly areas of public provision and to reconfigure the latter as a series of quasi-
> markets in services and expertise.[18]

Our conceptualization of political economy goes beyond the conventional
liberal idea of supply, demand, and markets. "Political economy" involves
the specific power-based relationships between politics and economics that

lead to order and discipline. Our concerns are not only "who gets what, where, and when," in Harold Lasswell's classic formulation,[19] but also who decides who gets what, which parties have used their influence and wealth to shape the environment in which those decisions get made, and how the power of both individuals and the discourses they proffer are reinforced through the shaping of that environment.[20] In political economy, what is central is the "economy of power" through which economic relations are produced and reproduced. Thus, we ask not only "how many rolls of duct tape and plastic sheeting have been sold?" but also "how do duct tape and plastic sheeting come to be a means of constructing and maintaining a particular social order?" The political economy of a discourse therefore involves the production of truth claims in ways that help to generate specified outcomes and develop the material base. The expansion of that materiality, in turn, funnels resources into that political economy and helps to reproduce the discourse.[21]

Let us be more specific: counterterrorism and terrorism constitute a discourse of the kind we have described in the preceding. "Terrorism" has many definitions.[22] In fact, the absence of a clear definition enhances the utility of the concept, for anything which involves destabilization of the normalized order of society can come under its rubric, including the destruction of skyscrapers, the detonating of car bombs, the defacing of SUVs, and the defamation of individuals and groups.[23] By contrast, military attacks by one state on another, or by a government against an internal or external opposition group, do not constitute "terrorism" because the target of the action is usually accused of attempting to destabilize the normalized order of society, whether national or international. There is, of course, a history and a genealogy of the apparent expansion of the concepts of "terror" and "terrorism," but space precludes an exploration of the terms' past.[24]

The discourse of "counterterrorism" cannot exist without "terrorism." An essential element of this discourse is the belief that the natural tendency of the world is toward chaos and that the forces of evil and disorder lurk everywhere, both within and without. This "truth" is articulated in the oft-repeated claim that "the world is a dangerous place." Military force can eliminate some of the dangers "out there," but it is ill-suited to management and discipline, as is evident in continuing violence in Afghanistan and Iraq. Counterterrorism constitutes a particular form of deployment of state power against those who seek to upset the social order. It is a form of "police," as Foucault describes it, not the organized forces of the "thin blue line" but, rather, something along the lines of the German *Polizeiwissenschaft*, which involved, among other things, "the maintenance of order and discipline" as well as the welfare and comfort of the citizen.[25] Consequently, labeling oppositional elements as "terrorists," whatever their politics and methods, serves two functions. First, it invokes protection, or counterterrorism, which includes a broad range of practices, as the appropriate means of response. Second, it alerts citizens to the omnipresence of danger, not only outside of society, but also within it.

This does not mean that attacks against social targets are, somehow, imaginary. Since the destruction of the World Trade Center, many more than one hundred car, truck, and suicide bombs have been detonated around the world, with concomitant injury and death.[26] But all of these have taken place outside the United States, and it is the individual's lived experience that is, most often, the basis for one's assessment of risk.[27] In the absence of repeated exposure to a stimulus, the effect of operant conditioning weakens. It must be periodically reinforced to maintain its effect. For counterterrorism to function as "police" and generate continued public support in the absence of material evidence (i.e., actual attacks), it must, as part of the discourse, create materiality where none exists, as we shall see in the following.

The political economy of counterterrorism is based, therefore, on two elements. First, through its economy of power, the discourse creates public demand for counterterrorist services, supplied through the material infrastructure: policing, intelligence gathering, espionage, reports, press conferences, alerts, and so forth. In the United States, these result in expenditures of tens of billions of dollars per year and help create a substantial private sector that provides all kinds of protective services. Second, the existence of this substantial material base confirms the need for counterterrorism, even in the absence of actual attacks, through both media and state publicity associated with counterterrorist activities. Examples are U.S. attorney general John Ashcroft's tour in defense of the Patriot Act in late 2003, as well as periodic practice drills by authorities and first responders who would react in the event of an actual attack.[28]

NO ONE IS SAFE, BUT NO ONE IS BEYOND SUSPICION

Given the paucity of bioterrorist attacks, how can the counterterrorism discourse be maintained? Why invoke biological terrorism when the statistical risk of such an attack would seem to be quite small? It has been common practice to invoke Aum Shinrikyo's release of chemical agents in the Tokyo subway in 1995 to illustrate the threat of biological agents, but such a citation is quite misleading.[29] In point of fact, there are no risk data for biological attacks and, in the absence of a statistical base, it is impossible to estimate how likely one is to occur. Moreover, because such attacks would not occur at random, risk assessment is not a reliable means of estimating the threat. Vulnerability plays a role in terms of risk, too, but given the large number of "soft" targets, there is no way to predict which might be most attractive. Crowds are often described as being especially vulnerable—for example, the police in Livermore, California, are worried about terrorist disruption of local parades—but not all crowds are equal; there is more to be gained by attacking elite targets than plebeian ones.[30]

The absence of risk data does not mean there is no risk, only that the magnitude of risk is unknown. Those who are wise in the ways of the world often point out that "the absence of evidence is not evidence of absence." Or, as defense secretary Donald Rumsfeld put it in a press conference in Brussels in June 2002:

> There are no knowns. There are things we know that we know. There are known unknowns—that is to say, there are things that we now know we don't know but there are also unknown unknowns. There are things we do not know we don't know. So when we do the best we can and we pull all this information together, and we then say well that's basically what we see as the situation, that is really only the known knowns and the known unknowns. And each year we discover a few more of those unknown unknowns.[31]

In the absence of evidence, there is a compelling logic for producing "truths" that account for the failure to confirm hypotheses. Despite the apparent absence of weapons of mass destruction in Iraq, one can never prove that they did not once exist, which also implies that they might still exist, albeit in some place other than Iraq.

An alternative approach to estimating the risk of biological terrorism is to look at capabilities: who could manufacture such agents? Here, we run into the problem of too much data and too many suspects (see figures 2.2 and 2.3). For example, according to the authors of a study prepared at the Belfer

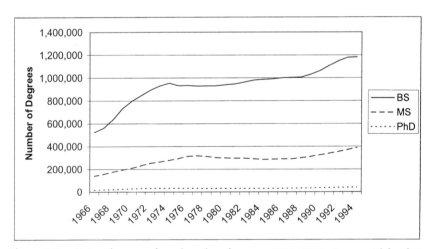

Figure 2.2.   U.S. science and engineering degrees, 1966–1994. Source: Richard A. Falkenrath, Robert D. Newman, and Bradley A. Thayer, *America's Achilles' Heel— Nuclear, Biological, and Chemical Terrorism and Covert Attack* **(Cambridge, Mass.: MIT Press, 1998), 172.**

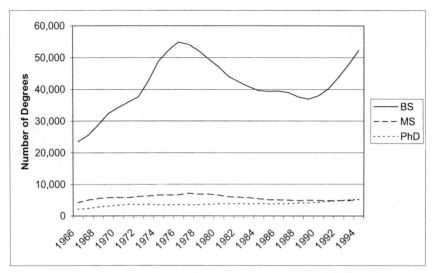

Figure 2.3. U.S. biology degrees, 1966–1994. Source: Richard A. Falkenrath, Robert D. Newman, and Bradley A. Thayer, *America's Achilles' Heel—Nuclear, Biological, and Chemical Terrorism and Covert Attack* **(Cambridge, Mass.: MIT Press, 1998), 173.**

Center for Science and International Affairs at Harvard University's Kennedy School of Government,

> How and why is the underlying capacity of nonstate actors to master the technical challenges of NBC [nuclear, biological, chemical] acquisition and use increasing? The first reason is that the basic science behind these weapons is being learned by more people, better than ever before. In the United States alone, the number of people receiving bachelor's, master's and doctoral degrees in science and engineering fields more than doubled between 1966 and 1994. . . . Over the same time period, the number of B.S. degrees awarded in biology increased by 122 percent, and the number of PhDs grew by 144 percent; more than 60,000 advanced degrees were granted in biology each year by 1994.[32]

And they continue,

> An even more important gauge of the ability of nonstate actors to build and use weapons of mass destruction is the increasing level of knowledge available even in high school science courses, not to mention undergraduate or graduate-level courses, as well as the sophistication of the laboratory and analytical tools, from computers to laboratory-scale fermentation equipment, that are now routinely available.[33]

There is no evidence available to indicate, however, that American high school students are manufacturing biological agents. Nevertheless, apparent possession of the capability to do so renders them objects of suspicion.

WHEN THE DOG BARKS, WHEN THE BEE STINGS,
WHEN I'M FEELING SAD

The discourse of counterterrorism represents, in other words, the articulation and implementation of a political economy of threats whose primary product is fear. And just as corporations must grow in order to remain competitive, so must the discourse of counterterrorism not be permitted to wane. Over time, a "yellow alert" no longer stands for a condition of "elevated" threat but becomes the normal state of affairs. Fear dies down, and the viability of the discourse itself comes under threat. No one notices the dog that doesn't bark, even if it might be there. But how are sleeping dogs made to bark?

All discourses possess a historical context, and so does that of T/CT. Over time, both actions and actors are categorized within this discourse as signifiers for particular events and identities that set in train a series of already fixed yet malleable responses. This process is organized and articulated by those who participate in the construction and reconstruction of the discourse, and it is reinforced through public response to the discourse, triggered by certain signifiers. For example, the words *alert, Middle Eastern, Islamic, illegal,* and *terrorist* are signifiers within the discourse of T/CT, whose articulation invokes the discourse and all that is associated with it. Recognition of these signifiers also suggests the validity of the discourse through the "facts" that have been established by particular historic events, actors, beliefs, and practices. Two such incidents illustrate this argument.

On December 30, 2002, the Federal Bureau of Investigation alerted all U.S. law enforcement agencies to be on the lookout for five Middle Eastern men who were "believed" to have illegally crossed the Canadian border "sometime around" December 24. The bulletin read, "Although the FBI has no specific information that these individuals are connected to any potential terrorist activities, based upon information developed in the course of ongoing investigations, the FBI would like to locate and question these persons."[34] Invoking the long history of its "Most Wanted List," the FBI posted what it "believed" to be the names, ages, and photographs of the men on its website, requesting assistance from both police departments and the public across the nation. The "all points bulletin" was ordered by President George W. Bush, who stated, "We need to know why they have been smuggled into the country, what they're doing in the country." The chief spokesperson of New York City's police department, Michael O'Looney, immediately announced that police have "increased their counterterrorist efforts" while, elsewhere, around the country, security was stepped up at "icon sites."[35]

But the vagueness of the "counterterrorist effort" and "potential terrorist activities" generated mass anxieties. Where were these five mysterious suspects who could attack at any given moment? What were their objectives? How could they elude capture? The "Big FBI Story," as CNN newscaster Paula Zahn reported on December 30, became a sensational terrorist possibility as New Year's Eve approached. The suspects were popping up everywhere and yet nowhere, triggering loud alarms of potential vulnerability.[36]

And then, as quickly as it began, the story was over. Nothing happened on New Year's Eve. On January 3, 2003, FBI spokesman Ed Cogswell announced, "There is no border-crossing information that would say they're here . . . and to say they came in from Canada is pure speculation."[37] Four days later, the *New York Times* reported that the FBI had discontinued the search for the five suspects, named in "bad information" from a "jailed tipster"[38] who had sought to "ingratiate" himself with the authorities.[39] The *Times* noted that the FBI nonetheless defended the alert because Canadian border crossings and New Year's attacks are serious realities, illustrated by al Qaeda's millennium attempt to bomb Los Angeles International Airport, foiled only by the perpetrators' capture near Seattle in 1999. The FBI also issued the following statement: "Based on all the information we had, we thought it was necessary to put these photos out there and err on the side of caution. In today's climate, if something had happened and we hadn't done anything, what would the public reaction have been?"[40] (Was the terrorist threat real or was it, as one Royal Canadian Mountie suggested, "a slow week at the White House"?[41])

Media reports during the first week of February 2003 dabbled in potential terrorist activity, even as the chatter level about the impending war in Iraq was rising. On February 6, U.S. intelligence analysts reported a "recent upsurge in possible terrorist threats" and alerted law enforcement to look for "potential Al Qaeda attacks in coming weeks, possibly timed for end of Muslim Hajj pilgrimage or war in Iraq."[42] On February 7, 2003, homeland security secretary Tom Ridge, attorney general John Ashcroft, and FBI director Robert Mueller declared a nationwide "orange alert." Based on "specific intelligence received and analyzed by the full intelligence community," and "corroborated by multiple intelligence sources," they reported that "Joint Terrorism Task Forces have been working 24 hours a day following up on information we *may* have received." The "specific intelligence," as Ashcroft told a press conference that day, was an "increased likelihood" that there would be an attack "in or around the end of Hajj." He "emphasized planning for attacks" on "soft targets," perhaps apartment buildings or hotels, and stated that the recent bombings in Bali, Indonesia, and Kenya "demonstrated continued willingness of Al Qaeda to strike peaceful, innocent civilians." He also cited the recent arrests in London, "where chemical ricin was discovered . . . [which] demonstrated Al Qaeda's interest in carrying out chemical, biological and radiological attacks."[43]

This manipulation of signifiers created anxiety, alarm, and a demand for counterterrorist activity. An orange alert indicates a "high risk of terrorist attacks" and requires that counteractions, precautions, and protective measures be taken by federal, state, and local authorities, as well as the "general public."[44] At the time the alert was issued, Ridge assured the press and public that relevant "information" was being provided to all "local and state law enforcement officials, federal agencies, members of Congress, governors, state homeland security advisers, and mayors" as well as "fire, emergency, health and public safety personnel."[45]

Reactions varied:

> National alert spurred extra patrols on Minnesota's northern border, increased Coast Guard stops along both coasts and added more eyes at theme parks in Florida and California. . . .
>   Massachusetts announced stepped up patrols at Logan International Airport, subways and in the waters off the Atlantic Coast. . . .
>   New York Governor George Pataki said specialized units of state police and the National Guard were activated [to provide] . . . extra security at bridges, tunnels, airports, subways, and many public buildings. . . .
>   Security was increased at the San Onofre [California] nuclear facility. . . .
>   And National Grid, the company that owns Massachusetts Electricity and energy providers in New York, New Hampshire and Rhode Island "asked employees to be extra vigilant."[46]

But what was the public expected to do? Ashcroft and Ridge counseled Americans to "remain aware and remain alert." For what? Where? When? Ridge's response focused on responsibility and protective duty.

> The thought occurred to me, traveling to join my colleagues for this public announcement, that when I step across the threshold of the front door at night I'm not sure I'm seen as the secretary of the Department of Homeland Security; I'm a husband and a father, a parent and a spouse. And I know a lot of parents and spouses are saying, "Well, what should we do? What does this mean for us?" And all I would say to you as a parent and a spouse is, take the time now to get informed.[47]

Was that all? What kind of attack? What should we *do?*[48]

Planning was the key for an event whose form, timing, location, and severity were unknown. To assuage growing levels of concern and frustration, the White House and the Department of Homeland Security released "disaster plans," or "guides," specifying how to respond during particular terrorist threats and "what to do" in response to the heightened terror alert.[49] The guides listed a series of "what to do" in all sorts of disaster situations, but the focal points were biological and chemical threats. The following instructions were issued:

How to prepare for a biological or chemical attack—
  *Assemble a disaster supply kit and be sure to include:
  —Battery-powered commercial radio with extra batteries
  —Nonperishable food and drinking water
  —Roll of duct tape and scissors
  —Plastic for doors, windows, and vents for the room in which you will shelter—this should be an internal room where you can block out air that may contain hazardous chemical or biological agents. To save time during an emergency, sheeting should be premeasured and cut for each opening.
  What to do during a chemical or biological attack—
  *Listen to your radio for instruction from authorities such as whether to remain inside or to evacuate.
  *If you are instructed to remain in your home, the building where you are, or other shelter during a chemical or biological attack:
  —Turn off ventilation, including furnaces, air conditioners, vents and fans
  —Seek shelter in an internal room, preferably one without windows—seal room with duct tape and plastic sheeting—ten square feet of floor space per person will provide sufficient air to prevent carbon dioxide build-up for up to five hours.[50]

But over the three days following the orange alert, uncertainty and fear were further heightened by more government warnings. During a television interview, Ridge assured the public that "the terrorism alert issued last week was 'the most significant' since the 2001 attacks. . . . The threat is real," he affirmed, "[and] we believe the threat has substantially increased in the last couple of weeks." Pressed to hand the public *something*, the Bush administration and Ridge recommended "that people keep a supply of duct tape and plastic sheeting in their homes to seal off windows in the event of a chemical or biological attack."[51] The administration's announcements were supported by a growing number of media reports and speculations. The FBI was searching, yet again, for a *Middle Eastern* man. This time he was Pakistani, which was important as "part of the decision to raise the alert level." And even as the FBI had "no specific information that the man is connected to any potential terrorist activities," hospitals were receiving reports of possible cyanide attacks, and the federal government claimed it had found connections between terrorism and a possible war in Iraq.[52]

The new objects of protection and, arguably, obsession became those of duct tape and plastic (DTP). With nothing else for people to do, it seemed completely rational that "Duct Tape Sales Rise amid Terror Fears"[53] and that New York residents might "consider temporary relocation to motels in New Jersey."[54] Why did the administration suggest DTP? Would DTP really protect you in a biological or chemical attack? Why did people actually buy DTP (the argument as well as the materials)? Among the many articles written after the government's endorsement of DTP, one from the *New York Times* stands out: "Protective Devices; Duct Tape and Plastic Sheeting Can Offer Solace, If Not Real Security."[55]

On the one hand, it seemed ridiculous to purchase the products, because they would not protect you. Randall J. Larsen, director of the nonprofit Anser Institute for Homeland Security in Arlington, Virginia, thought that "if it lowers your blood pressure, go ahead and do it, but do everything else first. . . . I don't think there's enough information out there for people to be locking themselves in airtight rooms." Dr. Monica Schoch-Spana, a senior fellow at the Johns Hopkins Center for Civilian Biodefense Strategies, explained that the utility of a "safe room" would be nil in a biological attack: "You won't be tipped off that something's going to happen. . . . You wouldn't have time to get that in place."[56]

On the other hand, the American Red Cross, ahead of the game, had recommended inclusion of DTP in an emergency safety kit "for a decade." David Paulison, a U.S. fire administrator in the Greater Washington, D.C., area advised the purchase of duct tape, plastic, and other emergency items because of the growing concerns of "Al Qaeda's interest in acquiring weapons of mass destruction." He believed that because "aid after an attack could be hard to come by," during "the first 48 to 72 hours of an emergency, many Americans will likely have to look after themselves."[57] Dr. John H. Sorensen, scientist from Oak Ridge National Laboratory and coauthor of the provocatively titled *Will Duct Tape and Plastic Really Work?*, written in 2001 for the Federal Emergency Management Agency, averred, "We think that from a purely engineering standpoint, they are effective. . . . Every little bit helps. What we don't know a lot about is how good people are at putting them up." The article continued:

> Though there is no direct evidence that a room sealed with duct tape and plastic would increase the chances of survival, experiments have indicated that chemical warfare agents take at least several hours to seep through such a seal. Some real-home trials found that sealing doors, windows and vents reduced airflow into the room by up to two-thirds. Even then, however, outside air completely cycled through the room within hours. . . . In the tests, some people were able to seal rooms in a few minutes; others took nearly 40 minutes.[58]

For those not sure about their abilities, companies such as the Regional Environmental Hazard Containment Corporation (based near Washington, D.C., but apparently an Israeli company with practical experience in such matters) made available inflatable plastic "safe rooms" for $3,200 to $5,000. Lester Lewis, a company executive, assured the *New York Times* that not only were they "getting more inquiries" but that they even had "sold some."[59]

The mutual production and reproduction of the discourse continued. To justify advice about seemingly useless protection, media reports focused on CIA director George Tenet's announcement that Osama bin Laden's most recent taped message was "similar" to previous statements made in 2001, which were followed by "deadly terrorist strikes against American and other targets overseas."[60] The arrest of two *Pakistani* men at the Canadian border in possession of "a container with perhaps a half a pound of a white powder and tools described as being consistent with those used in bomb-making, including wire cutters and Casio digital watches" was also widely reported.[61] Security continued to heighten, and people continued to buy and debate about DTP despite the fact that there was a greater "risk of dying in a car accident while driving to buy duct tape" than "dying because you lacked duct tape."[62] Now, homeland security kits, containing one hundred feet of plastic sheeting and a sixty-yard roll of duct tape, could be bought on eBay for $15.00 plus $15.80 for shipping and handling.[63] American counterterrorist efforts had successfully helped create "Panic City, USA," inducing the public to reproduce the discourse.[64] Finally, the end of the cycle arrived. The success of "getting through the week" enabled the Bush administration to reduce the alert level back to yellow on February 27, warning, however, that Americans needed to "continue to be defiant and alert." Ashcroft and Ridge both declared that "Al Qaeda will wait until it believes Americans are less vigilant and less prepared before it will strike again."[65] Not long after, the United States attacked Iraq, citing as one of its reasons linkages between the regime of Saddam Hussein and Al Qaeda and offering the possibility that the former might give weapons of mass destruction to the latter.

But vigilance is the cost of freedom. On September 5, 2003, the FBI issued a global alert seeking information on four Muslim Middle Eastern individuals "after intelligence corroborated by multiple sources, including foreign governments and law enforcement officials, indicated they might be plotting new attacks against the United States." As usual, these warnings were couched in conditional and nonspecific terms: "Federal law enforcement officials . . . have no evidence any are in the United States, but because they have all used false names and travel documents in the past, the possibility cannot be ruled out." The same officials, "speaking on condition of anonymity, cautioned that it was unclear if the four men were working together" and that "there was no information they were involved in a specific terrorist operation."[66] But recognizing perhaps that ridicule did not support the cause, the threat level remained at yellow.

FOLLOW THE MONEY

How, in this atmosphere of threat levels and constant chatter, can counterterrorism operate effectively? Why should anyone believe warnings of the "inevitability" of biological terrorism? And how can a doubting public remain convinced? An informative leaf can be taken from the American experience with Cold War strategic nuclear planning. As Andrew Grossman points out in his study of civil defense during the 1940s and 1950s,

> Information pertaining to nuclear war depended on complicated, abstract, *theoretical* modeling drawn largely from economic science. These formal models were used by civilian and military planners in their development of war-fighting scenarios. However, *since there was no baseline for nuclear war*, formal nuclear war-fighting models were, more often than not, an amalgam of two ontologies: an abstract hypothetical "reality" and the tangible reality of conventional warfare—specifically World War II.[67]

He also writes,

> When planners within the Truman administration reflected on the key role of the domestic population and its essential support for postwar U.S. grand strategy, they made almost no distinction between planning for a real war and planning for a Cold War. The central state's apparatuses for external and internal security worked together to investigate potential and real saboteurs and "fifth columnists" who might be preparing the country for a surprise attack.[68]

One could say that these two processes constituted the organization of a discourse that posited the inevitability of nuclear war, as depicted by the models, and required the selling of the need for constant mobilization to the population, threatened from not only external enemies but also internal ones.

Grossman argues that the state's proffering of this type of discourse is, at least in part, a consequence of the tension between democracy at home and threats from abroad. Democracy and liberalism cannot be allowed to stand in the way of national security and emergency planning. In a "state of emergency" (or "state of exception," as Carl Schmitt puts it in his critique of the Weimer Republic in the 1920s), security must come first. As Grossman frames the argument of the national authorities, "When state survival is measured against liberal constitutional protection of the individual, individual rights, and political parties, state survival supercedes all constitutional protection."[69] The agencies of the state must therefore overplay potential threats in order to receive public approval for antiliberal actions, claiming that these actions are essential to national survival.

Although Grossman's analysis seems on the mark, it offers only half of the story, saying nothing about political economy. There are two reasons for this omission. First, during most of the Truman administration, the defense budget was rather small, especially in comparison to wartime expenditures. Not until after the outbreak of the Korean War did defense spending rise from about $12 billion to $50 billion, much of which went for rearmament in Europe rather than the fighting in Asia. Second, in the late 1940s, the state's legitimacy was not as tightly linked to the economy as it is today. Keynesianism was only beginning to be institutionalized, and the market did not play the dominant social and cultural roles that it has come to occupy over the last two decades. Nor was the defense sector a central structural support for the national economy that it has since come to be. There was, to be sure, a "political economy" at work, but it was not yet completely a "capitalist tool."

Today, the legitimacy of the state is both more complex and more fragile. The attacks on Washington and New York were aimed at symbols of the homeland and did not seek to destroy the homeland itself. But the homeland has come to represent global capitalism as well as America's presence abroad (more people are exposed to the United States' commercial products and institutions than to its military power, although that might change in the future). The attacks on the Pentagon and the World Trade Center thus struck at the heart of the American state, protector not only of domestic society but also of global capitalism. The state cannot simply defend the economic system through military means: attempting to do so would confirm widespread cynicism about whose interests the government seeks to protect. It must, therefore, generate the conditions that make it possible to protect capitalism in the course of protecting society—hence, the never-ending "war on terrorism."

It is either ironic or inevitable that capitalist huckstering becomes the mode through which the manufacture of discourse, production of danger, and peddling of fear take place. After all, products promising to deal with the most mundane threats to everyday life are bought, guilelessly, all the time. Bad breath? Foot odor? Unstylish auto? Better be safe than sorry! Still, there's a limit to what even American consumers will believe and, aside from made-for-television disaster movies, Madison Avenue has yet to find a way to fully commodify imagined catastrophes. *Caveat emptor!*

NOTES

An earlier version of this chapter was published as "The Militarization of Inner Space," *Critical Sociology* 30, no. 2 (2004): 451–81.

The epigraphs to this chapter were taken from W. Seth Carus, *Bioterrorism and Biocrimes—the Illicit Use of Biological Agents in the 20th Century* (Washington, D.C.: Center for Counterproliferation Research, National Defense University, 1998), 9; and Paul S. Mead et. al., "Food-Related Illness and Death in the United States," *Emerging Infectious Diseases* 5, no. 5 (September–October 1999): 607–25.

1. William Miller, "Rajneeshpuram, 1981–1985—When It Was Crazy" (2001), www.empirenet.net/imageworks/Raj1.htm (accessed September 10, 2003).

2. Carus, *Bioterrorism*, 9.

3. Joshua Lederberg, ed., *Biological Weapons—Limiting the Threat* (Cambridge, Mass.: MIT Press, 1999). W. Seth Carus, "The Rajneeshees (1984)," in *Toxic Terror—*

Assessing Terrorist Use of Chemical and Biological Weapons, ed. Jonathan B. Tucker (Cambridge, Mass.: MIT Press, 2000), 115–37.

4. Judith Miller, Stephen Engelberg, and William Broad, *Germs: Biological Weapons and America's Secret War* (New York: Simon and Schuster, 2001).

5. The number of hoaxes was, however, quite large. Between October 1998 and October 2001, one scientist counted 120 anthrax hoaxes reported in the U.S. media. Paul Sperry, "Experts Debunk Bioterror Myths," *WorldNetDaily*, October 4, 2001, www .worldnetdaily.com/news/article.asp?ARTICLE_ID=24785 (accessed September 2, 2003). Between September 11 and December 22, 2001, fifty-eight individuals were arrested on charges of making anthrax hoaxes or threats. Karen Gullo, Associated Press, "For Anthrax Hoax Suspects, Arrests, Charges Are No Joke," December 22, 2001, http://multimedia.belointeractive.com/attack/bioterror/1222hoax.html (accessed September 2, 2003).

6. Biological agents are only one of the unholy trinity of "weapons of mass destruction" (WMD), along with nuclear and chemical agents (the three are frequently labeled CBN). A crude Google search of the Internet (March 8, 2005) using various combinations and search strategies reveals the following hits: terrorism, 17,100,000 websites; biological terrorism, 1,310,000; nuclear terrorism, 2,980,000; chemical terrorism, 1,540,000.

7. Peter Drahos, *Information Feudalism*, with John Braithwaite (New York: New Press, 2003).

8. Michael Dawson, *The Consumer Trap—Big Business Marketing in American Life* (Urbana: University of Illinois Press, 2003).

9. Michel Foucault, *Discipline and Punish—the Birth of the Prison*, trans. Alan Sheridan (New York: Vintage Press, 1977), 102.

10. Stuart Hall, "The West and the Rest: Discourse and Power," in *Modernity—an Introduction to Modern Societies*, ed. Stuart Hall et al. (Cambridge: Polity Press, 1995), 201.

11. Karen Litfin, *Ozone Discourses—Science and Politics in Global Environmental Cooperation* (New York: Columbia University Press, 1994), 13.

12. Antonio Gramsci, *Selections from the Prison Notebooks*, trans. Q. N.-S. Hoare (New York: International Publishers, 1971); and Stephen Gill, ed., *Gramsci, Historical Materialism and International Relations* (Cambridge: Cambridge University Press, 1993).

13. Ole Waever, "Securitization and Desecuritization," in *On Security*, ed. Ronnie D. Lipschutz (New York: Columbia University Press, 1995), 46–86.

14. For example, nuclear deterrence during the Cold War may have "worked" either because of fear of retaliation, beliefs about nuclear weapons' disutility in war, norms about the morality of using them, or all three.

15. Thomas Kuhn, *The Structure of Scientific Revolutions* (Chicago: University of Chicago Press, 1962).

16. Andrew D. Grossman, *Neither Dead nor Red—Civilian Defense and American Political Development during the Early Cold War* (London: Routledge, 2001).

17. Foucault, *Discipline and Punish*, 304, 308; and Hall, "West and the Rest," 204.

18. Mitchell Dean, *Governmentality—Power and Rule in Modern Society* (London: Sage, 1999), 171–72.

19. Harold Lasswell, *Politics: Who Gets What, When, How* (New York: P. Smith, 1936).

20. Drahos, *Information Feudalism.*

21. Note that this is not the same as arguing that the material base determines the social superstructure. The three elements in discourse—beliefs, practices, outcomes—are codetermining.

22. All who write about terrorism make an effort to define the term yet find it difficult to do so, especially inasmuch as there are over one hundred distinct uses recorded in the literature. The superfluity of definitions may be more a reflection of the epistemologies and proclivities of the individual author and the genealogy of the term than the refusal of "terrorists" themselves to conduct their practices in a specified fashion. Some try to finesse the problem, as has Harvey W. Kushner, by suggesting that they know terrorism when they see it: "Nowadays, a considerable number of books devoted to terrorism spend an inordinate amount of time discussing how difficult it is to define the concept. Guess what? Readers are usually left more confused than before they started. The authors who contributed to this book did not become bogged down in a morass of verbiage in trying to craft the universal definition of terrorism. They chose instead to discuss terrorism without detailed discussions about the problem with the problem definition." *The Future of Terrorism: Violence in the New Millennium,* ed. Harvey W. Kushner (Thousand Oaks, Calif.: Sage, 1998), vii.

23. Stacy Finz, "Activists See More Violence from Extreme Protestors," *San Francisco Chronicle,* September 6, 2003, www.sfgate.com/cgibin/article.cgi?file/chronicle/archive/2003/09/06/MN258847.DTL (accessed September 9, 2003).

24. Ronnie Lipschutz, "Terror in the Suites: Narratives of Fear and the Political Economy of Danger," *Global Society* 13, no. 4 (1999): 411–39; Heather Turcotte and Ronnie Lipschutz, "States of Terror: Framing Threats and Selling Texts" (paper presented at the forty-sixth annual convention of the International Studies Association, Honolulu, Hawaii, March 1–5, 2005).

25. Michel Foucault, *The Essential Foucault,* ed. Paul Rabinow and Nikolas Rose (New York: New Press, 2003), 262.

26. According to one report, 87 percent of the 776 attacks against U.S. interests between 1998 and 2002 involved bombs. Laura Parker, "Terrorists' Most Likely Weapons Here? Bombs," *USA Today,* May 15, 2003, www.usatoday.com/news/nation/2003-05-15-bombs-cover_x.htm (accessed September 2, 2003).

27. The problem of risk assessment is a complicated one. Most risk analysis assumes "rational action" in response to quantified risk data. For example, although the risk of injury or death is much higher from auto than air travel, people generally regard the latter as being more dangerous. But most people drive all the time without experiencing an auto accident. They fly much less often and have only a limited experiential basis on which to assess the risks of flight. What they know comes mostly from media reports about plane crashes.

28. Eric Lichtblau, "Ashcroft's Tour Rallies Supporters and Detractors," *New York Times,* September 8, 2003, www.nytimes.com/2003/09/08/politics/08ASHC.html (accessed September 8, 2003).

29. William Cohen, "Foreword," in *Biological Weapons—Limiting the Threat,* ed. Joshua Lederberg (Cambridge, Mass.: MIT Press, 1999): xi–xvi.

30. Erin Hallissy, "Livermore Vigilant about Security of Labs, City," *San Francisco Chronicle,* September 9, 2003, 6A, www.sfgate.com/cgi-bin/article.cgi?file=/chronicle/archive/2003/09/09/MN12449.DTL (accessed September 9, 2003).

31. Donald Rumsfeld, "Rumsfeld Baffles Press with 'Unknown Unknowns,'" *ABC News Online* (Australian Broadcasting Corporation), June 7, 2002, www.abc.net.au/news/newsitems/s576186.htm (accessed August 28, 2003).

32. Richard A. Falkenrath, Robert D. Newman, and Bradley A. Thayer, *America's Achilles' Heel—Nuclear, Biological, and Chemical Terrorism and Covert Attack* (Cambridge, Mass.: MIT Press, 1998): 171–72.

33. Falkenrath, Newman, and Thayer, *Achilles' Heel*, 173.

34. Neil Lewis, "FBI Issues Alert for Five Illegal Immigrants Uncovered in Investigation of Terrorism," *New York Times*, December 30, 2002, 9A.

35. The *New York Times* reported similar false identification of Mustafa Khan Owasi but did not acknowledge another name for the misidentified suspect. Eric Lichtblau, "Search for 5 Mideast Immigrants Was Based on Made-Up Story, FBI Says," *New York Times*, January 8, 2003, 11A.

36. The bad information included false identification of one of the suspects. Mustafa Khan Owasi, a Pakistani jeweler in Lahore, claimed he never visited the United States and that his real name is Mohammed Asghar. Peter Cheney and Victor Malarek, "The Case of the Five Vanishing Suspects," *Globe and Mail* (Toronto), January 4, 2003, www.globeandmail.com/servlet/articlenews/printarticle/gam/20030104/ufiven (accessed August 25, 2003).

37. Cheney and Malarek, "Five Vanishing Suspects."

38. The tipster was detained informant Michael John Hamdani. Hamdani was arrested in Canada in October 2002 for fraud charges where Canadian officials found fake passports, immigration documents, and counterfeit traveler's checks. United Press International, "FBI Removes Pictures of Five Suspects," January 7, 2003, www.newsmax.com/arch/2003/01/07/top4.htm (accessed August 28, 2003).

39. Cheney and Malarek, "Five Vanishing Suspects."

40. Lichtblau, "Search for 5 Mideast Immigrants," 11A.

41. Cheney and Malarek, "Five Vanishing Suspects."

42. Eric Lichtblau and David Johnston, "Alerts, Confidential Advisory Warns Officials of Rise in Possible Terror Threats," *New York Times*, February 6, 2003, 23A.

43. "Ashcroft, Ridge, Mueller Announce Threat Level Increase," *CNN*, February 7, 2003, www.edition.cnn.com/2003/us/02/07/threat.transcript/index.html (accessed August 28, 2003); "Excerpts from Ashcroft-Ridge News Conference on the Level of Danger," *New York Times*, February 8, 2003, final, 7A.

44. White House, "Are You Ready?" White House press release, February 7, 2003, www.whitehouse.gov/news/releases/2003/02/print/20030207-10.html (accessed August 25, 2003).

45. "Ashcroft, Ridge, Mueller."

46. "From Borders to Hotels, Security Up another Notch," *CNN*, February 7, 2003, http://edition.cnn.com/2003/us/02/07/alert.reax.ap/index.html (accessed August 28, 2003).

47. "From Borders to Hotels."

48. Sandman and Lanard analyze five polled responses to the advice: the mocking response, the fearful/dependent response, the numb/counterdependent response, the political response, and the skeptical/distrustful response. Peter Sandman and Jody Lanard, "Duct Tape Risk Communication," February 19, 2003, www.psandman.com/col/ducttape.htm (accessed August 25, 2003).

49. White House, "Are You Ready?"; "From Borders to Hotels"; Bruce Berkowitz, "Terror Alert 'To Do' List," *CNN*, February 7, 2003, http.edition.cnn.com/2003/us/02/07/alert.whatto.do.ap/index.html (accessed August 28, 2003).

50. White House, "Are You Ready?"

51. Philip Shennon, "Precautions; Administration Gives Advice on How to Prepare for a Terrorist Attack," *New York Times*, February 11, 2003, 16A.

52. Eric Lichtblau and David Johnston, "Alerts, Confidential Advisory Warns Officials of Rise in Possible Terror Threats," *New York Times*, February 6, 2003, 23A. Tina Kelley, "Medical Center Issues Memo on Possible Cyanide Threat," *New York Times*, February 11, 2003, 21A.

53. Jeanne Meserve, "Duct Tape Sales Rise amid Terror Fears," *CNN*, February 11, 2003, http://edition.cnn.com/2003/us/02/11/emergency.supplies (accessed August 28, 2003).

54. N. R. Kleinfield, "With Eyes and Noses Open, New York Lives with Threat," *New York Times*, February 11, 2003, 1A.

55. Kenneth W. Chang and Judith Miller, "Protective Devices—Duct Tape and Plastic Sheeting Can Offer Solace, If Not Real Security," *New York Times*, February 11, 2003, 21A.

56. Chang and Miller, "Protective Devices," 21A. John Leland, "Unraveling Duct Tape, Warts and All," *New York Times*, February 16, 2003, 1(9).

57. David Paulison, quoted in Chang and Miller, "Protective Devices," 21A.

58. John H. Sorenson, quoted in Chang and Miller, "Protective Devices," 21A.

59. Meserve, "Duct Tape Sales Rise."

60. David Johnston, "Intelligence; Bin Laden Tape May Hint at Attack, CIA Says," *New York Times*, February 13, 2003, final, 1A. Berkowitz discusses why intercepted communications are difficult to analyze. Bruce Berkowitz, "Terrorists' Talk; Why All That Chatter Doesn't Tell Us Much," *New York Times*, February 16, 2003, 5(4); Berkowitz, "Terror Alert 'To Do' List"; Berkowitz, "Official: Credible Threats Pushed Terror Alert Higher: FBI Seeking Pakistani Man for Questioning," February 9, 2003, http://edition.cnn.com/2003/us/02/07/threat.level/index.html (accessed August 28, 2003).

61. Adrian Humphreys and Stewart Bell, "White Powder, Tools Raise Border Alarm: Two Men Arrested after Incident at Bridge from US," *National Post*, February 15, 2003, www.drumbeat.mlaterz.net/Jan%20Feb%202003/2%20pakistanis%20arrested%20atborder.html (accessed August 25, 2003).

62. Gregg Easterbrook, "Home Security—the Smart Way to Be Scared," *New York Times*, February 16, 2003, 1(4).

63. Jeffrey Selingo, "For Some, the Jitters Help the Bottom Line," *New York Times*, February 20, 2003, 5G.

64. Mary McGrory, "Panic City, USA," *Washington Post,* February 16, 2003, www.washingtonpost.com/ac2/wp-dyn/A10604–2003feb14.htm (August 28, 2003).

65. John Lumpkin, "Terror Alert Level Lowered to Yellow," *Chicago Tribune*, February 27, 2003, www.chicagotribune.com/news/nationworld/sns-terror-alert,0,113028.story?coll=chi-newsbreaking-hed (accessed August 28, 2003).

66. Curt Anderson, "FBI Issues Worldwide Alert in Possible Terror Plots Involving Four Linked to Al-Qaida," Associated Press, September 5, 2003, www.sfgate.com/

cgi-bin/article.cgi?file=/news/archive/2003/09/05/national1634EDT0683.DTL (accessed September 8, 2003).

67. Grossman, *Neither Red nor Dead*, 4 (first italics in original, second added).

68. Grossman, *Neither Red nor Dead*, 12.

69. Grossman, *Neither Red nor Dead*, 111. This is also the rationale for torture at Guantanamo and Abu Ghraib.

3

Making Civilian-Soldiers:
The Militarization of Inner Space

Jackie Orr

OPERATION SCRAMBLE

WARNING: The following statement may contain secret coded messages intended to reach any of my allies who may reside within your borders.[1]

"Every American is a soldier" now, declared George W. Bush one month after September 11, 2001.[2] Speaking at the inaugural meeting of the Homeland Security Council, whose opening order of business was to beef up U.S. border operations by tightening immigration surveillance and control, Mr. Bush's pronouncement itself performed a consequential border crossing. His sweeping rhetorical induction of the entire U.S. citizenry into the ranks of military combatants obliterated the very boundary between "civilian" and "soldier" on which popular understandings of "terrorism" fundamentally depend: would future attacks on U.S. civilians now be acknowledged as a targeted assault on U.S. soldiers? Mr. Bush's border transgression, conducted in the midst and in the name of intensified border patrols, raises a few other urgent questions for the newly anointed civilian-soldier:

When was I trained for battle?

What are my weapons, and how do they work?

And where, precisely, stands this "home" that the new armies of civilians are asked to secure? Which borders are we really being asked to defend? What exactly is this war into which we have been involuntarily drafted?

The "war against terrorism" is the repetitiously proffered answer to this last query. But a little bit of history and the website of the U.S. Space Command suggest another story. The U.S. Space Command was established in 1985 as the coordinating military body unifying army, navy, and air force activities in

47

outer space. In *Joint Vision 2010*, the operational plan for securing and maintaining unchallengeable "space power," the U.S. Space Command describes how "the medium of space is the fourth medium of warfare—along with land, sea, and air." The end result of the pursuit of "space power" is the achievement of Full Spectrum Dominance or the capacity of the U.S. military to dominate "across the full spectrum of conflict," waged in any terrestrial or extraterrestrial medium.[3]

The battles for which the U.S. Space Command is prepared are not futuristic science-fiction scenarios. Satellite-mediated infotech warfare has arrived. The real-time military use of space-based satellites debuted in the U.S. invasion of Panama in 1989 and expanded during the first U.S.-led attack on Iraq in 1991 and in the killing fields of Kosovo.[4] In the current invasion and attempted military occupation of Iraq, "space-aided warfare" wires together U.S. military command centers from Virginia to Saudi Arabia with human soldiers on the ground and automated, unmanned planes in the air to create flexible networks of vision and destruction.[5] In the fall of 2004, the Pentagon announced the building of a global "war net" that will link space-based intelligence and communications satellites to new weapons technologies and to commanders and soldiers in the battlefield. The consortium of U.S. military contractors and information technology companies (including Microsoft, Sun Microsystems, Hewlett-Packard, and IBM) selected to develop the necessary technologies— with an estimated $24 billion budget over the next five years—plans to "weave weapons, intelligence, and communications into a seamless web," a web conceptually anchored in the ever less ethereal void of space.[6] Home to the imperial technohallucinations of a planetary war net, to an increasingly sophisticated and expensive infrastructure of satellites, and to a proposed network of (possibly nuclear-powered) space stations equipped with laser weaponry, "outer space" emerges as the U.S. military's final, fantastic frontier.

With Full Spectrum Dominance as its official doctrine, the U.S. Space Command clearly articulates its twenty-first-century mission: to ensure that the United States will remain a global power and exert global leadership during the current "globalization of the world economy."[7] The U.S. Space Command stands ready to serve. And we—we civilian-soldiers—where do we stand? In what space really do we wage our scrambled warfare, our civilian participation in the militarized state of the nation? Are we all soldiers now, in the battle for Full Spectrum Dominance of the globe? South Asia. Eurasia. East Asia. Central Asia. What boot camp has prepared us for the rigors of a perpetually ambiguous, infinitely expanding battlefield? Mosul. Ramadi. Najaf. Fallujah. Across what geography is the "war against terrorism" really mapped? In how many dimensions must today's civilian-soldier really move?

The Bush administration's first National Security Strategy document, published in September 2002, offers the inquiring civilian-soldier some indication of the full scope of the battle plans. Twelve months after launching its boundless war against terrorism, the administration introduced its new doctrine of preemptive strikes, unilaterally pursued, against the "perception" of threat. National security now depends, the civilian-soldier learns, on "identifying and destroying the threat before it reaches our borders. . . . We will not hesitate to act alone, if necessary, to exercise our right of self-defense by acting preemptively."[8] Released just as the Bush administration stepped up preparations for the invasion of Iraq, the document leads even mainstream media commentators to note, with measured alarm, its imperial posture. An editorial in the *Atlanta Journal-Constitution* calls the National Security Strategy statement a "plan for permanent U.S. military and economic domination of every region on the globe," with the war against Iraq marking "the official emergence of the United States as a full-fledged global empire."[9] By the November 2004 elections, when George Bush secures another four years of executive power, a significant stream of public political discourse embraces the "American empire" as a given: the question is no longer whether the U.S. is an empire but whether it can be a beloved—and cost-effective—empire.[10]

If the militarization of outer space is an essential component of Full Spectrum Dominance, and if the so-called war against terrorism must be situated within broader U.S. ambitions for global empire,[11] it is perhaps useful for today's civilian-soldier to wonder just how wide and deep a "full spectrum" of dominance is. Does dominion in outer space require the militarization of a somewhat more covert spatial territory—a territory more spectral and less smoothly operationalized but no less necessary to an extraterrestrial empire? What kind of militarized infrastructure is needed "inside" the soldierly civilian called upon to support the establishment of military superiority across the spectrum of spaces "outside"?

The psychology of the civilian-soldier, the networks of everyday emotional and perceptual relations, constitute an "inner space" that is today, I suggest, one volatile site of attempted military occupation. But the occupying forces I am concerned with here are not those of an invasive, enemy "other." Rather, a partial and urgent history of how the U.S. government, media, military, and academy has enlisted the psychological life of U.S. citizens as a military asset—this is the embodied story that occupies me here.

The militarization of inner space is now, as it has been before, a major concern of those responsible for the business of war. Militarization, defined by historian Michael Geyer as "the contradictory and tense social process in which civil society organizes itself for the production of violence," constitutes at its core a border-crossing between military and civilian institutions, activities, and aims. [12] The militarization of inner space can be conceived, then, as the psychological organization of civil society for the production of violence. It is not my intention to reify psychology or psychological processes as if they could be separated from social, historical, or economic contexts. Quite the contrary. My hope is to deepen contestations over the "space" of psychology as the radically social matter of political struggle, as one radically material weapon of war. Or its refusal.

While I refer to this psychological space as "inner," it is of course not irreducibly individual and is never confined to a neat interiority. Inner space both produces and is produced by deeply social ways of seeing, profoundly cultural technologies of perception. And though I want to reject any notion of a homogeneous collective psyche, I do want to conjure the dense sociality and historicity of psychology spaces. Psychological life occupies a difficult borderland, a "between-space" where the question and human confusions of what is "inner" and "outer" are repetitiously experienced and consciously and unconsciously lived. Indeed, the space of psychology is the very site where everyday sensations of what's "inside" and what's "outside," what's "them" and what's "us," what feels safe and what seems fatally frightening are culturally reproduced or resisted; it is an intensely border-conscious space. The politics of borders—how they are made and unmade, what they come to mean—is one shifting center of the politics of nationalism; of language; of memory; of race, gender, class; of terror. What has come in the modern West to be called the "psychological" plays a dramatic, power-charged role within each of these entangled political fields. The militarization of psychological space can be imagined then as a strategic set of psychological border operations aimed at the organization of civil society for the production of violence.

The historically specific confusion and reconfiguration of the borders between the psyche of the soldier and that of the civilian, between the practice of psychology and the prosecution of war, are the topic of several studies of World War II and its Cold War aftermath. "New languages for speaking about subjectivity," writes Nikolas Rose, emerged during World War II to address the new consensus that "winning the war was to require a concerted attempt to understand and govern the subjectivity of the citizen."[13] Research on "attitudes" and "personality," public opinion polling and statistical survey research, constituted new "sciences of the psyche" aimed at managing both military and civilian beliefs and behaviors; the human psyche itself became "a possible domain for systematic government in the pursuit of socio-political ends."[14] According to historian Laura McEnaney, with the rise of the U.S. national security state, the "ambient militarism" of Cold War culture translated the very meaning of national security into a "perception, a state of mind"—a profoundly psychological state in which the civilian psyche became a difficult but pervasive variable in military planning.[15] Ellen Herman recounts how efforts at "mass emotional control" in the name of national security led, by the late 1960s, to an unprecedented blurring of boundaries between public policy and private emotions.[16]

Today, one important contributing factor to civilian-soldiers' willingness to serve may be a sanctioned ignorance of this history of previous campaigns to effectively mobilize "inner space" in the interests of war and the organized production of violence. Remembering the militarization of psychic space as part of the full spectrum of tactics deployed in twentieth-century warfare may help us better grasp the multiple dimensions of danger in the present, post–September 11 contagion of terrors. "What one remembers of the past and how one remembers it depend on the social and cultural resources to which one has access," writes Fred Turner in his recent history of collective memory-making, cultural trauma, and the Vietnam War.[17] Consider this text as one attempt at a public remembrance of how the inner space of psychology has been already a calculated battlefield, a terrain of cultural combat where the measure of victory includes the possibility, or impossibility, of re-membering that a fight took place.

An orbiting U.S. doctrine of Full Spectrum Dominance calls for critical terrestrial practices of full spectrum demilitarization. Economy. Culture. Society. Psyche. Perhaps it is time for a few collective flashbacks. How hard would it be to publicly remember the civilian-soldier as a central, contested figure of twentieth-century hot and cold wars? What difference could it make to reframe and refuse today's "war against terrorism" as the most recent theater of operations for securing the psychological organization of U.S. civil society for the manufacture of mass violence? Insisting on a border-crossing between the past and present tense, asking you to live briefly in the question of the boundaries between "then" and "now," this text tries to contribute to an effective history of the present—one that might arrive in time for the fight for less-terrorizing future spaces.

TARGET YOU

At a time of national crisis, I think it is particularly apparent that we need to encourage the study of our past.

—Lynne Cheney (October 5, 2001)[18]

The concept of the U.S. civilian-soldier is at least as old as a New World conquered in part by volunteer armies of white settlers and constitutionally founded on the right to own lethal weapons. But not until the advent of twentieth-century military and communications technologies did certain contours of today's civilian-soldier begin to take shape. Terrorists, we are told, have training camps. The twenty-first-century civilian-soldier does, too. World War II and the early years of Cold War U.S. culture, I suggest, supplied one not-so-secret training camp where the civilian-soldier was experimentally shaped by not-so-civil lessons in "total war."

London. Dresden. Tokyo. Hiroshima. Nagasaki.

Launched during World War II to name the new strategic situation in which the civilian home front became as important militarily as the frontlines of battle, the notion of "total war" officially drafts the U.S. civilian-soldier into an active psychological role in the conduct of successful war.[19] In a special 1941 issue of the *American Journal of Sociology*, published on the eve of U.S. entry into World War II and devoted to the problem of civilian morale, sociologist Robert E. Park observes,

> Since war has invaded the realm of the spirit, morale has assumed a new importance in both war and peace. Total war is now an enterprise so colossal that belligerent nations find it necessary not only to mobilize all their resources, material and moral, but to make present peace little more than a preparation for future war. Under these conditions so-called psychic warfare . . . has assumed an importance and achieved a technical efficiency which . . . has profoundly altered the character of peace, making it much harder to bear.
>
>   The object of attack in psychic warfare is morale, and less that of the men in arms than of the civil population back of the lines.[20]

The wartime preoccupation with civilian morale marks an official recognition by the U.S. government and its professional knowledge makers that, as Ellen Herman writes, "the human personality and its diverse and unpredictable mental states were of utmost importance in prosecuting the war."[21] The problem of morale receives enormous, well-funded attention in the United States throughout the war years and becomes a pivotal concept in the construction of the ideal twentieth-century U.S. civilian-soldier.

Faced with the emergent challenges of total psychic warfare—in which the boundaries between soldier and civilian, home and combat zone, war and peace, are set spinning—U.S. social scientists in the *American Journal of Sociology* actively mobilize their civilian resources. Noted psychiatrist Harry Stack Sullivan argues for a program of "total defense" to be waged equally by the U.S. citizen and the military conscript. Preventing civilian demoralization in the United States will require, he urges, a suspension of democratic ideals and a reeducation in the "rigid discipline" of a distinctly "authoritarian" society. If the successful redisciplining of the population can be achieved, Sullivan writes, "we will then . . . have time and ingenuity to work out a little strategy of terror of our own."[22]

But most voices in the 1941 issue call for more "democratic" methods to maintain the psychological fortitude of the civilian-soldier. In a report on government-sponsored research on citizens' attitudes and opinions, sociologist Edward A. Shils identifies the kind of "'intelligence' activities" that distinguish a democratic government's efforts to shape civilian behavior from more overtly authoritarian information gathering: "For a democratic government which regards preferences not merely as objects to be manipulated but as a source of guidance . . . it is especially urgent to possess means of acquiring knowledge of the state of mind of its citizens." Shils celebrates the recent techniques of public opinion polling and survey research as intelligence activities befitting a democratic state. Reliable information about citizens' "state of mind" is a prerequisite for the government's effective management of "the population whose behavior it seeks to influence."[23] The social sciences—which, in close collaboration with market researchers, have by the early 1940s started to develop statistical techniques for gathering precisely such information—thus carve out for themselves a key role in the political administration of civilian psychology. Indeed, with the U.S. entry into the war, hundreds of sociologists, psychologists, anthropologists, and educators form a "new breed of policy-oriented psychological experts," employed by civilian and military agencies to study human attitudes, behavior, opinions, and emotions.[24]

Two entangled technological developments in the first half of the twentieth century create the historical context in which the psychology of the civilian home front becomes an obsessive variable in the political calculus of war. Both developments involve enhanced and accelerated "delivery systems"—for weapons and for words. Both developments heighten the permeability of geographic and psychological borders. First, the invention and deployment of airplanes as instruments of war, making aerial bombardment a key strategy of industrialized warfare, ushered in a new spatial-temporal rhythm of military attack. With virtually no warning, an enemy located many hundreds of miles away could launch an aerial attack on a targeted city. The speed of the attack, combined with the potential intensity of destruction, posed a potent new psychological as well as material threat to the everyday life of civilians.[25] But the delivery system that amplifies most dramatically the volatility —and military significance—of civilian psychology is the crackling black box with the numerical dial sitting in most U.S. households by the mid-1930s. As the first popularized form of electronic mass media, radio radically alters the spatial-temporal rhythm of the production and reception of news and information, erasing previous boundaries of both time and space. When the 1938 radio broadcast of Orson Welles's *War of the Worlds* reportedly creates mass panic among millions of listeners in the United States, news commentators quickly focus on the military implications of radio's power to influence the psychology of a mass audience.[26] While there is general agreement that "radio can spread and radio can control ideas and information essential to national defense," there is no consensus over how this newfound weapon should be wielded.[27] Should the state protect the public from its tendencies toward terror and initiate government control of the radio airwaves as the first line of national defense? Or is government control of radio actually a weapon of totalitarianism, securing a deadly monopoly on this powerful psychological medium? Perhaps most disturbingly, what to make of the potential for this new "delivery system" of words and world events to broadcast theatrics and simulations that can have just as much psychological force as real news? As one news columnist put it, if the electrified radio voice of Adolf Hitler was currently scaring much of Europe to its knees with "an army and an air force to back up his shrieking words," then what to make of the power of Orson Welles's radio theater to "scare thousands into demoralization with nothing at all"?[28]

U.S. social science takes note of the shifting technosocial terrain constructed by new mass communications technologies and their capacity to rapidly mobilize psychological movements. As Princeton psychologist Hadley Cantril writes up *The Invasion From Mars*, his famous study of the 1938 "panic broadcast,"[29] social scientists in the special 1941 issue of the *American Journal of Sociology* also grapple with the influence of mass media on civilian psychology, publishing essays by a movie studio executive and an employee of the National Broadcasting System (NBC). Movie industry executive Walter Wanger asserts that the "builders of morale must weave . . . a fabric of emotion around the rational aspects of democratic life. . . . Men must become emotionalized, to use a clumsy word, about their country and their country's goals." Filmmakers, Wanger promises, can contribute significantly to the national cause.[30]

How exactly will the coordinated efforts of the mass media, social scientists, and government officials to "emotionalize" and manage psychological investments on the civilian front of total war differ from the domestic propaganda techniques of totalitarian governments?[31] "The arts and devices of spiritual warfare are many and various and more subtle no doubt than any analysis has thus far disclosed," Robert E. Park enigmatically observes.[32] As the U.S. civilian-soldier materializes as a strategically conceived combatant in the crucible of a world war mediated by new mass communications technologies, the battle to establish psychological supply lines and defense systems for this most vulnerable and volatile of troops opens out onto an unforeseen future.

DISASTER ON MAIN STREET

America will not live in peace.

—Osama bin Laden (October 7, 2001)[33]

The end of World War II, rather than marking a demilitarization of U.S. civilian-soldiers, signals a deepening anxiety over their psychological and military roles in the sustained tensions and proliferating dangers of the Cold War. With the United States' invention and use of atomic bombs in 1945, the character of industrialized warfare prefigured in aerial bombardment becomes exponentially more terrifying for civilian populations. In their top-secret analysis of U.S. nuclear testing in the South Pacific in 1947, the Joint Chiefs of Staff decide that the primary value of the atomic bomb is its "psychological implication"—that is, its capacity to terrorize and demoralize an enemy population without ever actually being deployed. The panic that would accompany the threat or use of nuclear weapons, they report, is both a key strategic advantage for a nation on the military offensive and a problem of the highest order for the nation planning its own defense.[34] Military victory is ensured for the country best able to exploit this potentially nerve-shattering psychological situation.

In a series of both classified and public documents produced in the late 1940s to address the civil defense problems facing U.S. planners, the findings of the 1947 Joint Chiefs of Staff's evaluation become foundational assumptions for thinking about atomic weapons. Panic and the destruction of national morale are named repeatedly as the main obstacles to the successful conduct of nuclear war. In an early instruction manual subtitled *Panic Control and Prevention*, readers encounter the remarkable claim that "mass panic can produce more damage to life and property than any number of atomic bombs. . . . If war comes, it will be a total, absolute war. Fitness of the civilian will be of equal importance with fitness of the fighter."[35] The psychology of the Cold War U.S. civilian-soldier becomes burdened with nothing less than the success or demise of national security itself. The militarization of civilian psychology takes on a new urgency as national defense is coupled with psychic defenses. In this ongoing "imaginary war" for the civilian psyche, the resources of the U.S. government, the academy, and the corporate mass media all mobilize in an effort to "bring the public psychology into conformity with the requirements of national security policy."[36] The effort is neither a conspiracy nor an ensured success: it is experimental, creative, committed, and sustained. It does not equally target all civilians but rather a dominantly white middle-class, or upwardly mobile working-class, population who owns property, preferably a house, presumably in the suburbs.[37]

In 1951, the fledgling Federal Civil Defense Administration (FCDA) launches "one of the largest mass programs the nation has ever essayed": the public education and training of U.S. civilians in the "proper public attitudes and behavior" necessary to their own defense.[38] Created by presidential executive order, the FCDA's basic mandate, spelled out in the Federal Civil Defense Act of 1950, is to provide for the civilian defense of both life and property in the event of war, including emergency communications networks to warn of enemy attack and the nationwide organization of local volunteer civil defense corps.[39]

A major theme of the FCDA's mass information program underlines the dangers of civilian terror in the face of atomic threat or attack. A civil defense pamphlet written for local municipal leaders reads, "The fear reaction of the uninitiated civilian is . . . of such magnitude that it could well interfere with important military missions or civil defense in time of war."[40] With "Keep Calm!" as its easy-to-remember antidote to atomic panic, the FCDA sponsors a range of print, radio, television, and cinematic messages aimed at advising appropriate behaviors. Over twenty million copies of the FCDA pamphlet *Survival under Atomic Attack* are distributed in 1951. In folksy prose, the text calmly describes how to avoid "losing your head" and panicking, even if an atomic blast catches you unawares and you "soak up a serious dose of explosive radioactivity."[41] During the next several years, the FCDA's mass public education program produces an instructive litany of films, newsreels, and made-for-television series, including *Disaster on Main Street, Operation Scramble, Bombproof, Target You, What You Should Know about Biological Warfare, Take Cover,* and *Let's Face It.*[42]

But alongside government-sponsored encouragements to Cold War civilian-soldiers to "Keep Calm!" an apparently contradictory effort to frighten the U.S. public is simultaneously underway. From its inception, the FCDA identifies "public apathy" as a major obstacle to a successful civilian defense. In a public letter to President Truman in 1952, the first director of the FCDA explains, "Too few realize that the atomic bomb changed the character of warfare and that in future conflicts the man and woman in the street and in the factory will be the prime target—that they will be in the front line of battle."[43]

In the *Report of Project East River* (1952)—an extensive study of the problems of civil defense commissioned by the FCDA and the Department of Defense—the authors cite recent public opinion surveys to argue that "a major barrier to involvement and activity in civil defense" is the public's tendency to believe that an atomic attack cannot really occur in their hometown or that the U.S. military will successfully protect the country should such an attack take place. *Project East River* recommends a massive public information and training program to address public indifference and inculcate civil defense procedures as a "future way of life." Noting a dangerous heightening of military tensions with the Soviet Union, *Project East River* asserts that the entire edifice of national security rests on the psychological fortitude of the civilian population. The public needs to understand that national defense today "transcends the military's ability and responsibility."[44] *Project East River* researchers also consult with the Psychological Strategy Board, an agency established by secret presidential directive in 1951 and charged with the task of designing "psychological operations"—propaganda and psychological warfare planning—against enemies. The public information campaign outlined in *Project East River* can today be read as a retooling of the psychological strategies aimed at enemies abroad, now deployed for use as "emotional management techniques for psychologically manipulating" the U.S. public at home.[45] Public opinion polls, attitude surveys, and personality analyses were the techniques used simultaneously to conduct psychological warfare abroad and to promote "morale" among civilians in the United States.[46] And so the management of fear—avoiding the dangers of its excess (the chaos of panic) or its absence (the unpreparedness of apathy)—becomes a primary aim in constructing the ideal civilian-soldier.[47] In the *Pro-*

ject East River's plan for an informed public inoculated against the threat of mass panic, the encouragement of individual and group fear is acknowledged as a necessary strategy. Under conditions of atomic threat, the boundary between national security and national fear is reconfigured: national security *is* national fear. A nation whose civilians do not fear their own annihilation is a nation without an effective defense system.

But by 1953, according to the picture drawn by public opinion and survey research, little has changed in the psychology of civilian-soldiers: the public continues to be confused and psychologically distanced from the looming dangers of atomic warfare. Researchers summarize survey findings on a public uninterested in learning about the effects of atomic bombs, unaffected by conscious worry about atomic war, with unstable attitudes lacking any "logical structure" or well-developed thinking. Further research and systematic investigation are recommended.[48]

Now it's 1955. The byline reads "Survival City, Nev.," and the news report narrates the highlights of the first atomic bomb dropped on a "typical" U.S. town. Part laboratory experiment, part reality, part mass-mediated spectacle, the incendiary fate of Survival City is broadcast live on CBS and NBC to an estimated audience of one hundred million viewers who tune in to watch the blast. The climactic televising of the explosion is preceded by two weeks of live telecasts three times daily from the test site. The televised nuclear test is designed to demonstrate the ferocity of atomic power and, according to the FCDA, to bring "vast numbers of Americans face to face with the enormity of the problem of survival in the nuclear age."[49] Televised "interviews" with the city's "survivors"—an array of human-size mannequins placed throughout the test site—are carried out before and after the explosion.[50]

The alarming facts of nuclear threat and civilian survival continue in 1956 to be circulated in an array of dramatized forms, with over twenty-two FCDA-sponsored films available for showing on television or in schools and churches. One of the films, *Operation Ivy*, documents the secret military operation carried out in the Marshall Islands on November 1, 1952, when the United States detonates its first hydrogen bomb, producing the largest nuclear fireball in history. Superimposed against the horizon of flame is a replica of Manhattan's skyline: "The fireball alone," the film narrates, "would engulf about one-quarter of the island of Manhattan."

Public release of the *Operation Ivy* film is debated in early 1954 at a National Security Council meeting. Discussion veers from FCDA director Val Peterson's plea for something that could "scare the American people out of their indifference," to President Eisenhower's denouncement of fear tactics and his insistence that the film be aired only if it offers "real and substantial knowledge to the people." For one reason or the other, or perhaps both, *Operation Ivy* makes its public debut on April 2, 1954, and is broadcast repeatedly over television stations throughout the day. In the media package accompanying the film's release, Peterson and the FCDA emphasize the spectacular power of the new weapon while reasserting the capacity of current civil defense strategies to absorb the new threat.[51]

TAKE COVER

A bright line has been drawn between the civil and the savage.

—Attorney General John Ashcroft (September 21, 2001)[52]

But behind the scenes, the FCDA's assessment of the home front situation is not so sanguine. At a National Security Council meeting in January 1954, the FCDA director suggests a new strategy for testing civilians' psychological readiness for World War III. He argues for a nationwide civil defense drill that might serve as a risky but useful measure of the extent to which the U.S. public is indeed "subject to hysteria." The results of the exercise would reveal operational as well as emotional vulnerabilities in the civil defense infrastructure and could aid in more comprehensive civil defense planning. Other council members fear the "psychological impact" such an exercise might have, both in the United States and internationally, and worry over the possibility of producing a public panic.[53]

Ground zero is incinerated in sixty U.S. cities when sixty-one atomic bombs explode on their civilian targets in the early afternoon of Friday, June 15, 1955. The bombs range in explosive force from the equivalent of twenty kilotons to five megatons of TNT. By the end of the day, the massive nuclear attack on the United States kills an estimated eight million people, injures twelve million more, destroys seven million homes, and creates potentially deadly radioactive fallout conditions over approximately sixty-three thousand square miles.[54]

The event is called Operation Alert, a national civil defense simulation exercise designed by the FCDA in cooperation with federal and state agencies, the White House and cabinet members, the broadcast media, the military, organized labor, municipal governments, businesses large and small, and the U.S. public. First organized in 1954, Operation Alert exercises take place each summer for the next four years. These "series of annual rehearsals for World War III," writes Cold War historian Guy Oakes, "enacted simulations of a nuclear attack in an elaborate national sociodrama that combined elements of mobilization for war, disaster relief, the church social, summer camp, and the county fair."[55]

The FCDA's carefully planned protocols for Operation Alert direct each participating city to play out its assigned civil defense scenario as realistically as possible. During the three-day exercise in 1955, over eighty U.S. cities carry out some form of public evacuation. In Memphis, Tennessee, an estimated twenty-five thousand people are evacuated from downtown office buildings. In Atlanta, Georgia, thirty-five hundred government officials are evacuated, with two thousand of them transported outside the city, registered, and fed lunch. In Youngstown, Ohio, the entire city, led by the mayor, evacuates. At the center of the deserted city, "adding realism to the exercise," the 554th Explosive Ordnance Detachment detonates a mock bomb.[56]

But the climactic moment of the 1955 Operation Alert exercise is the three-day evacuation of President Eisenhower, his cabinet, and fifteen thousand federal employees to thirty-one undisclosed locations outside Washington, D.C. Situated somewhere in the mountains of Virginia, the secret emergency headquarters of the president become the preserve of operational continuity for the state after the nuclear obliteration of the nation's capital. Seated inside a makeshift tent before a microphone, President Eisenhower addresses the nation in a live television broadcast announcing the (simulated) nuclear emergency and the continuing survival of the nation.

After a cabinet-level evaluation of Operation Alert in 1956, concern is expressed over how the exercises are affecting public attitudes. President Eisenhower calls for a blue-ribbon panel of social scientists to convene and conduct a "thoroughgoing study of the effect on human attitudes of nuclear weapons." The top-secret report is delivered to the president in November 1956. The panel of experts speaks in a chorus of collective bafflement. They suppose that people are frightened by the dangers of atomic weapons and desire to avoid war. But they are unable to report with any certainty what the new weapons really mean to the U.S. public.[57] In a cabinet discussion held during the course of the extended Operation Alert exercises in 1957, secretary of defense Charles Wilson reports that, due to the realistic simulation of emergency government activities over a period of several weeks, "people were panic stricken in large cities and were paying no attention to Government orders." Any solution to the problem of panic risks exacerbating the potentially explosive mix of the real and the unreal composing the elaborate sociodrama of Operation Alert: if the panic were due to people's confusion over the reality of the simulated emergency operations, then a statement by President Eisenhower clarifying the simulated nature of the operations might calm the public but be mistakenly interpreted by the Soviets as a sign of real preparations for war, thereby touching off a defensive Soviet nuclear offensive. The fake civil defense drill, creating an actual panic, could then explode into a real war caused by the simulated preparations to defend against it.[58]

With the real and the imaginary, the savage attack and the civil defense, survival and extermination, terror and television, and war and its bureaucratic simulation imploding around the heads of U.S. civilian-soldiers throughout the 1950s, what historical sense can be made of this psychological battleground? Vertiginous efforts to regulate civilian psychology in the name of national security become institutionalized, everyday concerns within military and civilian government agencies, the university, and the mass media. The partial history I offer here of a domestic war for civilian psyches suggests that a militarization of psychology has been a self-conscious goal and official aim of U.S. policy for quite some time. And the shape of that militarization, as well as the perceptions and affects promoted by such policies, has not been only about seeding blind aggression or violent arrogance in dominant U.S. culture. Militarizing civilian psyches involves the strategic deployment of fear, a considered risk of panic and terror, and a productive construction of intense vulnerability and insecurity. Perhaps most maddeningly, a militarized civilian psyche is faced with a government that, while avowing its commitment to a secure national defense, wants you to know that it may not be able to protect you at all.[59]

LET'S FACE IT

We're going to start asking a lot of questions that heretofore have not been asked.

—George W. Bush (October 30, 2001)[60]

What role will we assume in the historical relay of violence, who will we become in the response, and will we be furthering or impeding violence by virtue of the response that we make?

—Judith Butler (January 2002)[61]

"Every American is a soldier"—a declaration of psychic and social fortitude announced in the absent shadow of two pillars of world trade, near the cold ashes of the nerve center of U.S. military planning and power. The militarization of inner space that such a proclamation incites and enforces is part of a history of imaginary and real constructions of the ideal U.S. civilian-soldier. Full Spectrum Dominance and its ambition to link a hegemonic multidimensional U.S. military superiority with a global economic reach can be built only within the psychological space of a population that produces the violence demanded by such a blind, visionary conjuring of the future.

The so-called war against terrorism takes its place within this historical theater of cultural wars over militarized and demilitarized psychic zones. But in the current cultural war, what difference does it make to know that once upon a time the U.S. government built and bombed suburban-style houses and their plastic inhabitants, ensuring that the fallout included live television broadcasts from ground zero and social science surveys of public opinion before and after the blast? Does a history of the present cross paths with a theory of politics that would tell us where to go from here, after having once been there?

"A military Babel has risen out of nuclear proliferation and generalized terrorism," writes contemporary theorist and historian of war Paul Virilio. "We're disoriented and can no longer find our way, not even in our theoretical work."[62] That was in 1999. The "we" Virilio invokes may not include all of you. But some of us, well before September 11, 2001, lost our way in the proliferation of real and perceived terrors—and in the difficulty of confidently deciding the border between them. For me, making histories out of not-so-private memories is one way to be lost without losing my mind. For me, making histories of panic and terror is one way to participate, however crazily, in contemporary cultural wars over whether and how psychic spaces will be militarized. Today, for me, it is not surprising to hear Patricia Williams, a "mad" law professor, describe the U.S. war on terrorism as a *"war of the mind,* so broadly defined that the enemy becomes anybody who makes us afraid."[63] I know that war. I have been there before. Its casualties are never precisely calculated, and the archive of its psychic and political effects is always poorly kept.

To historicize, as I try to do here, the call to psychic arms implied in George Bush's appeal to civilian "soldiers," to track how the psychology of U.S. civilian populations became an explicit target of the national security state, is to incite public memories in the place of privatized terrors. In the aftermath of the 1991 U.S.-led war against Iraq, Thyrza Goodeve writes that "making connections . . . thickening the present with future visions and past complexities, forcing edges to rub up against and through their rough boundaries" is one kind of "critical survival strategy" for progressive politics under siege.[64] So what does the present look like when its edges rub against past state- and media-sponsored spectacles of terror?

"Seattle, May 12" the byline reads, and the news article reports at least 150 casualties when a "dirty bomb" packed with radioactive agents explodes in an industrial area of south Seattle in the spring of 2003. "Plumes of toxic smoke fill the air for miles as firefighters in protective chemical suits milled through the scene . . . where overturned buses, police cars and fire engines could be seen, fake victims wandered in a daze, car fires smoldered and a few news helicopters flew overhead in the most extensive terrorism response training in the nation's history," reads the giddy report from ground zero.[65] Organized by the Department of Homeland Security at a cost of $16 million, and prepared for over an eighteen-month period, the simulated terrorist attack involves eighty-five hundred medical, police, fire, rescue, and other personnel nationwide. It is followed the next day by a covert biological attack on Chicago, where volunteer victims start to arrive in city hospitals with flulike symptoms consistent with pneumonic plague.

Manipulating the borders of the real and the imaginary, the present and the future—these are not new tactics in the battle to militarize civilian minds. If the militarization of inner space involves a strategic set of psychological border operations, then collectively remembering Cold War events such as Operation Alert may help us recognize how these borders are once again battlefields inhabited by well-planned theaters of terror and its control. Imploding a possibly horrific future into the tremulous present, radically confusing the real with a tightly choreographed imaginary of catastrophe—these forms of state-sponsored spectacle, networked through channels of mass communication, can be read as a form of domestic psychological warfare. A public memory that such spectacles have been used historically to promote a politically productive fear may offer some U.S. civilians one kind of psychological border defense against such massively mediated attacks.

For all the disturbing resonances increasingly noted by contemporary critics, there is of course no simple correspondence between the culture of the 1950s Cold War and that of today. Both moments involve a transition in the image of the "enemy": from fascism to communism in the early years of the Cold War, and from communism to terrorism today. Both moments see the intensification of authoritarian and repressive domestic politics in the name of routing an enemy who has infiltrated national borders and resides "inside" as well as "outside" the United States.[66] But today's so-called war on terrorism was launched in the wake of an unprecedented, successful attack on U.S. civilian and military targets on September 11, 2001. The context in which a militarization of inner space is taking place today includes—in a dramatic difference from that of the Cold War—the psychological relations to violent injury and mass death experienced "inside" the U.S. borders.

One remarkable feature of the militarization of inner space in the post–September 11 United States is how the language of psychology itself, of emotional and "inner" experience, was immediately deployed in public discourse about the attack and its aftermath. A reductive, repetitive discourse of trauma, healing, and recovery displaced the complicated realities of violent historical and political conflict.[67] A kind of "therapeutic patriotism," mixing political authority and the authority of television news, took hold as the mass media addressed issues such as how to talk to your children, how to manage stress, and how to express grief and mourning and begin the emotional work of healing.[68] Representative Jim McDermott, a psychiatrist, used a meeting of House Democrats in late September 2001 to explain the symptoms of posttraumatic stress disorder and suggest that he, many of his colleagues, and much of the country were probably suffering from it.[69]

The contradiction here is clear: when a highly, historically militarized U.S. civilian population encounters violence against it, produced by others, it has nothing but a psychologized language of inner experience to understand that violence. As feminist theorist Laura Kipnis writes (of the political scene prior to September 11), "With trauma narratives in one sphere occluding historical consciousness in the other, it seems all the more likely that repetition and amnesia are to triumph and prevail as the identificatory modes of citizenship, rolling out the red carpet for creepy political forms."[70] With objects of terror and fear defined in primarily nonpolitical terms, a kind of antipolitics of fear emerges to effectively background the politics of globalization; the politics of oil; the politics of Palestine and Israel; or the haunting politics of a Cold War that played out in many non-Western countries, including Afghanistan, Iran, and Iraq. The "creepy political forms" that Kipnis warns against appear to have arrived. They include a militarization of psychic space that rests in part on an experience of violence as a strictly psychological event. The psychological organization of civilian society for the production of violence proceeds today, it seems, by amputating the psychological experience of traumatizing injury from issues of power or history. This may be one militarized consequence of a "therapeutic culture" or the "therapeutic state," theorized since the 1960s as a new formation of power in which cultural and political authority is wielded by appeal to the psychology of the individual. But, even more ominously, therapeutic culture itself may be one effect of the rise of the national security state and a Cold War obsession with U.S. civilian psychology as a military playing field.[71]

Finally, perhaps most important, efforts to militarize post–September 11 civilian psyches lean heavily on a coded politics of psychological meaning. If militarization always depends on the successful construction of confident borders between an evil "them" and a good "us," then "we" must notice the particular kind of border work being done today by the word *terrorism* itself. "Terrorism" does not only name and condemn specific acts; it also promotes a specific kind of psychological relationship. The word encodes a set of psychological meanings; it not only names but performs a form of self–other relationship. "As a boundary marker, the terrorist at once unsettles and stabilizes, filling a position recently vacated by the Communist in a post–Cold War era," writes Lon Troyer.[72] The unsettling threat of the "terrorist" as radically outside cultural intelligibility and beyond moral understanding secures for the presumably "nonterrorist" self its own moral grounding and cultural membership. The "terrorist" is grotesquely, yet gratifyingly, "other."

The historical fact that the twentieth-century usage of the word *terrorism* emerged in the violent ambiguities of colonial occupation—in the violation of national, racial, ethnic, cultural, sexual, religious, linguistic, economic, and psychological borders—is not coincidental. Used by French colonial forces in the 1950s to name strategies of violent struggle by Algerian guerillas against French domination, the word *terrorism* became a linguistic policing of forms of violence conducted without recourse to nationalized armies or centralized military command.[73] *Terrorism* became a name for the violence deployed by people operating at an enormous military disadvantage, outside the boundaries of a mutually agreed-upon battlefield, who stage their theaters of war—by force and of necessity—inside the realms of everyday life and everyday imagination and everyday fear.

But the purportedly distinguishing features of "terrorism"—that civilians are the direct target of attack and that the attacks are designed to create extreme fear and terror in the broader population—are, as I have tried to show here, a routinely practiced, planned-for feature of twentieth-century warfare. No, the difference between "terrorism" and other forms of violence lies elsewhere. "Terrorists" are a species of civilian-soldier who could not exist without the psychological and historical disavowal by other civilian-soldiers who refuse to remember that the borders between civilian and military, between lethal violence and everyday life, have been breached and are bleeding into almost every psyche, every twenty-first-century civilian-soldier's nightmare of domination or sweet dream of social justice. The boundary that the word *terrorist* really draws is between some civilian-soldiers and certain other civilian-soldiers. Historically, it is often a racialized boundary, sedimented with histories of colonization and economic and symbolic exploitation. Currently in the United States, it is a racialized name used against some civilian-soldiers by other civilian-soldiers who refuse recognition of our own historical and contemporary role in the military manufacture of everyday violence. It is a name used today to mobilize and militarize U.S. civilian psychology for the production of continued, intensified violence—often against other civilians. It is a name used to describe an Iraqi citizen armed with a Kalishnakov rifle whose bullets bounce off the armored skin of a sixty-five-ton U.S. Abrams battle tank rolling through the bombed-out streets of Fallujah. It is a word that promotes violence across unacknowledged borders, in the name of borders that do not exist. It is a secret coded message sending covert psychological instructions through political and historical, ambiguous and bloody networks of terror and fear.

Are we all soldiers now?

Were we all soldiers before?

Are we all terrorists now?

Have we all been terrorists before?

Today, "we" must be attentive and resistant to the variety of border patrols being deployed to sustain the imaginary, as well as the material, violence of "our" not-so-united (psychic) states. Historically speaking, the U.S. civilian-soldier was primarily a white man or woman who lived in a house with a relatively steady income. The complexities of the militarization of psychic space are now being lived out daily—it remains to be seen what difference racial, gender, and class differences can make in the refusal of "our" role as loyal psychic soldiers. The cultural battle today to construct forms of "we" that will not submit "our" inner space to the demands of an ongoing production of violence, to a militarization of everyday life and feeling, is just that, a battle. How to practice other everyday forms of emotional and political collectivity, how to make and to feel other meanings of "we," is today a psychological struggle with enormous military consequences.

NOTES

An earlier version of this chapter was published as "The Militarization of Inner Space," *Critical Sociology* 30, no. 2 (2004): 451–81. My thanks for permission to reprint here in revised form.

1. On October 10, 2001, then U.S. national security advisor Condoleezza Rice made a request to all major television networks to carry only carefully edited versions of future videotaped statements from Osama bin Laden or his "followers." Rice suggested that the broadcasts could be used "to send coded messages to other terrorists." In an unprecedented joint agreement, described by one television executive as a "patriotic" decision, the networks complied. Bill Carter and Felicity Barringer, "Networks Agree to U.S. Request to Edit Future bin Laden Tapes," *New York Times*, October 11, 2001, 1A. See also, Bill Carter, "White House Seeks to Limit Transcripts," *New York Times*, October 12, 2001, 7B.

2. Quoted in Elisabeth Bumiller, "Bush Announces a Crackdown on Visa Violators," *New York Times*, October 30, 2001, 5B.

3. All quotes are from the website of the U.S. Space Command, www. spacecom .af.mil/usspace (December 2001). The website has since been altered, and several of the documents cited here are no longer displayed. Thanks to John Burdick for originally calling my attention to the U.S. Space Command in "Terrorism and State Terror," a public talk presented at the Socialist Forum, Westcott Community Center, Syracuse, New York, October 14, 2001.

4. See Chris Hables Gray, *Postmodern War: The New Politics of Conflict* (New York: Guilford, 1997); and Karl Grossman, *Weapons in Space* (New York: Seven Stories Press, 2001).

5. See William J. Broad, "Allies' Vital Supply Line Now Stretches into Orbit," *New York Times*, March 31, 2003, 10B; Eric Schmitt, "In the Skies over Iraq, Silent Observers Become Futuristic Weapons," *New York Times*, April 18, 2003, 8B; and Eric Schmitt, "6,300 Miles from Iraq, Experts Guide Raids," *New York Times*, June 24, 2003, 13A.

6. Tim Weiner, "Pentagon Envisioning a Costly Internet for War," *New York Times*, November 13, 2004, 1A.

7. From www.spacecom.af.mil/usspace (accessed December 2001).

8. A published version of the document is available as *The National Security Strategy of the United States of America* (Falls Village, Conn.: Winterhouse Editions, 2002).

9. Jay Bookman, "Bush's Real Goal in Iraq," *Atlanta Journal-Constitution*, September 29, 2002, F1. Bookman traces the agenda set out in the 2002 National Security Strategy document to a report published in September 2000 by the conservative

Project for a New American Century (PNAC), whose signatories included Dick Cheney, Donald Rumsfeld, Paul Wolfowitz, I. Lewis Libby, and Elliott Abrams.

10. For a recent critical historical and geopolitical treatment of the question of a U.S. empire, see Jan Nederveen Pieterse, *Globalization or Empire?* (New York: Routledge, 2004).

11. Connections between the ambitions of the "war against terrorism" and the space-based military imperatives of Full Spectrum Dominance are exemplified by the figure of Donald H. Rumsfeld. Until his appointment in December 2000 as secretary of defense, Rumsfeld chaired the Commission to Assess U.S. National Security Space Management and Organization. The commission, charged with constructing a blueprint for the future of U.S. "military space assets," made public its unclassified report in January 2001. Citing the threat of a catastrophic "Space Pearl Harbor," the report argues forcefully and in detail for the prioritization and reorganization of military, intelligence, and commercial activities in space. See the *Report of the Commission to Assess U.S. National Security Space Management and Organization* (Washington, D.C., 2001), www.space.gov.

12. Michael Geyer, "The Militarization of Europe, 1914–1945," in *The Militarization of the Western World*, ed. John R. Gillis (New Brunswick, N.J.: Rutgers University Press, 1989), 79.

13. Nikolas Rose, *Governing the Soul: The Shaping of the Private Self* (New York: Routledge, 1989), x, 21.

14. Rose, *Governing the Soul*, 7.

15. Laura McEnaney, *Civil Defense Begins at Home: Militarization Meets Everyday Life in the Fifties* (Princeton, N.J.: Princeton University Press, 2000), 12–15, 39.

16. Ellen Herman, *The Romance of American Psychology: Political Culture in the Age of Experts* (Berkeley: University of California Press, 1995), 241–42.

17. Fred Turner, *Echoes of Combat: Trauma, Memory, and the Vietnam War* (Minneapolis: University of Minnesota Press, 1996), xii. For an analysis of the psychological politics of remilitarizing, and remasculinizing, civilians as soldier "heroes" in the wake of the U.S. defeat in Vietnam, see Turner, *Echoes of Combat*, 71–95. See also, Avital Ronnel, "Support Our Troops," in *War after War*, ed. Nancy J. Peters (San Francisco: City Lights Books, 1992), 47–54, for a critical psychoanalytically inflected deconstruction of the 1991 war against Iraq as a "healing" war to repair the wounds of what became called the "Vietnam war syndrome."

18. Opening quote in Jerry L. Martin and Anne D. Neal, *Defending Civilization: How Our Universities Are Failing America and What Can Be Done about It* (Washington, D.C.: American Council of Trustees and Alumni, 2001). The American Council of Trustees and Alumni (ACTA) is the largest private financial contributor to institutions of higher education in the United States. ACTA members reportedly gave $3.4 billion to colleges and universities in 2001.

19. A succinct statement of the doctrine of total war was offered in 1945 by Vannevar Bush, director of the U.S. Office of Scientific Research and Development: War, he writes, is "increasingly total war, in which the armed services must be supplemented by active participation of every element of the civilian population." Quoted in Vannevar Bush, *Science: The Endless Frontier* (Washington, D.C.: U.S. Government Printing Office, 1945), 12.

20. Robert E. Park, "Morale and the News," *American Journal of Sociology* 47, no. 3 (November 1941): 360.

21. Herman, *Romance of American Psychology*, 29–30.

22. Harry Stack Sullivan, "Psychiatric Aspects of Morale," *American Journal of Sociology* 47, no. 3 (November 1941): 292–95.

23. Edward A. Shils, "A Note on Governmental Research on Attitudes and Morale," *American Journal of Sociology* 47, no. 3 (November 1941): 472.

24. Herman, *Romance of American Psychology*, 54.

25. While World War II saw the first mass use of aerial bombardment, the use of aerial warfare by Western industrialized countries against colonial territories had been launched by the United States in Nicaragua in 1933. Occupied between world wars by U.S. military forces and declared a "protectorate of the United States of America," Nicaragua was the site of U.S. experiments with aerial bombing against the "Bolshevik" threat of Augusto Cesar Sandino and his itinerate, largely rural, indigenous army of liberation. See Eduardo Galeano, *Century of the Wind* (New York: Pantheon Books, 1988).

26. For a cultural history of panic and its technosocial management in the twentieth-century United States, see Jackie Orr, *Panic Diaries: A Genealogy of Panic Disorder* (Durham, N.C.: Duke University Press, forthcoming 2005).

27. *Daily News*, October 31, 1938, quoted in Howard Koch, *The Panic Broadcast* (New York: Avon Books, 1967), 22.

28. Dorothy Thompson, "On the Record," *New York Tribune*, November 2, 1938, quoted in Koch, *Panic Broadcast*, 92.

29. Hadley Cantril, *The Invasion from Mars: A Study in the Psychology of Panic* (Princeton, N.J.: Princeton University Press, 1940).

30. Walter Wanger, "The Role of Movies in Morale," *American Journal of Sociology* 47, no. 3 (November 1941): 380–83.

31. For an excellent historical discussion of how social psychology grappled with this question, self-consciously constituting itself as a necessary "science of democracy," see Nikolas Rose, *Inventing Our Selves: Psychology, Power, and Personhood* (Cambridge: Cambridge University Press, 1996), 116–49.

32. Park, "Morale and the News," 363.

33. Quoted in John F. Burns, "Bin Laden Taunts U.S. and Praises Hijackers," *New York Times*, October 8, 2001, 1A. The translated quote, from a videotape released just hours after U.S. and British forces began bombing Afghanistan, reads in full: "I swear to God that America will not live in peace before peace reigns in Palestine, and before all the army of infidels depart the land of Muhammad, peace be upon him."

34. Guy Oakes, *The Imaginary War: Civil Defense and American Cold War Culture* (New York: Oxford University Press, 1994), 35.

35. Office of Civil Defense, *Instructor's Manual and Teaching Outline: Panic Control and Prevention* (Sacramento, Calif.: California State Printing Office, 1951), 71–72.

36. Oakes, *Imaginary War*, 33.

37. See McEnaney, *Civil Defense*, 88–151, for an excellent discussion of the gender, race, and class politics of Cold War civil defense discourse, including the proactive role taken by the NAACP and women's volunteer clubs to make a place for themselves as participants in civil defense programs.

38. Associated Universities, *Report of the Project East River* (New York: Associated Universities, 1952), v.

39. Federal Civil Defense Association, *Annual Report for 1952* (Washington. D.C.: U.S. Government Printing Office, 1953), 38.

40. Office of Civil Defense, *Instructor's Manual and Teaching Outline*, 63.

41. Federal Civil Defense Administration, *Survival under Atomic Attack* (Washington, D.C.: U.S. Government Printing Office, 1950), 12.

42. For a summary of media activities see Federal Civil Defense Association, *Annual Report for 1951* (Washington. D.C.: U.S. Government Printing Office, 1952), 10–15; *Annual Report for 1952* (Washington. D.C.: U.S. Government Printing Office, 1953), 43–49; *Annual Report for 1953* (Washington. D.C.: U.S. Government Printing Office, 1954), 67–77; and *Annual Report for 1954* (Washington. D.C.: U.S. Government Printing Office, 1955), 90–96.

43. Millard Caldwell, "Letter of Transmittal" to President Truman, April 18, 1952, in Federal Civil Defense Association, *Annual Report for 1951*, v.

44. Associated Universities, *Project East River*, 3, v.

45. Oakes, *Imaginary War*, 51. Legally restricted to psychological affairs beyond the U.S. borders, the Psychological Strategy Board's relations to *Project East River* remained unofficial and secret. See Oakes, *Imaginary War*, 50–51.

46. Herman, *Romance of American Psychology*, 31.

47. Oakes, *Imaginary War*, 62–71.

48. Elizabeth Douvan and Stephen B. Withy, "Some Attitudinal Consequences of Atomic Energy," *Annals of the American Academy of Political and Social Science* 290 (November 1953): 109–11, 114–17.

49. Federal Civil Defense Association, *Annual Report for Fiscal Year 1955* (Washington. D.C.: U.S. Government Printing Office, 1956), 6.

50. Carol Ahlgren and Frank Edgerton Martin, "From Dante to Doomsday: How a City without People Survived a Nuclear Blast," *Design Book Review* 17 (Winter 1989): 26.

51. Oakes, *Imaginary War*, 149–50.

52. Quoted in David Johnston, "At the Site, Ashcroft and Mueller Speak of Pushing Ahead," *New York Times*, September 22, 2001, 6B.

53. Oakes, *Imaginary War*, 148–49.

54. Federal Civil Defense Association, *Annual Report for 1955*, 32–33, 98.

55. Oakes, *Imaginary War*, 84.

56. Federal Civil Defense Association, *Annual Report for 1955*, 157, 182.

57. Spencer R. Weart, *Nuclear Fear: A History of Images* (Cambridge, Mass.: Harvard University Press, 1988), 135–36.

58. Oakes, *Imaginary War*, 151.

59. See McEnaney, *Civil Defense*, 37–39, 53–62, for a discussion of the discourse of "self-help" promoted by Cold War civil defense planners as they relegated responsibility for atomic survival from the bureaucratic state to the individual and family, transforming Cold War militarization into a personal responsibility.

60. Quoted in photo caption of first meeting of the Homeland Security Council, *New York Times*, October 30, 2001, 5B.

61. Judith Butler, "Explanation and Exoneration, or What We Can Hear," *Theory & Event* 5, no. 4 (January 2002), http://muse.jhu.edu/demo/theory_event/5.4butler .html, paragraph 19.

62. Paul Virilio, *The Politics of the Very Worst* (New York: Semiotext(e), 1999), 97.

63. Patricia Williams, "This Dangerous Patriot's Game," *The Observer* (December 2, 2001). Williams writes a regular column for *The Nation*, which she titles "Diary of a Mad Law Professor."

64. Thyrza Goodeve, "Watching for What Happens Next," in *War after War*, ed. Nancy J. Peters (San Francisco: City Lights Books, 1992), 53.

65. Sarah Kershaw, "Terror Scenes Follow Script of No More 9/11's," *New York Times*, May 13, 2003, 21A.

66. For one example of an analysis of the "eerie resonance" between dominant Cold War culture and today, see Corey Robin, "Primal Fear," *Theory & Event* 5, no. 4 (January 2002), http://muse/jhu.edu/demo/theory_events/5.4.

67. This aspect of the post–September 11 political landscape was immediately and incisively critiqued in a public statement coauthored by Paola Bacchetta, Tina Campt, Inderpal Grewal, Caren Kaplan, Minoo Moallem, and Jennifer Terry, "Transnational Feminist Practices Against War," later published in *Meridians: Feminism, Race, Transnationalism* 2, no. 2 (Spring 2002): 302–8.

68. Pat Aufderheide, "Therapeutic Patriotism and Beyond," *Television Archive* (2002), http://tvnews3.televisionarchive.org/tvarchive/html/article_pal.html (accessed June 2002).

69. Quoted in David E. Rosenbaum, "The Psychiatrist in the House Feels the Nation's Trauma," *New York Times*, October 1, 2001, 16A.

70. Laura Kipnis, "The Stepdaughter's Story: Scandals National and Transnational," *Social Text* 58, no. 17 (Spring 1999): 72.

71. Ellen Herman's history of the post–World War II rise of psychology as an expert and popular discourse provides the best evidence of the possible military origins of "therapeutic culture" (though this is not a term she uses; see Herman, *Romance of American Psychology*). For a recent discussion of the therapeutic state and the U.S. military, see James Nolan, *The Therapeutic State: Justifying Government at Century's End* (New York: New York University Press, 1998), 280–82.

72. Lon Troyer, "The Calling of Counterterrorism," *Theory & Event* 5, no. 4 (January 2002), http://muse/jhu.edu/demo/theory_events/5.4.

73. My thanks to Troy Duster, who circulated his unpublished essay "From Theater of War to Terrorism" after the attacks on September 11. Written in 1986, his overview of "the historical evolution of the very concept of contemporary terrorism," and the links between twentieth-century colonial battles and "terrorism," set much of my thinking here in motion. The essay is available at www.hereinstead.com/sys-tmpl/ htmlpage13.

Reflections

Consuming National Security

Paul A. Passavant

Jackie Orr's "Making Civilian-Soldiers: The Militarization of Inner Space" gives the reader historical perspective for understanding the psychological operations involved in the successful recruitment of subjects for a "war on terror." As Orr notes, the "end of World War II, rather than marking a demilitarization of the U.S. civilian-soldier," unfolded a Cold War in which winning a nuclear standoff with the Soviet Union required an urgent militarization and management of civilian psychology. Orr describes how the civilian population was enlisted in this war through such publications as the Federal Civil Defense Administration's "Keep Calm!" that sought to incite a quantum of fear necessary to produce active subjects willing and able to conduct civil defense practices, while not allowing the levels of fear to overwhelm the civilian psyche as unproductive and undisciplined panic. Orr argues that, much as the United States sought to enlist a militarized citizenry during the Cold War, the U.S. military's present Full Spectrum Dominance, as part of its war on terror, addresses the psychological space of the population.[1] Ronnie Lipschutz and Heather Turcotte describe the current political economy of terrorism/counterterrorism (T/CT). They point out that, as in any political economy, this discursive formation requires a sufficient level of demand for what it produces. This discursive formation must both produce its products and reproduce its conditions of possibility. For a political economy of T/CT to persist, there must be a sufficient level of fear to sustain the ongoing production of CT. As much as a Keynesian state can prime its political economy when there is concern regarding recession, the CT state can seek to manage demand as the Department of Homeland Security increases its threat level to orange or the Federal Bureau of Investigation circulates bulletins asking for vigilance regarding Middle Eastern men "believed" to have crossed the

Canadian border illegally, while acknowledging that it lacks "specific" information regarding any connection to "potential" terrorist activities.[2] Analogous to the Keynesian state that could count on its institutions to produce a multiplier effect, the CT state counts on its institutions for its multiplier effect. For example, the CT state can count on *FOX News* to remind its viewers constantly when the threat level is raised to orange; news programs, to report on a "run" by consumers on duct tape and plastic or to interview tourists about how airport security affects their travel plans; and publishers, to identify a market for publishing guides for those seeking jobs or contracts in the new-growth industry of homeland security.

Both of these chapters bring into focus the question of the state, and the American state, in order to begin to grasp the efforts to mobilize properly fearful American subjects who will support, if not demand, CT. Is the present fetish for CT merely a continuing extension of a surprisingly strong U.S. state that is largely unchanged since the 1950s, only with the "terrorist" substituted for the "communist," and the addition of updated computer technology?[3] Or is it inapt to speak of the new security-incited technologies of control as extending the power of the state now that the era of "big government" is over?[4] My argument is that neither position is fully correct. One of the ways that the current state formation differs from that of the Cold War is that the American state operates under post-Fordist conditions of neoliberalism. Politics is no longer organized around mass mobilization; political economy is no longer premised on the social welfare state; social logics no longer center on social security; and economic discourse has been relocated from being production centered to being consumption centered. One of the significant ways in which we are governed today, I contend, is through consumption.

GOVERNING THROUGH CONSUMPTION

Under the conditions of capitalism's post-Fordist phase, we are governed as consumers. The problem of surveillance is often associated with an intrusive state—and it should be. We should recognize, however, the ways in which consumer capitalism has been responsible for extending the sinews of surveillance, thereby creating the conditions of possibility for a notable growth in the power of the state.

When George W. Bush addressed the nation to do its part in face of tragedy, he tellingly asked the nation to go *shopping*.[5] Governing subjects as consumers, however, means inserting subjects into networks of surveillance that can vastly expand state power. This form of power, however, is not merely repressive. Governing through consumption also means inciting active consumers who, through their purchases, extend an aesthetics of consent for current state policies.

When we are mobilized as consumers, we are inserted into vast networks of surveillance, from "cookies"[6] placed on our Internet browsers, to supermarket discount cards, to credit and medical histories. Moreover, due to the post office's introduction of zip codes and the advances in computer technologies, consumers have been demographically stratified, and all of this information has been stored for reference and can be cross-referenced.[7] And while it is easy to view these surveillance technologies as a sinister plot—and they are—this would absolve us from the pleasures we experience thanks to these technologies. These technologies *are* consumer capitalism in today's society.[8] For good consumers, they make renting a car easier, writing a check easier, and paying our credit card bills easier since if your computer accepts cookies, you can pay your credit card debts online. By tracking who purchases what—often by zip code but sometimes also by name—businesses are able to respond to demand and satisfy consumer interests more efficiently. Indeed, part of creating spaces for consumers is to create an aesthetic environment that makes consuming subjects feel safe, and this is the function of private security and obviously placed surveillance cameras: to make us feel secure. That is, the security camera—and surveillance generally—constitutes, in part, consumerism's aesthetic environment.

But the technology that allows the supermarkets to track customer purchases and give discounts to even its customers who forget their discount cards is the same technology that creates masses of data that can be mined for any number of purposes in addition to customer discounts. The technologies that give us pleasure if we are good consumers are the same technologies that the state seeks to utilize to discover potential terrorists and preempt future terrorist action. Section 215 of the USA PATRIOT Act allows the Federal Bureau of Investigation (FBI) to utilize Foreign Intelligence Surveillance Act (FISA) warrants—warrants that are exempt from Fourth Amendment requirements of "probable cause" regarding criminal activity because they are used for foreign intelligence purposes—to require the production of "any tangible things (including books, records, papers, documents, and other items) to protect against international terrorism or clandestine intelligence activities."[9] The Act changes the former FISA requirement that the government specify "specific and articulable facts" that give reason to believe that the person being searched is actually a foreign power or an agent of a foreign power.[10] This means, first, that the person whose records are being searched need not be suspected of any criminal wrongdoing. Second, the FBI may search anyone under this provision, including U.S. citizens.[11] The USA PATRIOT Act does forbid searches of a "United States person . . . solely upon the basis of activities protected by the first amendment to the Constitution." Section 802 of the Act, however, creates the new crime of "domestic terrorism," which is defined as activities "dangerous to human life that are a violation of the criminal laws of the United States or of any state" and which "appear to be intended . . . to influence the policy of a government."[12] Therefore, the language of section 215 forbidding a search of a U.S. citizen *solely* on First Amendment grounds means that a nexus to some other suspected illegal activity must be drawn by the FBI—a nexus that the crime of "domestic terrorism" creates.[13] Powers that had been considered an "abuse" when Hoover was discovered to have exercised them have now been legalized under the USA PATRIOT Act. Moreover, because the warrants to compel the production of any tangible thing are FISA warrants, and because section 215 literally forbids any person to disclose to any other person that the FBI has sought or obtained anything, the person whose records have been searched at Barnes and Noble or any other business (or library) that keeps customer records will never know that they have been the object of surveillance by the government.[14] As this example shows, the surveillance technologies that facilitate and deepen consumerism have vastly expanded the powers of the state by allowing it to criminalize political action.

This expansion of state power through the networks of consumer capitalism is not merely a repressive power. We are governed as active subjects through consumerism as well. This, in turn, extends state power visually and perhaps ideologically. Others have described how the state under modern capitalist conditions utilizes institutions of civil society as mechanisms through which to generate consent for its order. Typically, the institutions noted for their capacity to extend and deepen state power include schools, families, churches, political parties, and the mass media. Today, we must add to this list the sites and commodities of consumer capitalism.[15]

On the one hand, we have been incited by Bush to show patriotism by being good consumers. On the other hand, capitalism requires new commodities to sell to new consumers lest a crisis of oversupply lead to the implosion of capitalism foreseen by Karl Marx.[16] September 11 and the war on terrorism have been functional for both—they have provided fuel for consumer capitalism, and they have enabled an extension of the state of being that seemingly authorizes support for Bush's policies, including the war in Iraq. After September 11, stores within shopping malls enabled a continuing articulation between shopping and patriotism through ubiquitous flags and posters memorializing September 11. To shop since September 11—and particularly during the holiday shopping season of fall 2002—is to be interpellated visually as a consenting subject to a continuing war on terror and, particularly, its Iraqi chapter.

September 11 has been functional for consumer capitalism because it has enabled the creation of new markets and differentiated commodities. Consultants for police departments offer four-day certification programs in media "self-defense" (media training "boot camps": "Souvenir PIO Boot Camp t-shirt included with registration"; learn the "art of talking without saying anything") to teach public information officers how to utilize the media more effectively, deflect attention from scandal (learn how "ambiguous public records laws can help you stall for time"), and deal with the public relations issues surrounding a possible terrorist attack.[17] State and local governments can subscribe to the *Homeland Security Funding Report* to get up-to-date on money available for homeland security programs.[18] And businesses can buy manuals to learn how to become USA PATRIOT Act compliant. Not only has the war on terrorism created new markets, but the availability of government money for state and local governments and private government contractors means that governments and businesses will become dependent, to varying degrees, on the homeland security regime. This money will shape which government capacities will be developed; it will stimulate demand for increased funding for these security-oriented programs; it will thus stimulate and institutionalize a discourse of homeland security to further access to these monies; and this homeland security regime of CT will become resistant to change through the production of stakeholders—those who hold a financial stake in this institutional arrangement and thus will resist efforts to diminish its funding or do away with it.

September 11 has also facilitated commodity differentiation that is so critical for consumer capitalism. Consumer capitalism requires and thrives on difference. The Time-Warner cable television company, for example, advertises an increase in international programming to a multicultural society, encouraging different groups to celebrate their distinctive ethnicities and lifestyles. A multicultural society celebrating difference is a market for sales of additional channel packages. From the perspective of consumer capitalism, difference, as we have learned well from Benetton's ad campaigns, is an opportunity rather than a barrier: it means that there is a potentially new market segment to be developed.[19]

The possibility of differentiated products helps to sustain consumer capitalism. While many households have a deck of cards somewhere, war on Iraq generates the conditions of possibility for a differentiated commodity to capture this moment, so to speak: a deck of cards with the faces of the fifty-two most wanted Iraqis—Saddam Hussein's face is on top, of course. In this way, consumer capitalism has generated a flood of new, war-on-terrorism commodities, from a George W. Bush action figure doll to a cap that lights up, reading "Let's Roll."[20] Recognizing the opportunity presented by the anniversary of September 11, consumer-goods producers developed a variety of products, the release of which were timed to coincide with this date and to take advantage of the holiday shopping season. Indeed, multiple video games utilizing post–September 11 themes were released during this period, including PlayStation 2's *Conflict: Desert Storm II—Back to Baghdad*, a simulation for computer gamers that preceded the real event by five months.[21]

By mobilizing the nation to become good consumers and to go shopping in the wake of September 11, Bush is calling into being a certain type of active subject—the consumer—that is useful not only for the present mode of capitalism but also for the reproduction of state power. By purchasing these products and inciting their continued production, consumers are enabling the extension of state power. By purchasing these commodities and by multiplying their presence on our bodies, in our living spaces, in the stores, and in our everyday lives, consumers create a visual culture that manifests support for the present state of affairs and its projects. The consumer capitalist machine is manufacturing consent for a state formation conducive to an endless war on terrorism.

CONCLUSION

In this reflection, I have argued that state policies of inciting fear, and hence demand for CT, raise questions regarding the contemporary state's capacities. Are fear and the ensuing demand for CT forms of political affect that miraculously coincide with state interests despite a notoriously weak American state? Or, is this environment the extension of the state's management of its militarized citizen-subjects during the Cold War, now bent toward antiterrorist objects? I have contended that neither approach is adequate. Although the present state formation achieves its ends through mechanisms that are distinct from state practices under the social welfare conditions of the Cold War national security state, the neoliberal post-Fordist state that embraces market-based solutions is not a weak state. Under neoliberal conditions of consumer capitalism, we are governed, in part, as consumers. Consumer capitalism has made extensive and intensive systems of surveillance, which, as these systems have been articulated to state technologies of governance, have vastly extended the state's surveillance powers. This form of state power, however, is not simply a repressive form of power. Rather, we are governed as active consumer-subjects who, through commodified acts, extend a visual culture of consent for this state's projects and projections.

Generally, consumption is positively correlated with consumer confidence —as consumers feel more confident about the future, they tend to become more active as consumers. Indicative of a significant shift in American political economy, however, retail sales increased in October 2002 (the month that Congress voted in favor of delegating its constitutional war-making powers to Bush) despite drastically low consumer confidence. Today, Americans have been persuaded to consume not out of confidence but out of fear.[22] This fear is manifested in polls finding that a majority of Americans surveyed—53 percent—"feel the country is less safe today than it was 10 years ago."[23] Fear thus proves itself.[24]

NOTES

1. Jackie Orr, "Making Civilian Soldiers: The Militarization of Inner Space," in *Making Threats: Biofears and Environmental Anxieties*, ed. Betsy Hartmann, Banu Subramaniam, and Charles Zerner (Lanham, Md.: Rowman & Littlefield, 2005).

2. Ronnie Lipschutz and Heather Turcotte, "Duct Tape or Plastic? The Political Economy of Threats and the Production of Fear," in *Making Threats: Biofears and Environmental Anxieties*, ed. Betsy Hartmann, Banu Subramaniam, and Charles Zerner (Lanham, Md.: Rowman & Littlefield, 2005).

3. Andrew Grossman, *Neither Dead nor Red: Civilian Defense and American Political Development during the Early Cold War* (New York: Routledge, 2001), 121–29.

4. Michael Hardt and Antonio Negri, *Empire* (Cambridge, Mass.: Harvard University Press, 2000), 348–50.

5. Office of the Press Secretary, "President Works on Economic Recovery During NY Trip," October 3, 2001, www.whitehouse.gov/news/releases/2001/10/20011003-4 .html (retrieved May 9, 2005); Office of the Press Secretary, "Remarks by the President to Business, Trade, and Agricultural Leaders," October 26, 2001, www.whitehouse .gov (retrieved December 4, 2002).

6. Cookies log one's visits to Internet sites.

7. Tellingly for my purposes, Jonathan Robbin created a computer program for correlating U.S. census data with information from credit firms and shopping outlets, among other sources, to disaggregate the mass market into clusters of lifestyle segments to produce a system of commercial profiling in 1974. See Christian Parenti, *The Soft Cage: Surveillance in America from Slavery to the War on Terror* (New York: Basic Books, 2003), 103–4.

8. Of course this is not to say that other periods of capitalism did not also involve surveillance. Surveillance at the factory was certainly an element of the Fordist mode of production, and, as Christian Parenti describes in *Soft Cage*, surveillance continues at our various work sites. For a discussion of communicative capitalism and the pleasures of being known through surveillance, see Jodi Dean, *Publicity's Secret* (Ithaca, N.Y.: Cornell University Press, 2002).

9. USA PATRIOT Act, sec. 215. For a discussion of the Foreign Intelligence Surveillance Act of 1978 and amendments made to this Act, including the USA PATRIOT Act, see David Cole and James Dempsey, *Terrorism and the Constitution* (New York: New Press, 2002).

10. These standards themselves were easily abused. See Cole and Dempsey, *Terrorism and the Constitution*, 21–33.

11. See Nancy Chang, *Silencing Political Dissent* (New York: Seven Stories, 2002), 53.

12. USA PATRIOT Act, sec. 802.

13. This nexus was apparently drawn in a grand jury subpoena that was issued against a student chapter of the National Lawyers Guild at Drake University that had sponsored a conference entitled "Stop the Occupation! Bring the Iowa Guard Home!" After the conference, some civil disobedience reportedly occurred, such as a demonstrator who climbed a National Guard fence. After an article appeared in the *New York Times*, however, the government backed down and withdrew the subpoena. For

a summary of the event, see David Cole, "Spying on the Guild," *The Nation* (March 1, 2004): 5–6.

14. Although section 224 contains a sunset provision stating that section 215 will cease to have effect after December 31, 2005, Bush has requested that Congress make this and other temporary provisions of the USA PATRIOT Act, permanent. See "President's State of the Union Message to Congress and the Nation," *New York Times*, January 21, 2004, www.nytimes.com (accessed January 27, 2004). The "gag order" aspects of the USA PATRIOT Act, are presently being challenged by the American Civil Liberties Union. See *Muslim Community Association of Ann Arbor, et al. v. John Ashcroft*, filed in the U.S. District Court, Eastern District of Michigan, Southern Division (court documents are available at www.aclu.org).

15. Joseph Femia, *Gramsci's Political Thought* (Oxford: Clarendon Press, 1981).

16. Karl Marx, "Manifesto of the Communist Party," in *Selected Works*, 3 vols., ed. Institute of Marxist-Leninism (Moscow: Progress Publishers, 1969), 1:114.

17. See www.homelandsecuritycourses.com (accessed January 27, 2004).

18. See www.cdpublications.com (accessed January 27, 2004).

19. On the development of market segments, see Lizabeth Cohen, *A Consumers' Republic* (New York: Knopf, 2003), 292–344.

20. "G.I. George: Bush Stars as Action Figure," *Atlanta Journal-Constitution*, August 12, 2003, www.ajc.com (accessed February 21, 2004); M. Higgins, "Retailers Build Inventories of September 11 Collectibles to Meet High Demand," *Washington Times*, September 5, 2002, www.lexis-nexis.com.

21. From www.walmart.com (accessed February 21, 2004).

22. D. Altman, "Optimism among Midsize Manufacturers," *New York Times*, November 29, 2002, 4C; *The Conference Board*, "Consumer Confidence Index Falls," October 29, 2002, www.conference-board.org/economics/consumer.cfn (accessed August 21, 2003).

23. Eric Lichtblau, "Terror Policy: Between Fear and Freedom," *New York Times*, January 11, 2004, 4(3).

24. Richard Ericson and Kevin Haggerty, "The Policing of Risk," in *Embracing Risk*, ed. Tom Baker and Jonathan Simon (Chicago: University of Chicago Press, 2002), 269.

II

SCARCITY

4

Malthusianism and the Terror of Scarcity

Larry Lohmann

> Clouds of Barbarians seemed to collect from all points of the northern
> hemisphere. Gathering fresh darkness and terror as they rolled on, the
> congregated bodies at length obscured the sun of Italy, and sunk the
> whole world in universal night. These tremendous effects . . . may be
> traced to the simple cause of the superior power of population to the
> means of subsistence.
>
> —T. R. Malthus, *Essay on the Principle of Population*

Since 1798, when the Reverend T. R. Malthus wrote these lines, Malthusianism has been one of the great scare stories: a tale of overnumerous Others menacing Us. For nineteenth-century French elites, these Others were German and British; for Prussian intellectuals, Jews; for late-Victorian English elites, the laboring classes of their own nation.[1] In the early twentieth-century United States, they were immigrants from southern Europe or China, or the "morons" and "unfit" infesting slums or backward rural areas. In the 1990s, the overpopulated Others included the "loose molecules" of disaffected west African youth.[2] Today they are immigrants captured at night on heat-sensing cameras as pale, leechlike blobs swarming over fences to take advantage of Britain's National Health Service or California's job opportunities; or arrogant, sly "welfare queens," breeding up to welfare budgets in U.S. cities;[3] dangerous post–September 11 "youth bulge" stirring up trouble in "Muslim countries."[4]

In the Malthusian story, how many of Us there are is not usually a problem. Crowding at Indian railway stations is due to Their wanton breeding; crowding at London stations, to Our government's poor transport planning. Covers of books on the "population problem" feature photographs not of the white middle class but of people of color, usually women and children. What typically worries Malthusians is the idea that everything We have had to work hard for—property, the fruits of intellectual and physical labor, political power, survival itself—will fall to feckless Others through mere fecundity. Yet as borders between Us and Them dissolve, shift and reform as different threats loom or recede, even We Ourselves can intermittently slip into the category of overpopulating Others. Women who are Us in some lights become Them in others. "Females create population problems," said one population control scientist a decade ago. "The common pathway to turn off having people is females."[5] And the Northern middle classes—the customary Us of the Malthusian story—periodically have to share the spotlight as part of the Other of nature, the mindless "human virus" infecting the planet. At the same time, people who are ordinarily Others sometimes attain temporary status as Us when both are faced with a more menacing Outside Other: two U.S. experts recently pointedly included "poor inner-city Americans" among those whose educational opportunities were threatened by "over-immigration."[6]

But Malthusianism is not only an ever-adaptable tale of "darkness and terror," "congregated bodies," and impending "universal night." That is only its werewolf side, the side that comes out after sunset, around the storytelling fire. There is also a daylight Malthusianism that draws in its claws and feels no need to show its teeth, that to its adherents "goes without saying." This is the Malthusianism that more visibly underpins a scaffolding of two centuries of productive thinking about private property, "free markets," government policy, development, and biology. From what it sees as a natural, quasi-logarithmic relationship between available food and the labor used to grow it, this Malthusianism derives or predicts a political regime featuring economic scarcity, enclosure, market-allocated food and labor, inequality, sharp divisions between owners and nonowners of land and sexuality and a zero-sum game between humans and nature, with the stakes being nature, economic scarcity, enclosure, market-allocated food and labor, and inequality—a game that especially includes sharp divisions between owners and nonowners of land and sexuality. It follows from this derivation that a whole range of social thinkers have been misinformed: not only revolutionaries, egalitarians, utopians, and do-gooders but also those who have feared that revolution would lead to permanent tyranny; not only commoners convinced of their own right to subsistence but also aristocrats persuaded that earning the poor's deference means fulfilling traditional paternalistic obligations to them.

Grim as it may be, this theoretical Malthusianism does its best not to present itself as a scare story of Others menacing Us. The man who invented it (this chapter's epigraph notwithstanding) was not a xenophobic demagogue but a courteous, cosmopolitan clergyman, theodicist, and mathematician who professed as much concern as many others of his genteel background about the plight of the poor. Even today his theory helps shape an enlightened middle class's sense that there is something "natural" about market discipline. To question it is typically not to run up against the fearful, closed-faced rage of obsessive bigots but rather to confront the blank-faced, bewildered anger of ordinary people who feel that common sense, even civility itself, is being challenged and who can't understand why.

What is the relationship between these two aspects of Malthusianism—the dark, often racist scare stories on the one hand and the polite establishment wisdom about how society must be analyzed and organized on the other? And what can this relationship tell us about how both aspects work in contemporary politics and about what the permanent appeal is of Malthusianism?

Obviously, some tension exists between the two sides of Malthusianism. Malthus himself tried to dissociate the two when he insisted his theory was actually on the side of the poor, pointing them toward the discipline needed for survival and success. He also famously withdrew an inflammatory passage in the 1803 edition of his major book in which "nature" bid the landless and jobless "begone" from her dinner table. So, too, contemporary Malthusians have periodically tried to dissociate themselves from the Us-and-Them narrative. Some have even pointed out, with some justice, that economists in the tradition to which Malthus belongs tend have a better antiracist record than do many virulent anti-Malthusians, such as Charles Dickens.[7]

Yet, equally obviously, the two sides of Malthusianism have affinities. Even if they appeal to somewhat different audiences, they serve many of the same purposes. In Malthus's own time, the objective was a defense of private property and inequality against the assaults of utopian intellectuals at a time of popular unrest and revolution in Europe. It was also to loosen, among elites, the residual grip of a culture of respect for subsistence rights that was blocking a fuller commodification of labor and a sharper divide between owners and workers. In our own time, when what the late Ivan Illich called the "war against subsistence" has entered a new stage, the common objective of the two Malthuisanisms has expanded to include a defense of technocratic management of peoples and their reproductive organs and genes in the service of Our economy and environment.

In addition, both aspects of Malthusianism are often found in the same places. The same book that talks about "darkness and terror," Malthus's *Essay on the Principle of Population*, also broaches technical ideas in economics that are still being worked through today. A contemporary neo-Malthusian such as Paul Ehrlich, similarly, is capable of writing in one book about the "feel of overpopulation" brought on by encounters with the Others he found in Delhi—"People eating, people washing, people sleeping. People visiting, arguing, and screaming. People thrusting their hands through the taxi window, begging. People defecating and urinating. People clinging to buses. People herding animals. People, people, people, people, people"[8]—while discoursing in the next on technical themes in population biology.

Both aspects of Malthusianism, finally, have always been jointly subject to suspicions from the Left. In the early nineteenth century, William Cobbett satirized Malthusian "feelosophy" as a cover-up for "parson"-ish Us-and-Them prejudices:

> What ignorance, impudence and insolence must those base wretches have, who propose to *transport* the labouring people, as being *too numerous*, while . . . they say not a word against the prolific *dead-weight* [of] pensioners, placemen, soldiers, parsons, fund holders, tax gatherers or tax eaters![9]

More recently, feminists have criticized Malthusianism as being masculinist in both theory and practice: undermining cooperation and discussion while inspiring population control programs that amount to "something like a war" against women and the poor.

In this chapter, I want to suggest that the Malthusian "darkness and terror" narrative about Us and Them and the Malthusian economic model are united by more than common authorship, common purposes, and common critics. Though they seem on the surface to belong to different genres, the two Malthusianisms strengthen and complement each other structurally.

The first part of this chapter retells the would-be predictive Malthusian political economy story against its historical background. The second part describes how the economic model contained in the story needs Us-and-Them fear narratives and metaphors to get itself out of conceptual trouble and to distract or rally the troops in times of cultural confrontation, social upheaval, or theoretical uncertainty. The final section details how the Us-and-Them narratives also need the Malthusian mathematics: to displace and elevate themselves into ritual and tragedy and perpetuate and reconstitute themselves as civil common sense.

THE MALTHUSIAN STORY

In a sense, Malthus was for one revolution but against another. Despite having reservations about manufacturing, he stood mostly behind the revolution that in his time was trying to turn commons into resources—that is, to commodify labor, privatize common land, replace "fair" food prices set by local magistrates with market prices, and so forth.[10] At the same time, he opposed the political and intellectual upheavals that, coinciding with the French Revolution, were stressing equality (including gender equality) and the overthrow of hierarchical institutions.

The first revolution was only partly underway at the time he was writing (and, as Karl Polanyi argues more than a century later, could never be fully carried out anyway),[11] and Malthus's stance could not be but controversial. His particular point of attack was the felt right to subsistence or survival—an aspect of commons structures that interferes with market mechanisms because it tends to override exclusive individual rights to possess, exchange, and accumulate. It was a timely target. The formal welfare system of his time, still administered under a 1601 law by local authorities, was in disrepute. Confined to their parishes at the mercy of the growing power of rural capitalism, laborers were being paid at a rate below that of subsistence. Local elites resorted to using parish-poor rates to top up their wages to levels at which they could buy all their children enough bread to live on. But there was little need for farmers to pay laborers a full subsistence wage if local ratepayers could pick up part of the salary bill. More and more people claimed relief. It became hard to tell poor laborers from dependent paupers. Productivity dropped. Individuals and small families were especially disadvantaged. Poor rates rose, seemingly without making a dent in pauperism. Even capitalists were demoralized. Other elites resented the "insolence" of boozy welfare dependents who were failing to live up to the picture of the destitute they wanted to see—industrious poor widows and orphans responding to the "unexpected favours" of rich, benevolent landowners with "uplifted hands . . . bursting tears . . . [and] unfeigned gratitude."[12] With figures such as Malthus tugging at the thread consisting of the idea that everybody had subsistence rights, the tattered fabric of the commons ethic was even closer to coming apart than it had been before.

Malthus's stance pitted him against both elite traditionalists, who still valued subsistence rights as part of a paternalistic system ensuring their own status, and commoners who were adversely affected by the commercial revolution. But it also set him against the democratic currents whose influence was helping to shift modes of popular protest used under the older paternalism toward new ones informed by utopian and anti–private property currents of thought. Malthus's method was to assure his peers that the bitter suffering they were seeing around them was not something that anybody could do much about. Scarcity was not a sometime thing resulting from periodic natural disasters. It was a permanent feature of nature, always impinging disproportionately on the poor. Privatization was a necessary adaptation to it. It was not subsistence rights that were natural but private property rights. The poor laws might as well be abolished outright. Nobody should be compelled to take care of those who had lost out through privatization. Charity should be voluntary, not an obligation. Laborers had a right only to the food they could buy with their labor. The sooner they got that into their heads, the sooner they would learn to appreciate any benevolence that did happen their way. And the sooner that landed elites got it into *their* heads that the subsistence ethic was untenable, the quicker they would realize that they would gain neither the poor's deference nor national prosperity by pretending to respect it.

Malthus tried to establish his case by telling a story about nature and the way it acts on humans to create private property, inequality, and monogamous marriage. Imagine, Malthus says, a benevolent utopia without property, possessiveness, inequality, misery, marriage, vice, or luxury. Everybody would be supplied with what they needed out of available surplus. Leisure would be plentiful. People would not need to take responsibility for the future welfare of their children. It would be of no consequence who their fathers were; they would be provided for regardless. Unconcerned about status, people would have no reason not to form attachments early and have plenty of children. But this would lead to scarcity. Crops would be stolen or harvested before they were ripe. People would sicken. Murder would threaten. People would begin worrying about self-preservation. Benevolence would be banished. Strife would reign. Nor would there be any chance of people's realizing their intellectual abilities.

To get themselves out of danger, people would seek ways of increasing produce and allocating it only to selected people. The only solution: private property. Land previously held in common would be divided up, and every man's parcel secured against violation by anyone else. To check population growth, the costs of raising children would have to be made to fall on individuals, who would then be compelled to take responsibility for their children's upkeep—or, rather, on individual men, who were society's property owners: Malthus writes that women could not be expected to "have resources sufficient to support their own children."[13] Men would then be more inclined to hesitate before fathering children. Delay, of course, would have a feedback effect: older people would have fewer children. Yet all this meant that men would have to know who their children were; it went without saying that they would never consent to helping raise anyone else's. But that created a problem: unlike women, who are seldom in much doubt about which children are theirs, men can never be quite sure. Human survival therefore dictated a sexual double standard under monogamy, by which women, Malthus said, could "be almost driven from society for an offence which men commit nearly with impunity."[14]

But with private property and unequal marriage would come inequality in wealth. "Those who were born after the division of property would come into a world already possessed,"[15] writes Malthus. If their parents had not tailored their family size to their properties, they would have no land for themselves and could not legitimately demand it from others. Because benevolence had been wiped out during the first phase of subsistence crisis, smaller families—or families who had been lucky enough to extract more from their land—would be willing to share their surplus only with those whose labor could be used to produce yet more surplus. This could then be offered to still more property-less people in return for yet more labor. If there was a huge supply of laborers, shares would be small; sickness and misery would grow; and population would be checked. But after more food was produced with the cheaper labor, wages would increase, as would the population of the lower orders. The surplus the upper classes made available to the lower would be the limiting factor on population. Giving in to humanitarian impulses when the laborer population was high and when suffering was great, by undertaking a radical redistribution of property—for example, luxuries and manufacturing capital—would just encourage the poor to breed. The supply of laborers with insufficient work to do would grow, keeping wages low. Food prices would increase, impoverishing willing and active laborers. And the educated class would be deprived of the leisure needed to develop their thinking on liberty and the market, as well as their role in creating demand for luxury goods.

Revolution, the tale suggests, should be neither hoped for nor feared.[16] Contemporary society did not rest on anything as mythical as a social contract. Scarcity, poverty, private property, inequality, food and labour markets, and unequal marriage were inevitable given any starting point whatever. Nature and God dictated that society ultimately be divided into owners and nonowners of land and sexuality alike. Subsistence rights for all were physically impossible to defend, making further moral debate about them pointless. If work was by nature a commodity with the same price across the country, any worker unable to command wages enough to live on would have to starve. Private property, not welfare legislation—and not commons either—would provide the best possible deal for the poor, the best hope for allowing people to realize their potential, and the best guarantee that the lower orders would continue to defer to the higher. Malthus's tale of an endless return to nature's equilibrium promised to abolish feminism, radical politics, and progress toward equality in one go.

Like most great narratives, Malthus's tale can also be read as a metaphor. The overarching image is an old one comparing society with a machine hooked up to nature and tended by wise elites. Already in the fourteenth century, Aristotelian commentator Nicole Oresme had introduced the idea of God as clockmaker (replacing the old figure of potter), and the image was passed down through Leibniz and Voltaire to the theologian William Paley, whose books were Oxford texts for both Malthus and Charles Darwin. The comparison reassured religious believers that bits of a device that seemed of little virtue in themselves could serve a higher purpose. Hunger, vice, and profitmaking might all be part of a mechanism necessary for the achievement of a greater good. What's more, a clock, once set in motion, drives itself. It needs only to be wound, adjusted, and repaired once in a while. Today, this literary figure of economy, as machine occasionally wound up and adjusted by the state, dominates policy thinking around the world. Economists —always "inordinately fascinated by machines"—continue to develop the metaphor.[17]

Long before Malthus wrote, moreover, machine metaphors had also been formulated explaining how numbers of people could be regulated. In the mid-1700s, the theologian and statistician J. P. Sussmilch had posited a sort of population thermostat correlating availability of farmland with rate of, and people's age at, marriage.[18] In 1767, James Steuart, another clergyman-economist, had come up with a metaphor according to which

> the generative faculty resembles a *spring* loaded with a weight, which always exerts itself in proportion to the diminution of resistance. . . . If . . . food be increased, . . . people will begin to be better fed; they will multiply, and in proportion as they increase in numbers, the food will become scarce again.[19]

Malthus famously upgraded this metaphor through a mathematical analogy, which is itself a novel narrative. Population, he claimed, tends to increase geometrically (1, 2, 4, 8, 16, 32, 64, 128, 256, 512, . . .), while, even with ever-increasing applications of labour to land, food supply at most increases only arithmetically (1, 2, 3, 4, 5, 6, 7, 8, 9, 10, . . .). The disparity between the two series increases extremely rapidly:

> The germs of existence contained in this spot of earth, with ample food and ample room to expand in, would fill millions of worlds in the course of a few thousand years.[20]

By force or by foresight, the geometric power of population—the immensely powerful natural spring that drives Malthus's machine narrative—had to be constantly and strongly restrained.

Today many other metaphors jostle with Malthus's for attention: population bombs and explosions, human floods, tides and swarms, tiny lifeboats sinking under their human cargo, petri dishes overwhelmed with the putrid toxins from proliferating bacteria, lemmings charging off cliffs, automobiles smashing into brick walls at high speed, and so on. But these catastrophe metaphors are not nearly as fertile as the seed from which they are derived: Malthus's diverging curves $y = 2x$ and $y = x + 1$. A bomb goes off only once. A lifeboat sinks only once, and a car can only be smashed into a brick wall once. But Malthus's mathematical metaphor emphasizes that there is no need to wait for a bomb to go off or a lifeboat to sink. Pressure is *always* being exerted by abstract humans against an abstract "nature." Humans, at least the lower grade of humans (Malthusianism has always turned on this equivocation), are *in principle* opposed to the rest of nature. Scarcity is built into their very interaction. Even one couple is potentially "too many."

WHY THE POLITICAL ECONOMY MODEL NEEDS THE US-AND-THEM FEAR NARRATIVE

In a celebrated article, the legal scholar Carol Rose argues that the classical property theories of Locke, Blackstone, and others were, logically speaking, incapable of doing what they aspired to do: to predict the development of a private property regime "from a starting point of rational self-interest":

> There is a gap between the kind of self-interested individual who needs exclusive property to induce him to labor, and the kind of individual who has to be there to create, maintain, and protect a property regime.[21]

In order to account for the existence of such a property regime, Rose maintains, Locke, Blackstone, and the rest had to reach outside their models for a narrative that would allow their audiences to imagine themselves one with characters taking risks for an imagined common good. They plugged the analytical lacuna in their theories with a story. Only a narrative could render plausible the transformation of economic individuals whose nature is supposed to be to maximize short-term self-interest into vulnerable, imaginative seekers after cooperation, capable of learning from the past long enough to join with others in setting up a civil society capable of securing and protecting property rights.

Malthus, a late arrival among these political economists, also hoped to find a scientific, "natural" basis for private property, as well as for inequality. But his theory, too, survives only if it is propped up with an extraneous story. As many of his contemporaries noticed, Malthus's argument is circular. His model, which posits human actors behaving as "plants and animals" in an egalitarian utopia, always ends up in an inegalitarian scenario. But it is only by booby-trapping the initial setup with extra narrative ingredients derived from contemporary middle-class mythology that Malthus can make it turn out that way.

One of these ingredients is a preexisting class division between a Them who breed up to subsistence and an Us who do not. Without this division, it is hard to understand how one group of humans in Malthus's egalitarian starting scenario, after having gotten lucky with their crops or their family size at one point in the narrative, suddenly become a permanent upper class obsessed with conserving their high status, while others never seem to learn; but fortunately for Malthus, such a story seemed natural to his audience. Another ingredient is a preexisting gender divide between men, who can have "resources sufficient to support their own children," and women, who cannot. This divide, with its associated "marriage market" narrative, again seemed a commonplace to most of Malthus's peers. A third ingredient is a polarity between a security-ensuring private property regime and a

commons regime viewed as little more than its Other: an absence of ownership; an inability to accumulate; a license for freeloading, antisocial behavior, and endless baby making; an emblem of Their disorder. While con-
testable, the resulting narrative again dovetails with stories familiar to
Malthus's middle-class readers. As a traditional English popular rhyme com-
plains, tales emphasizing the security value of commons to the poor were no
match, in the elite imagination, for stories stressing the security value of private property to the rich:

> They hang the man and flog the woman
> That steal the goose from off the common,
> But let the greater villain loose
> That steals the common from the goose.

A final mythological patch on Malthus's otherwise untenable theory is his
mathematical narrative of diverging numerical series that bring about
scarcity, property, and class society. As Malthus himself admitted in the end,
these series are not observable in society. They are a romance out of a mathematics classroom—merely an illustrative metaphor for a fearful "power"
controllable by Us but not by Them. Just as Locke and Blackstone paper over
their theories' incoherence by smuggling in a narrative their audiences respond to instinctively without realizing its extrinsic nature, so Malthus lends
flesh to his own theory's emptiness by helping himself to Us-and-Them narratives that made plausible his audience's preexisting prejudices and terrors.

Critics puzzle over the fact that Malthusianism perennially rises from the
dead. But to wonder why repeated demonstrations of its circularity, factual
incorrectness, and inconsistencies do not defeat it is like wondering why
people still look at the fashionable paintings of Malthus's age. Both endure
less because they are true to life than because they are well made. In
Malthus's age, they helped tell elites how to look (or not look) at paupers
and women, see beggary and hard labor as natural fixtures of society, and
feel a benevolence toward the victims of the transition from paternalism to
capitalism that remained disconnected from any sense of responsibility.
Graphs derived from the most striking metaphor of Malthus's narrative could
usefully be exhibited as successors to paintings such as Thomas Gainsborough's *Cottage Girl with Dog and Pitcher, The Woodcutter's Return*, and
Charity Relieving Distress. Cottage Girl, for example, dating from 1785 and
evidently found "natural and pleasing" by its well-off buyer, portrayed a
poverty that was felt to be ordained by nature—neither the responsibility of
the rich nor an incitement to social change. Such children, it was thought,
had to become inured to hard labor as a condition for sympathy. The role of
the rich—benign spectators of laborers' struggle to survive, unable to raise
their wages or lower their rents—was to encourage them to work hard
enough to feed their many dependents. The more oppressed the subjects of

such paintings were, the bigger the opportunities for benevolence and philanthropy.[22] Malthus's picture of the life of the lower classes (see figure 4.1), first set out thirteen years later, set a steeply rising curve representing the "power of population" against a line representing the far feebler power of food supplies to increase. Whereas for the rich, and for "civilized" societies, the upward thrust of the top curve is held in check by abstinence grounded in worries about loss of status, for the poor (and for "savage" and egalitarian societies) it strains more directly against the dark line representing subsistence. The picture, although as much a product of imagination as Gainsborough's painting, helped give the old attitude that the "pressure of distress" on "the lower classes of society . . . is an evil so deeply seated that no human ingenuity can reach it" a new scientific lease on life as a "provable" proposition.[23] In this way, Malthus helped reinforce the idea that Our right to exclude Others from Our property in times of scarcity comes not only out of an unequal natural order but also out of Our hard work and Our socially beneficial abstinence. Challenges to Our right to accumulate indefinitely become threats not only to Our goodies but also to, among other things, Our self-image and identity as disciplined abstainers. In a newly vivid way, the Malthusian narrative asked its audience whose side they were really on. Like all narratives, metaphors, and pictures, it had the additional advantage in a debate of not colliding, logically speaking, with propositions or with opposing narratives, metaphors, and pictures. Removing or changing premises in arguments is often a tacit admission that they are invalid. Importing or switching narratives is safer in that it amounts only to quietly changing the subject or replacing background with foreground.

To audiences other than the one for which it was intended, of course, the appeal of Malthus's art was limited and his images of the poor insulting. In many ways, his concepts of social life looked as empty to the lower orders as their notions of subsistence, commons, and proper behavior looked to him. But how to communicate this to those who found their own identity and struggles expressed and idealized through Malthus's narrative? Malthus's acutest critics lived in a world so far removed from his that to them his views often seemed mad and evil, a bizarre stew of tautologies and falsehoods. Saying so did little to advance the debate. The success of Malthus with his chosen audience and his failure with others are two sides of the same coin, and one reason that his theories have so often seemed to be simultaneously common sense and nonsense.

Contemporary neo-Malthusian arguments, too, owe much of their imperviousness toward rational or scientific criticism to their artistry in papering over logical gaps with stories of Us and Others central to their audience's identity. They are able to arrive (with great shows of regret) at "conclusions" unfavorable to the underprivileged partly because, by deploying extrinsic narratives, they smuggle in assumptions prejudicial to them at the outset.

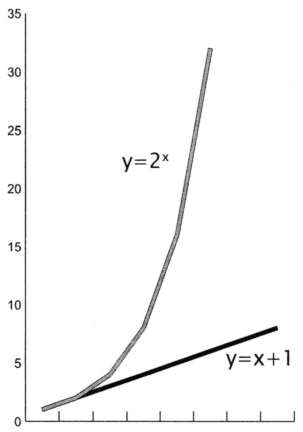

Figure 4.1.   T. R. Malthus's picture of the life of the lower classes. The steeply rising curve is the "power of population" to rise when unchecked, the dark line the far feebler power of food supplies to increase. Whereas for the rich, and for "civilized" societies, the upward thrust of the top curve is held in check by worries about loss of status, for the poor (and for "savage" and egalitarian societies) it strains more directly against the dark line representing subsistence. The picture helped turn the attitude that the "pressure of distress" on "the lower classes of society . . . is an evil so deeply seated that no human ingenuity can reach it" into a "provable" proposition.

For instance, immigration to Northern countries is sometimes criticized on the ground that "immigrants will adopt wasteful Northern lifestyles." This argument is advertised as nonracist and is backed with impressive numbers. Yet the conclusion relies on the premise that changing Northern lifestyles is a lower priority, or less achievable, than preventing others from sharing them. Those who already follow those lifestyles are treated as being entitled to them. This questionable premise escapes notice when embedded in stories of undeserving Others moving into Our space; or of the commons being overexploited by free riders; or of population bombs going off; or of Our overloaded lifeboat in the middle of a lake in a storm being faced with the prospect of Others from surrounding shipwrecks trying to clamber aboard. Among middle-class environmentalists, such stories have always enjoyed an appeal greater than that of other possible, equally cogent narratives: of human beings in faraway places being displaced or their commons enclosed by Our arms exports or corporate enterprises; of their lifeboats being sliced in two by industrial fishing trawlers or oil tankers; of "consumption bombs" going off in their midst; of people who walk around lakes when they see a storm coming rather than jump into leaky rubber rafts. Similarly, if population control programs have been disproportionately directed at women of color, it is not out of any scientific logic. Social problems are not caused by the XX chromosome, nor have women been engaging in parthenogenesis all these years.[24] It is rather that today's middle-class folk narratives about "population" put black females in the dramatic role of helplessly fertile Others in much the same way that Malthus's own narrative starred poor commoners.

WHY THE US-AND-THEM FEAR NARRATIVE NEEDS THE POLITICAL ECONOMY MODEL

If Malthus's political economy model needs an Us-and-Them terror framework to get off the ground, the Us-and-Them scare story also ultimately needs the political economy model. The model makes at least two contributions to the story. It helps construct a suitably alien Them for the narrative. And it conjures up a Fate that strives to lift a tale that scapegoats the poor for their own predicament to the level of tragedy.

The era in which the Malthusian discourse came of age—an era when the confines that had previously hedged in the market were being broken down, with all too few new constraints rising up to take their place—was one of stupendous suffering. It was suffering that was felt to be new in its volume, intensity, and possible consequences. "Within three miles of the house where I am writing these pages," wrote Gilbert Wakefield, Malthus's former tutor, in the same year that his old student was composing his *Essay on Population,*

> There is a much greater number of starving miserable human beings . . . than on any equal portion of ground through the habitable globe.[25]

Such suffering could not be ignored. It had to be addressed if not eased, accounted for if not justified. During Malthus's lifetime, explanations and proposals for action flooded the public realm. Added to old theories attributing pauperism to the poor's indiscipline or God's plan were new ones citing drug addiction, bad administration, primogeniture, maldistribution, inequality, and so on. The ferment over mass poverty and the poor laws shaped the minds of every intellectual of the time and for long afterward: from Mary Wollstonecraft to Charles Darwin, from Harriet Martineau to Karl Marx, from Robert Owen to Herbert Spencer.[26]

Malthus's code-predictive mathematics built on the elite tradition of blaming the poor for their plight by reducing the tensions of their culture to a seesaw battle between geometric and arithmetic series. This was more dehumanization than demonization. But if it scorned the sentimentalization of the poor practiced by Gainsborough and other painters, it had a similar effect of distancing the Other. Helping edit out the social background against which scapegoating of the poor might be seen for what it was, it pushed aside paternalistic observation or interaction only to replace it with calculation. The relentless Othering it enabled continues today whenever explanations of present scarcity invoking inequalities, land takeovers, wars, or erosion of commons are brushed aside with the riposte "Yes, but what about *future* human numbers?" (This reply usually means future numbers of Them.) This invitation to leave aside the details of who We and They really are and jump to a mathematical terror myth of abstract, inexorable, monolithic future tensions between Them and Nature functions, as Malthus's own narrative did, to obscure the politics of both the past and the present.

Yet, however successful it was in making the poor and women into Others, the story Malthus told, as he was well aware, still has a morally ugly sound to it. Benevolence and equality die an early death; the impulse to provide welfare is to be resisted; misery, disease, and vice provide the only cure for population crisis: it is difficult not to see the harsh measures the tale advocates as a kind of violence or aggression. Uglier still are the events that the narrative sanctions. As welfare was chipped away and poor rates were held down, workhouses were made as like prisons as possible in accordance with Malthusian ideals of instruction. Historian E. P. Thompson writes that the Poor Law Amendment Act of 1834, enacted with a respectful nod to Malthus, accompanied

> perhaps the most sustained attempt to impose an ideological dogma, in defiance of the evidence of human need, in English history.[27]

Equally ugly have been many subsequent applications of Malthusianism: the withholding of relief in times of famine in the nineteenth century, forced sterilization in the twentieth, and the persistent defense of overconsumption among the well-off.

At some point, responsibility for this order of violence, even against Others, needs to be denied. The denial, far from being merely individual, as in Freud, becomes one of the necessities of power and the tasks of culture: a collective, public, ongoing, recurring ritual denial transformed into a kind of civility, a denial that stunts reasoning about violent institutions and presents aggression as its virtuous opposite. Malthus modernized the elite fashion of identifying the poor's plight as their fate by using mathematics to explain why the killings troubling his society were unavoidable. The oppressed were recast as sacrifices, and those who scapegoated them as upholders of society. While the dead may have meant no harm, their nature victimized the community. Recalcitrant yokels, unmannerly Others, irreverent commoners undisciplined into infinite needs—all had to be either reformed or expelled from a rapidly marketizing social order. In the process, many were degraded into even more contemptible beings in need of still harsher measures of exclusion. On a Malthusian view, there was no malevolence in these killings. Paupers died from neglect, work, or their own nature. If they were treated brutally, it was for their own good and that of others. Relief would only cause more suffering. Abolishing it could be no crime. During the nineteenth and twentieth centuries, the Malthusian administration of poverty became a ritual in which millions were subjected to violence as the scapegoats for a social pestilence of which they themselves were the worst victims. As "overpopulation," they were offered up to an implacable nature in everyday ceremonies preserving the idealistic image of a self-regulating market. In the process, Malthus's dry mathematics acted as a ritual denial of the discrimination in the terror myths and of the persecution that they both gilded and sanctioned. It is no contradiction that one *Economist* cover from the time of the 1992 Earth Summit stirred population fears by picturing a crowd of African children behind the headline "The Question Rio Forgets," while a cover of a few years later presents similar African children as representatives of a deprived mass, clamoring for sweeping privatization, "free markets," and globalization. In one light, the "concern for the poor" to be found in Malthus and his followers can be seen structurally as that of a priest ridding the community of a plague through a sacrifice whose victims are open to later rehabilitation. The fact that the Malthusian story's implausibilities seem common sense to so many becomes less puzzling when the story is compared with other myths featuring what literary critic René Girard calls a "scapegoating delusion narrated from the standpoint of the deluded persecutors."[28] Such myths, as Girard points out, very often feature unbelievable premises, which are nonetheless unanimously accepted. Beginning as panicky free associations, which spread instantly through mobs in times of crisis, the premises are later remembered as established fact.

From this angle, too, it is easy to see why Malthus and Malthusians have often classified their narratives as tragedies. As Girard suggests, many tragedies can be read as sophisticated retellings of myths about the necessary sacrifice of troublemakers. In one variant of Malthus's tale, well-intentioned heroes are allowed briefly to enjoy equality and material improvement, only to come to grief through the enmity of nature and the tragic flaw of failing to acknowledge their own incorrigible individualism. Their strivings temporarily disturb an eternal system, which, after a short time of tragic upheaval, resettles into a "darkly tinted" equilibrium resembling modern capitalist society. The best-known neo-Malthusian narrative, authored by the eugenicist and plant biologist Garrett Hardin in 1968, even bears the title "tragedy."[29] Reviving nineteenth-century critiques of commons regimes, Hardin's "Tragedy of the Commons" traces how a common pasture is destroyed when its users, a group of stick figures who, deprived of the benefits of private property, all try to maximize their own individual short-term gain from the unpriced grass by grazing as many cows on it as they think they can get away with. Such tragedies are reimagined daily in the brains of influential economists eager to attribute environmental degradation to over-numerous commoners rather than their own policies and exploitation, or social breakdown to insufficient rather than excessive privatization. Most would be astonished and offended by accusations of scapegoating, racism, or ethnocentricity, which are in fact almost never made. Throughout, a modern sense of tragic destiny is provided by the Malthusian mathematics and the hard crust of economics and biology that has formed around it, although the mathematics, economics, and biology must all be seen as being continuous with the theodicy that animated Malthus's original writings. The same model that helps construct a Them easier to scapegoat also crafts a Fate that dresses up the scapegoating as a tragedy suitably ennobling to the ritual's participants.

CONCLUSION

Malthusianism has never really worked as a science. Nor does it amount to much as history. But it has always succeeded brilliantly as a prismatic compound of practices in which mathematics, economics, and Christian theology cannot be separated from metaphor, middle-class scare story, sacrifice ritual, and tragedy. It is partly through this inner breadth that Malthusianism has been able to organize so many productive scientific and bureaucratic enterprises and enter common sense through so many doors. Malthus's triumph, and the triumph of his successors, is that of conjoined poet, priest, and rationalist.

Malthusianism lives on, ubiquitous, resilient. Among its adherents, it is a part of both manners and identity. It writes the rules for how human beings are to contend with nature and how the blood of the past is to be commemorated to sanctify the violence of the future. But those who refuse to be its scapegoats struggle on as well, in alliances challenging neoliberalism as well as old and new forms of prejudice. To stand their ground, they need a narrative intensity and virtuosity to match its own.

NOTES

T. R. Malthus, *Essay on the Principle of Population* (Oxford: Oxford University Press, 1993 [1798]), 25.

1. Ian Hacking, *The Taming of Chance* (Cambridge: Cambridge University Press, 1990), 22.
2. Robert D. Kaplan, "The Coming Anarchy," *Atlantic Monthly* 273, no. 2 (February 1994): 44–76.
3. Dorothy Roberts, *Killing the Black Body: Race, Reproduction, and the Meaning of Liberty* (New York: Vintage Books, 1999); Jael Silliman and A. Bhattacharjee, eds., *Policing the National Body: Race, Gender, and Criminalization* (Boston: South End Press, 2002).
4. Betsy Hartmann and Anne Hendrixson, "Angry Young Men: The Strategic Demography and Geography of Threats," in *Making Threats: Biofears and Environmental Anxieties*, ed. Betsy Hartmann, Banu Subramaniam, and Charles Zerner (Lanham, Md.: Rowman & Littlefield, 2005).
5. Annette Burfoot, "An Interview with Dr Hugh Gorwill: Potential Risks to Women Exposed to Clomiphene Citrate," *Issues in Reproductive and Genetic Engineering* 5, no. 1 (1992): 22–30.
6. Ben Zuckerman and Stuart Hurlbert, "Is Overimmigration in the U.S. Morally Defensible?" *San Diego Union Tribune*, August 3, 2001.
7. David M. Levy and Sandra J. Peart, *The Secret History of the Dismal Science: Economics, Religion, and Race in the 19th Century* (Library of Economics and Liberty, 2001), www.econlib.org/library/Columns/LevyPeartdismal.html (accessed January 15, 2002).
8. Paul Ehrlich, *The Population Bomb* (New York: Ballantine Books, 1968), 1.
9. William Cobbett, "The Valley of the Avon," in *Rural Rides*, reprinted in A. Pyle, *Population: Contemporary Responses to Thomas Malthus* (Bristol, Eng.: Thoemmes, 1994 [1826]), 316–17, 299–321.
10. On commons, see James Acheson and Bonnie McCay, *The Question of the Commons* (Tucson: University of Arizona Press, 1990); and Ivan Illich, *Gender* (New York: Pantheon, 1983).
11. Karl Polanyi, *The Great Transformation* (Boston: Beacon, 2001 [1944]).
12. Joseph Townsend, *A Dissertation on the Poor Laws* (Berkeley: University of California Press, 1971 [1786]).
13. Malthus, *Essay*, 84
14. Malthus, *Essay*, 84.
15. Malthus, *Essay*, 85.
16. A. M. C. Waterman, *Revolution, Economics, and Religion: Christian Political Economy, 1798–1833* (Cambridge: Cambridge University Press, 1991), 27–28.
17. Philip Mirowski, *Machine Dreams: Economics Becomes a Cyborg Science* (Cambridge: Cambridge University Press, 2002), 9.
18. Hacking, *Taming of Chance*, 21.
19. James Steuart, *An Inquiry into the Principles of Political Oeconomy: Being an Essay on the Science of Domestic Policy in Free Nations* (London: Pickering and Chatto, 1998 [1767]).

20. Malthus, *Essay,* 14.

21. Carol Rose, "Property as Storytelling: Perspectives from Game Theory, Narrative Theory, Feminist Theory," *Yale Journal of Law and the Humanities* 2 (1990): 52, reprinted in Carol Rose, *Property and Persuasion: Essays on the History, Theory, and Rhetoric of Ownership* (Boulder, Colo.: Westview Press, 1994), 37–57.

22. John Barrell, *The Dark Side of the Landscape* (Cambridge: Cambridge University Press, 1980); Martin Postle, *Thomas Gainsborough* (London: Tate, 2002).

23. Malthus, *Essay,* 43.

24. I owe several of these examples to Christine von Weizsäcker and Sarah Sexton.

25. Quoted in E. P. Thompson, *The Making of the English Working Class* (London: Penguin, 1980 [1963]), 192.

26. Polanyi, *Great Transformation*; Barbara Kerr, *Bound to the Soil: A Social History of Dorset, 1750–1918* (London: John Baker, 1968), 96; R. Ashcraft, "Lockean Ideas, Poverty, and the Development of Liberal Political Theory," in *Early Modern Conceptions of Property*, ed. J. Brewer and S. Staves (London: Routledge, 1996), 43, 3–61.

27. Thompson, *English Working Class*, 295.

28. René Girard, "Generative Scapegoating," in *Violent Origins: Ritual Killing and Cultural Formation*, ed. R. G. Hamerton-Kelly (Stanford, Calif.: Stanford University Press, 1987), 79; see also, Paul Connerton, *How Societies Remember* (Cambridge: Cambridge University Press, 1989); Richard Wollheim, *The Sheep and the Ceremony* (Cambridge: Cambridge University Press, 1979); Pierre Bourdieu, *Outline of a Theory of Practice* (Cambridge: Cambridge University Press, 1977); Hermann Rebel, "Dark Events and Lynching Scenes in the Collective Memory," in *Agrarian Studies: Synthetic Work at the Cutting Edge*, ed. J. C. Scott and Nina Bhatt (New Haven, Conn.: Yale University Press, 2001), 44–65.

29. Garrett Hardin, "The Tragedy of the Commons," *Science* 162 (December 1968): 1243–48.

Reflections

Scarcity, Modernity, Terror

Michael Watts

> Scarcity: The quality, condition, or fact of being scarce. 1. Frugality, parsi-
> mony; niggardliness, stinginess, meanness . . . 2. Insufficiency of supply
> . . . 3. Insufficiency of supply in a community, of the necessaries of
> life . . . a period of scarcity.
>
> —*Oxford English Dictionary*

> The whole of human development, at least up until now, has been a bitter
> struggle against scarcity.
>
> —Jean Paul Sartre, *Critique of Dialectical Reason*

The word *scarcity* does not appear as one of Raymond Williams's keywords
in his historical semantics of modernity *Keywords*.[1] Perhaps this is not surprising, because the very triumph of the modern stands as a crushing victory
over premodern want and dearth. It is abundance, surplus, and conspicuous
consumption—what Thorsten Veblen calls "pecuniary capitalism"—and an
economy of waste that distinguishes the modern epoch and contemporary
capitalism.[2] Yet *scarcity*'s absence in *Keywords* must confront the obvious
fact that scarcity—as dearth, as threat, as the very condition of the material
world—is very much with us. Its presence is not simply reflected in the ap-
palling fact that currently one in seven people in the world goes hungry[3]—
the brute fact of basic want—but also in the way that scarcity operates as a
principle of rule and of personal conduct. Indeed, one might say that scarcity
represents a sort of precondition for the modern, an epistemological principle on which our lives are built. It operates as part of a powerful discursive
formation of the modern world. I want to argue that scarcity is central to the

operation of liberal governmentality. Fear and terror, at least since the eighteenth century, are the bedfellows of scarcity. And this raises necessarily the question of how this unholy trinity—scarcity, fear, and terror—operate in the name of improvement, government, and freedom.

* * *

Here are three scarcity narratives taken almost at random from the press. A new report, *The Security Demographic*, by Population Action International, one of the most important and influential policy and advocacy groups for family planning and population programs, concludes that high population growth and resource scarcities (water and land in particular) are closely associated with civil conflicts.[4] A demographic transition can "actually reduce the risk of civil violent conflict." About half of the world's countries exhibit demographic characteristics that add to their risk of civil conflict during the current decade (as a prediction, this may strike you as not terribly robust, but that's another matter). Twenty-one countries in east and west Africa, south Asia, and the Middle East are seen to be likely sites for "future upheaval"— not surprisingly, in countries that represent the core of the post–September 11 U.S. military strategy. The report makes clear that there is no demographic determinism at work but that population growth is a driving force that produces key "stresses": a youth bulge in rapidly growing cities and an intense competition for scarce and strategic resources.

On January 4, 2004, Royal Dutch/Shell, the transnational oil major, announced that it was reducing its proven oil and gas reserves by 20 percent (almost 50 percent from Nigeria and Australia).[5] The announcement raised questions about the health of the company and, more generally, about the tabulation of oil and gas reserves throughout the industry. Shell's reassessment feeds into an ongoing anxiety, inside and outside of the petroleum industry, over the purported oil shortage. Oil scarcity, as a nonrenewable resource, has—like population—a long lineage. Periodic oil "crises" pockmark the annals of petroleum's historic rise to strategic eminence in the global economy. The threat of short-term dislocation of markets (compounded by growing import dependency in the case of the United States) and the long-term challenge of diminishing reserves are omnipresent. Hubbert's peak— the idea that oil product has peaked or is about to peak—encapsulates the compelling notion of an impending world oil shortage.[6] Indeed, this notion of oil scarcity has substantial currency across political and sectoral lines. Oil analysts and consultants, environmentalists, resource economists, government regulators, and antiglobal activists can, and do, participate in the oil scarcity narrative. The very idea of "blood for oil"—the rallying cry of the antiwar movement—turns on the fact that Iraq sits on the second largest oil reserves on the planet. In the context of growing scarcity (driven by U.S. consumption and the vast projected increases associated with future industrial growth in India and China), the occupation of Iraq was driven by the structural need to "liberate" 112 billion barrels of scarce oil running from Kirkuk to Basra.

The *New York Times* headline reads, "Why Americans Must Keep Spending."[7] Consumer spending as a proportion of gross domestic product is currently higher than that of any period since the pent-up postwar boom of the late 1940s. The proportion of consumer spending on "basic necessities" has fallen by 50 percent since 1949, but there has been a massive proliferation in other arenas. The bottom line, say the experts, is that consumers will keep spending no matter what: "Consumers in America spend because they feel they must spend. . . . They have too many needs, some that were luxuries yesterday." What might the relentless upward curve of consumer spending have to do with scarcity? One aspect of the *Times* story addresses the process— cultural, ideological, and economic—by which commodities become "necessities"; another speaks to the means by which this conversion is infinite, why needs are endless and why spending cannot stop. The *Times* had stumbled across a much larger historical shift, the great arch leading from an ancient Greek world of fixed "natural" needs to the seventeenth-century Hobbesian notion of desiring beings in continual motion ever seeking what we do not have. The fact of "economizing" is central to rule and government, to the very forms of freedom associated with liberal governance.

* * *

There is a way, a genealogy in fact, in which a discourse of scarcity and fear encompasses all three newspaper accounts I have sketched here. Malthusian scarcity, the artificial scarcity of rents, and the social world of scarcity are differing threads in the rise of a discourse (a set of ideas, institutions, and political practices) that is central to liberal government as we know it.[8] Malthus is present, one might say, at the birth of modern scarcity, of a discursive formation capable of weaving these threads together and of extending into other seemingly unrelated arenas of modern political economy.[9] Malthus was a radical presence in the rendering of new forms of welfare rooted in individual responsibility—to what Karl Polanyi calls the "discovery of society"[10]—but more profoundly to the exercise of modern rule and to modern forms of discipline, sovereignty, and government.[11]

It is hard to underestimate the enormous impact and legacy of Malthus and what has been called his "theology of scarcity."[12] Darwin, Wallace, Ricardo, J. M. Keynes—to say nothing of such lesser luminaries as Paul Ehrlich—have all acknowledged the legacy, the critical influence, of his ideas on their thinking. Malthus's influence was probably at its height in Britain in the second decade of the nineteenth century, when the debate over the abolition of the poor laws was at its most intense; but the suturing of his name to any discussion of demographic growth and poverty has persisted in a way that exceeds the legacies of many of his contemporaries—Adam Smith, David Ricardo, David Hume, William Godwin, Tom Paine, and perhaps even Marx himself.[13]

Malthus was a voice of *reaction*—recognizing that his reactionary views necessitated reform and indeed a quite radical reform by which the old moral economy of the eighteenth century was displaced by new forms of liberal governance and forms of personal responsibility.[14] And furthermore this reaction must be seen in class terms: only in this way can one understand that Malthus himself invokes the "passion of the sexes" and its checks operating in two socially distinctive ways. For the wealthy, the preventive checks to growth are compelled by their desire to avoid, as it were, downward mobility (i.e., compromising their wealth): that is to say, "fear of misery" is beaten out by hope for betterment. The poor, conversely, are shackled by vice and misery and must be goaded by necessity and insecurity as a spur to industry. Malthus's concern with political liberty is, as with all of his work, seized by a sort of paternalism and a class fear.

Malthus's ideas were put to work at a moment of political crisis. Karl Polanyi saw the debates over Speenhamland (the poor law reforms following the hardships of the early 1790s), and what he called pauperism and political economy, as "a great whole—the discovery of society."[15] The figure of the pauper was, in other words, part of a conversation—in which Malthus was a central presence—in which poverty and scarcity came to be thought about as part of a form of liberal governance; it became a social problem to be regulated. In a sense, then, population per se was less central to Malthus than the shift from an Elizabethan moral economy (a paternalist system of policing to relieve and employ the poor, as Edward Thompson sees it)[16] to a liberal mode of government in which poverty was a product of individual responsibility. Implicit in the shift from Speenhamland in 1795 to the repeal of the poor laws in 1834 is marked by a parallel tectonic movement, namely, a redefinition of state action: a retraction of state obligations to those without property and correspondingly new forms of state control and bureaucratization of relief. As Mitchell Dean puts it,

> If this liberal mode of government is distinguished by its aim of incorporating self-responsibility and familial duty within the lives of the propertyless, it does so by multiplying the institutional and administrative networks which surround poverty.[17]

To the extent that this was part of a sometimes acerbic debate over ethics, the historic role of Malthus was to root them in the overwhelming bioeconomic laws of population and subsistence.

The liberal mode of government, scarcity as an object of regulation and discipline, and Malthus's bioeconomic laws can be productively understood as a totality. Government for Foucault referred famously to the "conduct of conduct," a more or less calculated and rational set of ways of shaping conduct and of securing rule through a multiplicity of authorities and agencies in and outside of the state and at a variety of spatial levels. In contrast to forms of pastoral power of the Middle Ages, from which a sense of sovereignty was derived, Foucault charted an important historical shift, beginning in the sixteenth century, toward government as a right manner of disposing things "so as to not lead to the common good . . . but to an end that is convenient for each of the things governed."[18] At the center of government lay a complex notion of the governance of things. As he puts it,

> The things, in this sense, with which government is to be concerned are in fact men, but men in their relations, their links, their imbrication with those things that are wealth, resources, means of subsistence, the territory with its specific qualities, climate, irrigation, and fertility; men in their relation to those other things that are customs, habits, ways of acting and thinking; and finally men in relation to those still other things that might be accidents and misfortunes such as famines, epidemics, death, and so on.[19]

Foucault was concerned to show how government constituted differing expressions of "governmentality," which he articulates in terms of the pastoral (classically feudal in character), the disciplinary (the institutions of subjection from the prison to the school), and biopower (the administration of forms of life). Modern governmentality was rendered distinctive by the specific forms in which "the population" (the poor, the welfare mother) and "the economy" (as a separable and regulable entity) was administered. What was key for Foucault was not the displacement of one form of power by another, nor the historical substitution of feudal by modern government, but the complex triangulation involved in sustaining many forms of power put to the purpose of security and regulation. In reality, he notes, one has a triangle, sovereignty–discipline–government, "which has as its primary target the population, and as its essential mechanism the apparatuses of security." Three movements—government, population, political economy—came to constitute from the eighteenth century onward a solid series.[20]

How then do Malthus and liberal government speak to the question of scarcity and the modern? Malthus was the scientific theorist of antiradicalism, opposing not simply the French Revolution. He proposed an alternative in which scarcity—limited means and infinite needs—provided a mode of governing, a calculus for shaping the conduct of conduct. Scarcity shifted from a premodern sense of periods of necessary dearth to a generalized condition of insufficiency. By the mid- to late-nineteenth century, after Malthus's pessimism lost some of its power, scarcity came to hold what Xenos calls "the promise of abundance."[21] But this promise required choice, discipline, and above all a rational economic man capable of "economizing": making choices to allocate scarce resources among competing ends.[22] Scarcity in this generalized sense was present in the debate of the poor laws and entered into modern government with a broad discursive resonance. It became central to economics, which of course was significant not simply in the rise of neoclassical free market thinking but in the entire arena of economic policy and the very idea of a national economy.[23] Sartre famously claims that "the whole of human development, at least up until now, has been the bitter struggle against scarcity."[24] Scarcity became, one might say, a condition of possibility for modern rule. It represents a "discursive formation" precisely because it operates across many domains in and beyond the state (think of the army of family-planning nongovernmental organizations or famine-relief agencies).

Finally, why is it that scarcity and terror are, as a constitutive part of liberal governmentality, so tied to terror and fear. It is too superficial to simply say that there is a deeply held culture of fear in which "immense power and money await those who tap into our moral insecurities and supply us with symbolic substitutes."[25] The Malthusian tradition raises the specter of how scarcity breeds competition, conflict, famine, and death; and there is, of course, an academic industry purporting to chart the relations between deprivation and rebellion or even genocide. And ideas about scarcity have been the *source* of terror: Malthus saw no need to run from the deployment of state terror, and Malthusian famine policy in the late Victorian empire laid the foundation for what Davis has rightly called a holocaust.[26] But perhaps one must go deeper. Scarcity should be seen as a deeply modern concept, at heart contradictory, as is the experience of modernity itself. On the one side is the harbinger of death and catastrophe, and on the other that of abundance and wealth. Perhaps, as Malthus understood, there is something Freudian at work here pushing us into the realm of drive and instinct. If society was in a constant state of "rutting," Malthus accepted that the passion of the sexes was inevitable, necessary, and pleasurable. But these libidinal drives contained the possibility of challenging social order. Unlike Adam Smith, however, for whom the desire to accumulate was boundless (and, hence, could tear society apart), for Malthus "bodily cravings are fixed and permanent." As a result, the problem is not so much that there is no upper limit but that there is no lower limit. Desire could wither away and, hence, Malthus's concern with sloth and listlessness among the poor, with the calamity of men without drives. It was only fear of insecurity and scarcity— driven by population growth—that could act as a spur to industry, indeed to progress itself. What troubled Malthus was precisely that the poor laws were "a kind of systematic and certain relief on which the poor could confidently depend" (it was a sort of *right*). And this confidence carried two enormous burdens: first, it was antithetical to the spur of fear and insecurity (of the disciplining effects of the labor market); and, second, it encouraged the poor to stand up for the subversive notion of the right to subsistence. The renewal of the poor law debate between 1830 and 1834 was in this sense about a simmering crisis of social control and class hegemony. Scarcity then returns us to the question of fear and terror through class (and imperial) power.

Perhaps there is a homology between Malthus's figure of the pauper and President Bush's stigmatization of the Islamist militant or the Palestinian suicide bomber. Both are rooted in demographic growth and high-fertility regime; each driven by passions and drives peculiar to their class; one grounded in a discourse of poverty, the other in Orientalism. Both, in their own ways, are figures of terror. In the poor house, scarcity has its origins in "the superior power of population to the means of subsistence."[27] In the West Bank or among the recruits of Islamic jihad, scarcity draws its sustenance from the superior power of Islamic radicalism over failed secular nationalism. The echo of Malthus's "gathering fresh darkness and terror" in the present moment of danger is deafening.

NOTES

Oxford English Dictionary (London: Oxford University Press, 1990), 578–79. P. Sartre, *Critique of Dialectical Reason* (London: Verso, 1973), 23.

1. Raymond Williams, *Keywords* (London: Oxford University Press, 1973), 11–26.
2. T. Veblen, *The Theory of the Leisure Class* (London: Penguin, 1979 [1899]).
3. United Nations, *World Hunger* (Rome: United Nations, 2003).
4. Population Action International, *The Security Demographic* (Washington, D.C.: Population Action International, 2003).
5. Louis Uchitelle, "Why Americans Must Keep Spending," *New York Times*, December 1, 2003, 1C.
6. Kenneth S. Deffreyes, *Hubbert's Peak* (Princeton, N.J.: Princeton University Press, 2001).
7. Uchitelle, "Why Americans Must Keep Spending."
8. M. Dean, *The Constitution of Poverty* (London: Routledge, 1991).
9. T. Malthus, *Essay on the Principal of Population* (London: Oxford University Press, 1990 [1798]).
10. Karl Polanyi, *The Great Transformation* (Boston: Beacon Press, 1947), 103.
11. M. LeMahieu, "Malthus and the Theology of Scarcity," *Journal of the History of Ideas* 40, no. 3 (October 1979): 467–74.
12. His book on population was the most widely read tract in the wake of Adam Smith's *An Inquiry into the Wealth of Modern Nations* (New York: Modern Library, 1937).
13. E. P. Thompson, *Customs in Common* (London: Penguin, 1991).
14. Dean, *Constitution of Poverty*.
15. Polanyi, *The Great Transformation*, 103.
16. Thompson, *Customs in Common*.
17. Dean, *Constitution of Poverty*.

18. Michel Foucault, *Power*, vol. 3 (New York: New Press, 2000), 208–9.

19. Foucault, *Power*, 219.

20. Nicholas Xenos, *Scarcity and Modernity* (London: Routledge, 1989), 67–84.

21. Xenos, *Scarcity and Modernity*, 67–84.

22. L. Robbins, *The Nature and Significance of Economic Science* (London: MacMillan, 1932).

23. T. Mitchell, *The Rule of Experts* (Berkeley: University of California Press, 2000).

24. Sartre, *Critique of Dialectical Reason*, 23.

25. B. Glassner, *The Culture of Fear* (New York: Basic Books, 1999).

26. Mike Davis, *Late Victorian Holocausts* (London: Verso, 2001).

27. Malthus, *Population*. Quoted in Larry Lohmann, "Malthusianism and the Terror of Scarcity," in *Making Threats: Biofears and Environmental Anxieties*, ed. Betsy Hartmann, Banu Subramaniam, Charles Zerner (Lanham, Md.: Rowman & Littlefield, 2005).

III

PURITY

5

Decoding the
Debate on "Frankenfood"

Hugh Gusterson

Since the development in the early 1990s of the world's first genetically modified (GM) crop (a pest-resistant tobacco plant in China), the industry for bioengineered food has become big business. At the start of the new millennium 72 percent of the world's GM crops were grown in the United States, where sixty million acres—25 percent of all U.S. cropland—were planted with GM seeds. One-half of all the soy and one-third of all the corn and cotton grown in the United States are GM, and it is estimated that thirty thousand products, or about two-thirds of all processed foods in the United States, are GM. Since it costs between $30 million and $50 million to bring a GM crop to market, most GM crops have been developed primarily with Western markets in mind, rather than those of the less-lucrative Third World.[1] This has led Luiz Antonio Barreto de Castro, the head of Brazil's National Technical Committee on Biosafety, to remark ironically that "for the first time, populations of the First World will serve as the guinea pigs for the countries of the Third World."[2]

First-generation GM crops have been bioengineered to produce their own pesticides, to have immunity from selected pesticides, to resist selected pests, to resist frost, to stay fresh longer, or to be sterile. These include strains of corn that produce within their own cells *Bacillus thuringiensis* (Bt), a "natural" pesticide sometimes used by organic gardeners to repel bollworms; strains of soy bean that are immune to particular pesticides (such as Monsanto's Roundup Ready soy bean, which is resistant to Monsanto's own Roundup pesticide); squashes designed to resist particular viruses; tomatoes and strawberries implanted with a cold-resistant gene from Arctic flounder so that they can be grown in colder climates than usual; Calgene's Flavr Savr tomato, in which the gene that activates rotting has been reversed; and Monsanto seeds equipped with a "terminator" gene to render them infertile.[3]

Second-generation GM crops may focus more on "value enhancement" of crops.[4] There is already a strain of "golden rice" designed to boost metabolization of vitamin A, as well as "super" catfish and salmon that grow to maturity unusually quickly. Also in development are better-tasting, more-digestible soybeans and higher-oil strains of corn. And there are attempts underway to develop fruits and vegetables that would vaccinate those who eat them against particular viruses, thus obviating the need for cumbersome vaccination programs, which, in the Third World particularly, have proved difficult to mount. There is even a project to engineer a nonallergenic cat.[5] The agricultural biotechnology industry and its allies claim that such developments constitute a new "Green Revolution" in the making that will improve the practice of agriculture and enable us to feed more people with less land. Saying that GM technology will be essential in the fight against global hunger, they argue that GM crops will enable us to achieve higher yields with less pesticide and less artificial fertilizer; to grow crops at times of year and in places where they would have failed before; to bring crops to maturity more quickly; and to amplify the nutritional and medicinal value of selected crops. With regard to vitamin A–enriched "golden rice," for example, they point out that one hundred million children under the age of five currently suffer from vitamin A deficiency, which is implicated in blindness, chronic diarrhea, and measles. Over three million children die of measles and diarrhea in the Third World each year.[6]

Such optimism notwithstanding, recent years have seen the emergence of a burgeoning social movement, first in Europe and more recently in the United States, of protest against GM foods.[7] This movement includes major name-brand environmental organizations (Greenpeace, Friends of the Earth, and the Earth Island Institute); scientists' groups (the Union of Concerned Scientists and the Council for Responsible Genetics); and less-well-known organizations, such as the Native Forest Network, the Indigenous Peoples Council on Biocolonialism, the Organic Farmers Association, Genetix Snowball, Genetix Food Alert, the Rural Advancement Foundation, Food First, and the Foundation on Economic Trends. The Genetic Engineering Action Network has emerged as an umbrella group to coordinate the efforts of many of these groups. While activists in Britain and France have been conspicuously (often theatrically) militant, invading farmers' fields in white decontamination suits to rip up their GM crops and vandalizing McDonald's franchises, their American counterparts have tended to eschew such tactics in favor of street protests, conferences, and letter-writing campaigns.

Those opposed to GM crops make a number of arguments. They say that genetic engineering can introduce allergens into food that will be eaten by unsuspecting consumers.[8] Citing the controversial research of the English scientist Arpad Pusztai, who was fired after going to the media with his claim that rats' digestive and immune systems were harmed by GM potatoes in his experiments, they argue that GM foods may have harmful effects on human health.[9] They maintain that the antibiotic-resistant "marker genes" used to determine whether gene transfers have been successful could hasten the development of antibiotic-resistant bacteria. They point out that Bt crops (crops that produce their own Bt) will accelerate the development of pest resistance to the organic Bt pesticide, while herbicide-tolerant crops will cross-pollinate with weeds, producing "superweeds" that cannot easily be destroyed by common pesticides. And they cite another controversial study, this one at Cornell, which found that feeding on pollen from Bt corn killed larvae of the monarch butterfly.[10] Finally, pointing out that we already produce enough food for everyone on the planet, they argue that hunger is caused not by agricultural underproduction but by political and economic systems that deprive the hungry of access to food. The promise of an end to hunger, these critics say, is a rhetorical smokescreen that conceals the agrobiotech industry's real agenda: increased profits and control over farmers.[11]

Such arguments against GM foods have made more headway in Europe than in the United States. (Indeed, studies show that most Americans are surprised to learn that they are already eating GM foods, and many believe that tomatoes do not contain genes at all until they have been genetically modified).[12] In Europe, although GM crop trials continue, under pressure from the European public, the European Union instituted a moratorium on GM food imports from 1999 to 2004. At the time of writing, the European Union has only licensed one GM food for import (a pest-resistant corn developed by Syngenta) since the termination of the moratorium and, unlike the United States, it mandates strict labeling of all GM foods.[13] Many mainstream European supermarkets now refuse to stock any GM food. In the United Kingdom, for example, Sainsbury's, Tesco's, Safeway, the Co-op, and Marks and Spencer's are all GM-free. This European resistance to GM crops has in turn hurt the U.S. GM crop industry, since American farmers cannot sell GM food to the European market and must incur the additional expense of separating GM from non-GM food when exporting to Europe. This has led the United States to file a World Trade Organization complaint against the European Union for illegal restraint of trade.

While the debate about GM food has received extensive media coverage, relatively little has been written about it by sociologists, anthropologists, or practitioners of science studies.[14] In thinking how to analyze this debate as an anthropologist of science, I have taken as my starting point Ann Murcott's plea for a "considered sociology" of the GM food debate that, "rather than taking sides . . . requires concentrating on how the sides came to be the way they are."[15] Such an analysis asks, "What are the knowledges of GM food? How is knowledge of GM food declared? On what claims is knowing based?"

In this chapter, I map and analyze the discursive formations that have grown up around the GM food debate. In the next section, I map the discourse of anti-GM activists, using material culled from anti-GM flyers, talks, and articles in the media. Next, I sketch the contours of pro-GM discourse, drawing on pro-GM commentary in the media and on material provided to me by Monsanto. Then, in the more detailed analysis that follows this exercise in discursive mapping, I select two themes from this field of discourse for more detailed discussion: I ask how we are to understand the fact that critics of GM foods are so concerned about the pollution of something they call "nature," and I ask what it means that those who defend GM crops are so concerned about the authority of something they call "science." Finally, by way of conclusion, I assess the benefits and limitations of discourses that rely so heavily on, respectively, an idealized view of nature and an idealized view of science, and ask whether it would be possible to discuss risk in a different way.

In mapping the discourses that have arisen to contest and defend GM foods, I am interested in the way claimed facts and arguments are made meaningful by recurrent metaphors, symbols, and narrative themes. In his work on narratological tropes in policy analysis, Emory Roe has argued that "stories commonly used in describing and analyzing policy issues are a force in themselves, and must be considered explicitly in assessing policy options."[16] What makes factual claims about, for example, global warming plausible, Roe argues, is the broader narrative about the world within which they are embedded. As Carol Cohn and Emily Martin have shown in their work on the discourse of defense intellectuals and biologists, respectively,[17] it is particularly important in undertaking this kind of discourse analysis to pay attention to metaphors, to the subject position from which a story is told, and to strategies for presenting a contested position as obvious or natural.[18]

Finally, I assume here that a field of discourse must be seen as a whole and that the discourses of those for and against a particular technology cannot properly be understood in isolation from the other. Anthropologists have traditionally sought, when doing fieldwork abroad, to make the strange familiar and, when doing fieldwork at home, to make the familiar strange. For the anthropologist seeking to make the familiar strange in domestic debates about science, the juxtaposition of opposed discourses in policy debates offers a particularly effective strategy for relativizing and dramatizing the cultural construction of policy positions that claim simply to represent the world as it is. Of course, the price that must be paid here is that the relativizing effect of this strategy makes itself felt as much upon political positions with which one is inclined to sympathize as upon those one may dislike.

Discourse analysis does have its limits as an analytical tool. It tends to abstract speech from other kinds of practices and to reframe power struggles as debating contests. As Martin Teitel writes in his own commentary on GM food, "we are not faced with 'two sides' of an issue who are having a debate but, rather, an industry with a product to sell and huge sums of money at stake seeking to impose its views on the public."[19] Nevertheless, discourse analysis is a powerful tool for revealing the overarching structure and foundational assumptions of a political controversy and, in making assumptions visible, it may make it easier to transcend them and move debate forward.

THE DISCOURSE AGAINST GM CROPS

The discourse that is crystallizing in opposition to GM foods on both sides of the Atlantic emphasizes the undemocratic way in which GM products have been introduced into our food supply, the greed and unaccountability of agricultural biotechnology companies, images of irreversible contamination, and the destruction of "nature." Although it is often portrayed by its opponents as an "antiscience" movement, the movement against GM foods does draw for its authority on the pronouncements of scientific experts.

Democracy and Corporate Greed

Jose Bove, the charismatic leader of the "Confederation Paysanne" in France, on trial for destroying a shipment of Bt corn, turned the tables on the court, saying, "When were farmers and consumers asked what they think about this? Never. The decisions have been taken at the level of the [World Trade Organization]. . . . GM maize is . . . the symbol of a system of agriculture and a type of society that I refuse to accept. . . . Political choices are swept aside by the power of money."[20]

It is a recurrent theme in the anti-GM literature that citizens in a democracy, and consumers in a capitalist economy, should have a "right to choose" that has been taken away from them because "quietly and with very little media attention, giant 'biotechnology' corporations have rapidly introduced genetically engineered foods into our food supply."[21] The invisibility of modified genes in foodstuffs on the shelves of supermarkets compounds the problem: "by looking at these tomatoes you have no way of knowing that they may include the DNA of flounder or North Atlantic shellfish," says one flyer.[22] In the United States, this sense of injury is magnified by the government's refusal to mandate the labeling of GM foods.

Anti-GM activists have called for citizens to organize and demand the labeling of GM foods and for consumers to stage boycotts of stores that refuse to disclose whether or not they stock GM foods.[23] Their target is what one publication refers to as "a powerful, profit-driven industry, comprised largely of the same companies that have made their fortunes in chemical pesticides," and is now effecting "corporate capture of the food chain."[24] One flyer states that "biotechnology promotes a view of living beings with no greater value than as industrial product."[25] "If the trend is not stopped," says another broadsheet, "the patenting of transgenic plants and food-producing animals will soon lead to universal 'bioserfdom' in which farmers will lease their plants and animals from biotech conglomerates such as Monsanto and pay royalties on seeds and offspring."[26]

Pollution

The companies that seek to commodify nature in this way are frequently identified in this literature with pollution. The fact that they also manufacture pesticides is emphasized repeatedly. One flyer, for example, describes Monsanto as "the company that brought us Agent Orange and PCBs."[27]

The anti-GM discourse is full of metaphors and images of mutation and contamination. Anti-GM flyers are often decorated with pictures of corn stuck with syringes or potatoes and tomatoes that look mutant and abused, some sporting stitched Frankenstein-like scars on what have been turned into faces in the images. At street protests, some demonstrators even dress up as mutant vegetables. Meanwhile the discourse is full of references to "frankenfood," "frankenfish," and "frankencorn" and to the mutant "superbugs" and "superweeds" that these products are expected to produce in time. In keeping with the Frankenstein theme, when British prime minister Tony Blair boasted that he eats GM foods, he was promptly rechristened the "Prime Monster."[28]

Anti-GM literature also talks about "contaminated DNA," "genetic pollution," the intrusion into our food of "alien genes" and "foreign genes," and the need for farmers to segregate GM from non-GM corn. Greenpeace has described raids on GM crops in British farmers' fields as "decontamination" exercises, and those participating often dramatize the point by wearing white decontamination suits of the kind worn by those responding to toxic spills of chemicals.[29]

The comparison with more familiar kinds of pollution is recurrent. A full-page advertisement in the *New York Times* speaks of the biotechnology industry's plans to "dump" plants and animals into the environment—"dump" being a word more commonly associated with toxic waste than living organisms.[30] A newsletter quotes Jeremy Rifkin, a prominent critic of the biotechnology industry, as saying that "genetic pollution will loom as significantly on the political agenda of the twenty-first century as chemical and nuclear pollution have in the twentieth."[31] Another flyer says that, in the hands of the biotechnology industry, food becomes a form of toxic waste, and it points out that, in the case of Bt corn, consumers are confronted with a "food that is itself a pesticide registered with the EPA."[32] The association of transgenic food with allergies in anti-GM discourse only compounds this sense that there is something inherently toxic about the food.

Finally, the pollution inherent in GM foods is presented in terms of a transgressive confusion of categories that may arouse disgust. The following quotation even goes so far as to identify the practice of eating GM foods with the most disgusting practice of all—cannibalism:

> Vegetarians may not wish to eat vegetables that have been engineered to contain animal genes. Jewish people who keep kosher may not wish to eat products that have been engineered with pig genes. Many consumers may not wish to consume foods containing human genes.[33]

The Assault on "Nature"

The confusion of categories that genetic engineering involves is, above all, presented as "unnatural." Calling genetic engineering a "highly unnatural technology," one flyer says, "For the first time, humans are able to manipulate the very fabric of life, shuffling the genetic deck that controls every aspect of every living organism in ways that nature never intended."[34] Another flyer says that "genetic engineering is a radical departure from traditional plant and animal breeding. . . . Genetic engineering breaks down natural barriers between humans, animals, and plants."[35]

But nothing in anti-GM discourse quite symbolizes the propensity of GM technology to violate the integrity of nature as powerfully as Monsanto's "terminator" gene: "The terminator gene, which renders corporate seeds sterile . . . is an unconscionable technology because it destroys life."[36] Here transgenic biotechnology is presented not as a way to reshape life but as the means toward a sacrilegious assault on the fertility of the natural world and on the essence of life itself: the will to reproduce. Where pro-GM discourse valorizes genetic engineering as the means to creating unprecedented abundance, a superfertile natural world, anti-GM discourse associates transgenic technology with death and sterility—stressing the prospect of species extinctions, plagues of superpests, and plants programmed like the androids of *Blade Runner* to die at their appointed hour without reproducing.

The Appeal to Science

The sociologist Phil Sutton observes that "established environmental organizations such as Greenpeace and Friends of the Earth have over time become increasingly professionalized and dependent on rational modes of argumentation which rely heavily on scientific knowledge as a way of gaining credibility and respectability."[37] One might add that, in the debate about genetically modified organisms (GMOs), even the less-mainstream environmental organizations lean heavily on the authority of science, at least when it suits them. Thus, in anti-GM discourse, although it is science that is said to be destroying the natural world through GM technology, it is also scientists who speak for nature about the dangers of what is being done: "Mounting scientific evidence suggests that genetically engineered foods may present serious hazards for human health and the environment. The British Medical Association has called for a ban on genetically engineered foods."[38] "In one survey 100 environmental scientists in the United States warned that genetic engineering's 'imprudent or careless use . . . could lead to irreversible, devastating damage to the ecology of the planet.'"[39]

THE DISCOURSE IN DEFENSE OF GM CROPS

Those who support GM crops argue that the technology of genetic modification merely renders more targeted and deliberate a practice that humans have practiced for generations—the improvement of crops. They argue that GM technology promises to save the lives and improve the diets of the poor in the Third World and that we therefore have a moral responsibility to move forward with it. They also accuse those who oppose GM crops of being impervious to scientific evidence, maybe even opposed to science itself or, if they are scientists, of practicing "junk science."

Genetic Technology as the Embellishment of Tradition

One of the principal arguments used by those defending the genetic engineering of crops is that, while the precise technique used in the laboratories of agribusiness might be novel, the enterprise of experimentation to improve plant genetics is as old as farming itself, giving us crops today that never existed in "nature." For example, Prince Philip of England told a reporter, "Do not let us forget that we have had genetically modified animals and plants ever since people started selective breeding. People are worried about genetically modified organisms getting into the environment. What people forget is that the introduction of exotic species—like for example the introduction of the grey squirrel into this country—is going to, or has done, far more damage than a genetically modified piece of potato."[40] Writing in the London *Times*, another commentator said, "The only time and place where there were no GM plants was in the Garden of Eden. . . . Ever since then nature and husbandry have been creating hybrids by genetic engineering. . . . These single-issue Green zealots cause as much harm as the Luddites of the Captain Swing riots 170 years ago."[41]

James Watson, one of the discoverers of DNA and a fierce defender of GM food technology, points out that it is not new for plants to contain insecticides either. Arguing that biotechnologists are simply taking over where the invisible hand of evolution left off, he says, "Seeds have always been bred to be bug-resistant by natural selection. Plants that didn't have these compounds died out. Plants are naturally full of a variety of components which kill insects; that's their protection against being eaten."[42]

Hunger

Florence Wambugu is director of the International Service for the acquisition of Agri-Biotech Applications in Nairobi. The journalist Madeline Nash, writing in *Time* magazine, says,

> For Wambugu, the flap in the U.S. and Europe over genetically modified crops seems almost ludicrous. In Africa, she notes, nearly half the fruit and vegetable harvest is lost because it rots on the way to market. "If we had a transgenic banana that ripened more slowly," she says, "we could have 40% more bananas than now." Wambugu also dreams of getting access to herbicide-resistant crops. Says she: "we could liberate so many of our people if our crops were resistant to herbicides that we could spray on the surrounding weeds. Weeding enslaves Africans; it keeps children from school.[43]

Some commentators point to crops such as the new vitamin A–enriched "golden rice" and argue that anti-GM activists' espousal of the "precautionary principle" is irresponsible, even immoral. (According to the precautionary principle, new plants should not be introduced until the consequences of their introduction are fully understood, in order to ensure that ecological systems do not sustain irreversible damage). "Turning our back on lifesaving bioengineered products would irresponsibly condemn millions of people to unnecessary suffering and early deaths," said one commentator, arguing that it is more appropriate to evaluate the balance of probabilities in a GM and a non-GM world than to demand impossible guarantees of perfect safety as the precautionary principle does.[44]

Pro-GM commentators also often accuse their opponents of a hypocritical elitism that condemns the poor to suffer and starve in the service of First World environmental correctness. "I shuddered recently," says former Senator George McGovern, "when I read that a prosperous chef of a chic Manhattan restaurant denounced this lifesaving technology."[45] Hassan Adamu, saying that "starving people . . . want food and nourishment, not lectures" and that "it is wrong and dangerous for a privileged people to presume they know what is best for everyone," calls this willingness to deny biotechnology to the poor "colonialist."[46] This is an interesting inversion of anti-GM activists' repeated claim that companies such as Monsanto are engaged in economic neocolonialism by turning Third World farmers into "bioserfs" dependent on such companies for expensive seeds.

Science

Above all, pro-GM discourse presents the safety of GM crops as scientifically validated and represents its critics as irrational and even hostile to the entire enterprise of science.

While anti-GM discourse often presents humans as "guinea pigs" being forced to eat GM foods in a massive uncontrolled global experiment, it tends to be taken for granted in pro-GM discourse that the safety of GM foods has already been scientifically established.[47] Thus, pro-GM commentators often say, in passing usually, that GM foods have been tested and their safety scientifically validated—"as safe as every test by the FDA, the Agriculture Department and the EPA has shown these foods to be," begins one sentence in a *Boston Globe* editorial.[48]Similarly, Paul Krugman, in one of his regular opinion columns in the *New York Times*, refers to the safety of GM crops as "extensively tested."[49] These matter-of-fact presumptions in the opinion pages of two of the most prestigious newspapers in the United States that GM foods have been tested and found safe are interesting not least because they are quite untrue. U.S. regulatory agencies decided in the early 1990s to exempt GM foods from mandatory safety testing, and "food companies are on their own to test and verify the safety of their own products."[50]

Those who oppose GM crops are often presented as ignorant, superstitious, and unscientific. The same editorial in the *Boston Globe*, for example, says, "This page supports the genetic modification of crops as a service to mankind and believes that most of the protest against it is unscientific and wrong."[51] On the other side of the Atlantic, writing in the London *Times*, Mick Hume avers,

> In scientific terms, the anti-GM panic remains, literally, a lot of fuss about nothing. Nobody is known to have suffered so much as an upset stomach as a result of eating GM foods, and there is still no hard evidence of any environmental damage caused by growing GM crops. . . . Unaccountable little influence groups [are] puffing their influence by reinforcing a climate of irrational fear. In private, many politicians will admit that they are appalled by the growth of superstition and anti-experimental prejudices, so evident over the GM food issue. Yet none of them seems prepared to stand up to the new forces of darkness.[52]

An editorial in the *Minneapolis Star Tribune* characterizes a local protest against GM food as "a muddied Luddite yawp."[53]

Where those arguing that GM crops are unsafe are themselves scientists, they are often accused of practicing "junk science" or politicized science. Paul Krugman, writing in the *New York Times*, dismisses the Pusztai study, suggesting that GM potatoes harmed rats, with a reference to "supposed independent scientists who were actually political activists."[54] James Watson dismissed the same study by saying simply, without elaboration, "These were bad experiments."[55] The Nobel Prize–winning biologist and "father of the Green Revolution," Norman Borlaug, compared anti-GM scientists to the infamous Soviet biologist Trofim Lysenko, who insisted in the face of contradicting empirical evidence that plant biology conformed to the principles of Marxist dogma. The consequences were disastrous for Soviet biology and agriculture.[56]

Elsewhere Borlaug has accused the opponents of GM crops of being opposed to science itself, referring to "small, well-financed, vociferous, antiscience groups."[57] Despite the fact that anti-GM groups often cite scientists in their literature, this characterization of the movement against transgenic crops as "anti-science" is quite common. The columnist Debra Saunders refers to them as "anti-technology groups."[58] Another commentator, a professor of agriculture, responds to Prince Charles's observation that use of antibiotics and pesticides creates problems of pest and bacterial resistance by saying, "Yes, they do lead to problems of resistance. But would the Prince abandon antibiotics and return to bloodlettings? Nature did not provide smallpox vaccinations, electricity, flight or contraception. However, all of these aids to living required expanding our knowledge of nature."[59] This broad claim, that the critics of GM food are opposed not just to transgenic crops but to science itself, has a special resonance at a moment when the mainstream press has presented science as an institution under attack by an unholy alliance of postmodernists and New Agers in the context of the so-called science wars of the 1990s. By framing the debate as one between "science" and its opponents, commentators also efface the fact that a number of the critics of transgenic crops are themselves scientists who have published in peer-reviewed scientific journals.[60]

A European Disease

Finally, a number of American commentators identify hostility to GM crops as a form of superstition that is particularly likely to afflict Europeans. Speaking in a congressional debate, U.S. Representative Kenny Hulshof (R-MO) said, "I find it ironic that today as world scientists are heralding the breakthroughs and mapping human genetics that the EU remains in the dark ages regarding advancements in plant science."[61] Describing what it is like to be on the receiving end of such judgments, the technical manager of a British frozen-food chain, Iceland, recalled what an American biotechnology company executive said upon hearing that the manager planned to buy GM-free foods for his customers: "You are a backward European who doesn't like change. You should accept that this is good for your customers."[62]

American commentators have found various reasons for this European backwardness. Warren Hoge, writing for the *New York Times*, attributes it to a failure in European government institutions, saying, "There is no government agency in Europe of the regulatory rigor of the United States Food and Drug Administration to build consumer confidence."[63] (There is a certain pathos to this judgment in view of recent revelations that the FDA endangered public health by ignoring evidence that the drugs Vioxx and Celebrex increase the risk of heart attack.) U.S. Representative Roy Blunt (R-MO) sees more sinister reasons: saying that "the Europeans are clearly trying to protect their farmers from superior products that we can send into that market," he calls for the WTO to take action against European protectionism masquerading as environmental concern.[64] Many other commentators see in European unease with GM crops an irrational displacement onto GM foods of anxieties produced by the eruption of "mad cow disease" in Britain in the mid-1990s—a calamity that has made the British in particular paranoid about the safety of the foods they eat.

CONSTRUCTING "NATURE"

Although the discourses for and against GM foods evince a number of themes, there are two that I want to highlight in the remainder of this chapter. At the center of gravity of anti-GM discourse lie claims about contamination, confusions of categories, and disruptions of the balance of "nature." At the heart of pro-GM discourse is the claim that critics of transgenic crops are unscientific, if not hostile to science itself. Let's begin by looking at anti-GM claims that GM crops pollute "nature."

The environmental movement against GM foods is vitally concerned with purity.[65] While defenders of genetic engineering argue that scientists in their laboratories are only doing more efficiently what farmers have been doing for centuries—cross-breeding to produce improved crop strains—those who oppose transgenic crops point out that farmers and plant breeders never did, indeed could not, mate a tomato with a flounder or a soy bean with a Brazil nut. Their language of "foreign" and "alien" genes and "genetic contamination" highlights the "unnaturalness" of such couplings.[66] The hybrid entities created by genetic engineering are what anthropologists have called "liminal objects."[67] They are, to use Victor Turner's famous phrase, "betwixt and between," or, more colloquially and more to the point perhaps, "neither fish nor fowl." In her now classic analysis of liminal objects—objects such as the fish without scales prohibited for eating in Leviticus—Mary Douglas argues that notions of pollution and taboo are our responses to liminal or hybrid objects whose ambiguity disrupts our categorical systems. She says, "Ideas about separating, purifying, demarcating and punishing transgressions have as their main function to impose system on an inherently untidy experience. It is only by exaggerating the difference between within and without, above and below, male and female, with and against, that a semblance of order is created."[68] Calling dirt "matter out of place," she argues, "Where there is dirt there is system. Dirt is the by-product of a systematic ordering and classification of matter."[69]

Stephen Crook, noting the obvious relevance of Douglas's work for the debate on GM foods, argues that the liminal qualities of transgenic foods makes them "culturally risky."

> Pollution threats arise when boundaries that define a sociocultural order are breached: when non-food species are eaten, when the milk is mixed with the

meat. This conception of pollution connects with the principle that sociocultural order is built from basic binary oppositions: nature-culture, male-female, raw-cooked. Biotechnology is a culturally risky threat to order because it breaches boundaries between "natural" and "cultural/artificial" that have served as ordering principles in Western cultures.[70]

From this perspective, the technology of genetic modification is "culturally risky" because it breaks down the very distinction between animal and vegetable or between formerly distinct plant species. Thus the anti-GM impulse to taboo transgenic foods represents an attempt to reaffirm the categorical system threatened by hybrid objects. Seen in this light, anti-GM activists are not so much progressive defenders of the environment against the depredations of greedy corporations (though they may still be that) as they are reactionary defenders of an established order that is threatened by the unlicensed border crossings of migrant genes.

No one has seen this irony more clearly than the poststructuralist social theorist Donna Haraway, whose writing establishes numerous cross-cutting, often elusive, connections between discourses on biotechnology and discourses on race, class, and gender in Western society.[71] Although politically predisposed to sympathize with the environmental movement, she also finds herself "especially drawn by such engaging beings as the tomato with a gene from a cold-sea-bottom-living flounder" and "the potato with a gene from a giant silk-moth."[72] As George Myerson puts it, "She is intuitively sympathetic to all campaigners against the global powers. Yet her work also suggests a reservation about any demand for a return to lost purity."[73] Haraway's thought is built around the central figure of the cyborg, which she deploys as an ambiguously utopian figure that dramatizes the dangers and possibilities of life in a globalizing technoscientific age. Espousing a deconstructive feminism that challenges established categories in the name of liberation, Haraway embraces the hybrid figure of the cyborg as her icon and, to use her own word, as her "kin." For her, a cyborg is not just a combination of human and machine but, more elusively, any hybrid entity that rewrites our sense of the possible, by reworking relationships between any combination of animal, human, vegetable, microbe, and machine. For Haraway, "cyborgs are beings in whose presence the categories themselves break down."[74]

It is in the context of this postmodern political vision celebrating miscegenation, hybridity, and border-crossing that Haraway has expressed reservations about the rhetoric of anti-GMO activists—a rhetoric of endangered purity and genetic contamination that is haunted by histories of eugenics, segregation, and genocide in the West. "It is a mistake," she says, "to forget that anxiety over the pollution of lineages is at the origin of racist discourse in European cultures." She adds, "I cannot help but hear in the biotechnology debates the unintended tones of fear of the alien and suspicion of the mixed."[75] Perhaps this explains why the anti-GM movement in Britain has found support not only on the Left but also from the right-wing, anti-European tabloids the *Daily Mail* and the *Daily Express* and from such prominent members of the inbred classes as Prince Charles.

Haraway's work reminds us that animals, humans, and plants have for centuries constituted a complex web whose components and relationships have constantly shifted and evolved, partly through chance, partly through conscious experimentation and design. Indeed, as Richard Lewontin points out, activists' evidence of the dangers of invasive species and pest-resistant hybrids all comes from the pre-GM past they figure as "natural" in their discourse.[76]

It is in this context that we should be suspicious of noisy calls to defend "the natural." For, as Henry Miller asks, "what does 'natural' mean? The mutant peach we call a nectarine? The tangerine-grapefruit hybrid we call a tangelo?"[77] Humans are constantly modifying the natural world and forgetting that they have done so, making national parks and looking there for pristine nature, breeding wolves into dozens of species of dog and treating the poodle as if it came from the Garden of Eden. The "natural," then, is a fiction, a word that freezes the world around us, unnaturally, at a moment in time, after—or maybe before—the last set of changes we made, a way of erasing the traces of our own agency in our environment. If we are to use the term *nature*, it can only be to denote something that is constantly shifting rather than an idealized reification of a set of relations presumed to embody an immutable teleological wisdom.[78]

DEFENDING THE AUTHORITY OF "SCIENCE"

Scientists tend to construe public discussions of technological risks in terms of a "deficit model" of understanding: lay people lack the rigorous and objective understanding that scientists themselves have of the risks associated with, for example, nuclear reactor technology, and the role of scientists is therefore to educate the public. Stephen Crook has observed that "irritation at the ignorance and irrationality of those who cannot grasp the logic of risk assessment is widespread among risk specialists and promoters of new technologies."[79] The promoters of GM crops are no exception here. However, we might ask whether their rhetorical insistence that the opponents of GM crops are superstitiously opposed to science itself does not suggest, by implication, that at stake in their own stance is an anxious, quasi-religious faith in the authority of science and the project of technological progress at a moment when these are, to some degree, in crisis—a crisis manifested in such heterogeneous symptoms as the "science wars," the rise of alternative medicine in the West, the appearance of social movements opposed to nuclear energy and genetic engineering, the eruption of "mad cow disease" in the United Kingdom, the loss of two space shuttles in the United States, and the cancellation of such big-ticket science projects as the Superconducting Supercollider.

Behind the statements of those who deride GM technology's critics as "irrational," "unscientific," and "Luddite" is an assumption, which is part of the common sense of contemporary Western society, that "science" is a reliable means for producing objective, consensual facts about the world. However, this assumption is particularly problematic in the context of the debate over GM food. While the proponents of GM food like to speak as if all of science is ranged on one side of the scales against the irrational forces of darkness on the other, the truth is that there are scientists on both sides of the debate —an arrangement of forces that is, of course, profoundly at odds with science's idealized presentation of self as an efficient machinery for the production of consensus through the application of reason to empirical facts. This puts scientists in the awkward position of speaking in the name of a consensus that does not, in fact, exist.

In one of the foundational texts in science studies, Bruno Latour suggests that, rather than take a science-textbook view of scientific knowledge as the unproblematic accumulation of proven facts, those seeking to understand science as a social practice should focus more closely on the conduct of scientific disputes and on the process by which these disputes are brought to a close, when they are, and facts established.[80] Latour describes these disputes as "trials of strength" between contending scientists attempting to turn their own facts and theories into black boxes whose contents, everyone agrees, can be accepted without further debate. The double helix structure of DNA is an example of something that has been black boxed; the safety of cultivating GM crops is not.

According to the popular view of science, disputes are often cleanly resolved by experiments or by measurements that clearly validate one theory over its rival. The problem with this view is that, in reality, the reliability and meaning of experiments and measurements can themselves be open to dispute—sometimes protracted dispute, which Collins and Pinch refer to as "the experimenter's regress."[81] Collins and Pinch give the almost comical example of two scientists, James McConell and Georges Ungar, who spent the best part of their professional lives defending claims that worms and rats that ate the brains of other worms and rats that were trained in a skill showed greater mastery of the skill than did those of a control group. They believed that knowledge stored biochemically in the brain could be transmitted through ingestion. The two scientists spent years debating critics who failed to replicate their experiments over whether their theories were disproved (as the critics claimed) or whether the critics were not handling the animal subjects and administering tests properly. Numerous rounds of experimentation failed to bring about surrender by either party.

In the case of the debate over GM crops, one clearly sees the "experimenter's regress" in operation. For example, some scientists claim that, in his study of rats that were fed GM potatoes, Arpad Pusztai was rigorous neither in his design of the experiment nor in his analysis of the data. Although the *Lancet*, Britain's most prestigious medical journal, did publish the study, its peer reviewers were divided in their evaluation of its scientific rigor, and some later complained that it should never have been published. Similarly, environmentalists said that John Losey's laboratory data on Bt pollen's ability to kill monarch butterfly larvae in the laboratory clearly showed that the widespread planting of Bt corn in the Midwest threatened the monarch butterfly with calamity; however, those on the other side of the debate wondered whether the Bt in GM corn might not obviate the need to use pesticides that are even more damaging to the monarch butterfly, and they questioned the relationship between the events witnessed in a laboratory at Cornell and those of the "real world." One such person said acidly, "The well publicized experiments with the Monarch butterfly show that under laboratory conditions caterpillars force-fed pollen are damaged."[82] There were complaints that *Nature* should not have published the study.

One might argue that the debate on the safety of GM crops, like so many scientific debates in the past, is currently passing through a normal phase in the genesis of scientific knowledge in which debate and disagreement between scientists precedes the eventual closing of the black box. The debate about GM crops may, however, present special difficulties for those seeking to close the black box, because scientific discussion of the safety of GM crops is complicated by open-ended questions about the relationship between controlled laboratory experiments and "natural" environments; because the debate is so dependent on modeling; and because ecological systems embody chaotic and nondeterministic feedback loops quite different in character from the more regular behaviors charted by earlier bodies of scientific theory (the orbits of the planets, chemical reactions, and so on). I have argued elsewhere that, where the conduct of scientific disputes is heavily dependent on modeling—for example, in contemporary debates over global warming and the reliability of nuclear weapons in the absence of nuclear testing—facts, theories, and predictions get sucked into a vortex of "hyperconstructibility."[83] The debate on GM crops offers another example of hyperconstructible science. Putting the same idea a little differently, George Myerson writes,

> The Facts have become more complicated. They have changed their nature. A fact about Flavr Savr is just not the same kind of thing as a fact about oak trees, or rubber, or the moon. It has more in common with facts about, say, Black Holes, or programming "languages." These are 'mutated' facts—full of theories, full of uncertainties and ambiguities. You have to grasp these new facts as much with your imagination as with your calculator.[84]

For scientists seeking to convince the public of the authority of scientific pronouncements on such matters as GM crops—an authority predicated on the special ability of scientists to speak with one voice—the current situation presents a dilemma. One option is to reassert the unanimity of science by excommunicating those with whom one disagrees. In this case, if one supports GM crops, one calls their work "junk science" or "ideological science"; if one opposes them, one says their science has been bought and corrupted by biotechnology corporations.[85]

Such strategies carry their own cost in exacerbating the very unease among the public about the authority of science that the strategy is supposed to help reestablish. And that unease is already bad enough since, in the words of one British journalist, "We have had three decades of assurances by scientists about the safety of the nuclear industry—something no one can believe now. Then there is the BSE fiasco [bovine spongiform encephalopathy, or "mad cow disease"]. It is not surprising that people view the assurances of scientists with great skepticism."[86] Ulrich Beck spoke for many when he said that science is increasingly perceived as "the protector of global contamination of people and nature. . . . The sciences have squandered until further notice their historic reputation for rationality."[87] After Love Canal, after Chernobyl, after Three Mile Island, after Bhopal, after BSE, and after an epidemic of cancer in Utah and in the Pacific caused by nuclear tests that scientists at the time insisted were safe, we can say that, if members of the public are sometimes unduly afraid of new technologies, it is also the case that scientists —especially those employed by state military-industrial complexes and corporations—are sometimes unduly sanguine about new technologies, making pronouncements that they are clearly safe that later become embarrassments to the reputation of science.

CONCLUSION: A DEBATE WITHOUT "SCIENCE" OR "NATURE"?

At the beginning of this chapter, I speak of the way that arguments about public policy become persuasive as they embed themselves in narratives of the world. The opponents of GM foods have created a narrative centered on the greed of biotechnology corporations, the unnaturalness of genetic couplings effected in Dr. Frankenstein's laboratory, and the danger to "nature" of unleashing new hybrids into our fragile and complex ecological environments. This narrative has tremendous appeal among some segments of the modern Western public and has succeeded in mobilizing and unifying a new social movement against GM foods, especially in Europe, where public opinion about the risks of science had already been softened up by the BSE crisis. On the other side, the proponents of GM foods have created a narrative centered on the power of modern technoscience to ameliorate social problems such as hunger and on the primitive irrationality of Luddites and quaint aristocrats who question the authority of science, the ultimate institution for the production of truth in modern society. This narrative has been effective in staunching the damage inflicted by anti-GM commentators and in ensuring continued public consent for transgenic experimentation, especially in the United States, where techno-utopian discourses have always had more resonance than on the other side of the Atlantic.

While both of these narratives have been effective in generating partial public support for their exponents' positions, neither has been able to defeat the other, and both the narrative of "nature" and the narrative of "science" embody flawed accounts of the world. Jean-Francois Lyotard has argued that it is the essence of the "postmodern condition" that metanarratives— narratives that seek to ground themselves as totalizing and objective accounts of the world—are doomed to fail, imploding upon themselves or colliding painfully with the ambitions of rival metanarratives that they cannot finally defeat.[88] That certainly seems to be the case with regard to the two rival narratives of risk in the transgenic age that I have anatomized here. But if attempts to ground authority in appeals to "nature" or to "science" are only partially persuasive in the transgenic age, can we speak about risk in this context without invoking the authorization of an essentialized nature or science? What would a policy debate look like that did not invoke these categories? Would it be intelligible or compelling? Can we find a way of talking about the unintended, sometimes disastrous, consequences of introducing new agents into ecological systems without speaking as if those systems embody a frozen teleological wisdom? Can we find a way of taking seriously the learning and expertise of scientists without compounding unrealistic and, frankly, superstitious expectations that scientists are capable of oracular foresight and should always agree?

A more nuanced and productive debate about GM foods would be one that, first of all, disaggregated the category of GM food itself, acknowledging that rice with enhanced nutritional content may not carry the same risks as, for example, corn that synthesizes pesticides in its own cells or soy designed to withstand the strongest pesticides yet developed. Thus we might decide that we like some GM products but not others. Second, if we stopped speaking in the name of fairy-tale versions of "nature" and "science," we could ask not whether a GM product will despoil a mythological nature but whether it poses risks beyond the fluctuations that have proved tolerable, even beneficial, in the past; not whether the product's critics threaten the foundations of modernity but whether the science in support of the product is robust enough that we can be sure it is not like the science that claimed Vioxx as a new wonder drug with no harmful effects. Finally, a more productive and insightful debate about GM food would be one that foregrounded some of the political economic issues that have been submerged by the appeals to "science" and "nature." The debate about GM food is partly a debate about whether we want to live in a society where food production is dominated by a few large corporations and whether the solution to global hunger is (as the supporters of GM food maintain) a technical fix in the biology lab or whether it is (as the critics of GM food maintain) a distributional fix that empowers the poor to buy food that already exists in sufficient quantity to feed all the world's citizens. To raise such political economic issues is to put questions about values and power at the center of the debate on GM food, which is properly where they should be.

NOTES

This chapter grew out of a paper presented in 2001 to the Environmental Politics Colloquium at University of California, Berkeley; the meetings of the Society for Cultural Anthropology; and MIT's Symposium group. My thanks to all who poked and prodded at the paper in those settings. Special thanks go to Chris Walley for her close reading of the paper and to Xaq Frolich for interrupting his vacation to give editorial input at the eleventh hour.

1. Fred Buttel, "Agricultural Biotechnology: Its Recent Evolution and Implications for Agrofood Political Economy," *Sociological Research Online* 4, no. 3 (1999), www.socresonline.org.uk/4/3/buttel.html (accessed February 2, 2005). John Grogan and Cheryl Long, "The Problem with Genetic Engineering," *Organic Gardening* (January/February 2000): 42–47. Mac Marshall, "An MAQ Innovation: Editorial," *Medical Anthropology Quarterly* 15, no. 1 (2001): 3–8.

2. Mark Strauss, "When Malthus Meets Mendel," *Foreign Policy* 119 (June 29, 2000): 105–12.

3. While Monsanto defended its "terminator" seeds by saying that the terminator gene would prevent genetic modifications in its GM crops from moving through cross-pollination into the genome of wild plant life or that of crops owned by farmers who had not chosen to grow GM foods, the terminator gene also had the commercially beneficial consequence that it would force farmers to buy new seeds from Monsanto every year.

4. Buttel, "Agricultural Biotechnology."

5. Jeff Hecht, "More Doubts over Plan for Allergen-Free Cats," *NewScientist.com*, October 29, 2004, www.newscientist.com/article.ns?id=dn6594 (accessed May 9, 2005).

6. On "golden rice," see J. Madeline Nash, "Grains of Hope," *Time*, July 31, 2000; Debra Saunders, "A Golden Opportunity for Planet," *San Francisco Chronicle*, December 19, 2000, 31A; and Saunders, "Food for Thought," *San Francisco Chronicle*, May 7, 2000, 9. Critics argue that the nutritional benefit of golden rice has been oversold by boosters who do not point out that the rice does not contain vitamin A but a precursor, beta carotene, that cannot be converted into vitamin A by the malnourished. Richard Lewontin, "Genes in the Food!" *New York Review of Books* 48, no. 10

(June 21, 2001); Nina Schnapp and Quirin Schiermeier, "Critics Claim 'Sight-Saving' Rice is Over-rated," Nature 410 (March 29, 2001): 503.

7. One study found that 2 percent of American consumers consider GM issues when making consumer purchases, versus 20 percent of British consumers. Mark Henderson, "America Is Given GM Food for Thought," *London Times*, April 28, 2000, www.lexis-nexis.com.

8. In 1996 a group of Nebraska researchers who were splicing a Brazil nut gene into soybeans discovered through casual testing in the laboratory that it could trigger reactions among those allergic to nuts. Plans to commercialize this transgenic soy were promptly shelved. Marion Nestle, "Allergies to Transgenic Foods—Questions of Policy," *New England Journal of Medicine* 334, no. 11 (March 14, 1996): 726–28; Julie A. Nordlee, "Identification of a Brazil Nut Allergen in Transgenic Soybeans," *New England Journal of Medicine* 334, no. 11 (March 14, 1996): 688–92.

9. See Stanley W. B. Ewen and Arpad Pusztai, "Effects of Diets Containing Genetically Modified Potatoes Expressing Galanthus Nivalis Lectin on Rat Small Intestine," *Lancet* 354, no. 9187 (1999): 1353–54; and Sheldon Rampton and John Stauber, *Trust Us, We're Experts!* (New York: Putnam Books, 2001), 152–94. More information on Pusztai's verified research can be found at www.rri.sari.ac.uk/gmo/ajp.htm (accessed May 9, 2005); see also, *The Hindu*, "Call for Detailed Studies on Genetically Modified Foods," September 27, 2000.

10. See John Losey et al., "Transgenic Pollen Harms Monarch Butterfly," *Nature* 399, no. 6733 (May 20, 1999): 214. Critics of the Cornell study have questioned whether results from the laboratory where monarch larvae were compelled to eat Bt pollen can be extrapolated to the wild, and they point out that monarch larvae are also killed by the pesticides whose use Bt crops are intended to diminish. Meanwhile, subsequent studies suggest that it was not the pollen itself but parts of the plant not usually eaten by caterpillars that caused the monarch larvae to die. See Paul Brown, "Sowing Seeds of Doubt: U.S. Public Opinion on GM Crops Is Rattled by New Research," *Guardian*, August 9, 2000, 7; George Myerson, *Donna Haraway and GM Foods* (Cambridge, U.K.: Icon Books, 1999), 43; and Andrew Pollack, "New Research Fuels the Debate over Genetic Food Altering," *New York Times*, September 9, 2001, 28A. Losey himself has said that the laboratory experiment was only intended to be suggestive and that the jury is still out on the real-life consequences for the monarch of Bt crop planting. See also Nash, "Grains of Hope."

11. See Douglas Boucher, ed., *Paradox of Plenty: Hunger in a Bountiful World* (Oakland, Calif.: Food First, 1999); Mike Davis, *Late Victorian Holocausts: El Nino Famines and the Making of the Third World* (New York: Verso, 2002); and Amartya Sen, *Poverty and Famines: An Essay on Entitlement and Deprivation* (New York: Oxford University Press, 1984).

12. See Brenda Derby, "Consumer Perceptions of GM Food Labelling Issues in the U.S.: A Focus Group Study" (paper presented at the conference of the Society for the Social Study of Science, Vienna, September 30, 2000); and John Palfreman, *Harvest of Fear* (PBS film, Nova/Frontline, 2001). Derby also reports that the U.S. public is more concerned by the genetic modification of animals than that of plants, that men are more supportive of GM crops than are women, and that those who know the least about GM technology focus on its health effects while those who know the most focus more on its environmental consequences.

13. *Economist.com*, "Another Gene Genie out of the Bottle," May 19, 2004, www.economist.com/displaystory.cfm?story_id=2685115 (accessed May 9, 2005).

14. Exceptions include Barbara Adam, "The Temporal Gaze: The Challenge for Social Theory in the Context of GM Food," *British Journal of Sociology* 51, no. 1 (2000): 125–42; Stephen Crook, "Biotechnology, Risk, and Sociocultural (Dis)order," in *Altered Genes: Reconstructing Nature*, ed. Richard Hindmarsh, Geoffrey Lawrence, and Janet Norton (St. Leonards, Austral.: Allen and Unwin, 1998), 132–46; Crook, "Length Matters: A Note from the GM Debate," *Anthropology Today* 16, no. 1 (2000): 8–11; Arturo Escobar and Chaia Heller, "From Pure Genes to GMOs: Transnationalized Gene Landscapes in the Biodiversity and Transgenic Food Networks," in *Genetic Nature/Culture*, ed. Alan Goodman, Deborah Heath, and Susan Lindee (Berkeley: University of California Press, 2003); Claire Marris, "Between Consensus and Citizens," *Science Studies* 12, no. 2 (1996): 3–32; Mac Marshall, "An MAQ Innovation: Editorial," *Medical Anthropology Quarterly* 15, no. 1 (2001): 3–8; Ann Murcott, "Not Science but PR: GM Food and the Makings of a 'Considered Sociology,'" *Sociological Research Online* 43, no. 3 (1999), www.socresonline.org.uk/4/3/murcott.html (accessed February 4, 2005); Murcott, "Public Beliefs about GM Foods: More on the Makings of a Considered Sociology," *Medical Anthropology Quarterly* 15, no. 1 (2001): 9–19; Myerson, *Donna Haraway and GM Foods*; Janet Norton, "Throwing Up Concerns about Novel Foods," in Hindmarsh, Lawrence, and Norton, *Altered Genes*, 173–85; Bob Phelps, "Genetic Engineering: The Campaign Frontier," in Hindmarsh, Lawrence, and Norton, *Altered Genes*, 186–198; Glenn Davis Stone, "Both Sides Now: Fallacies in the Genetic-Modification Wars, Implications for Developing Countries, and Anthropological Perspectives," *Current Anthropology* 43, no. 40 (2002): 611–19 (and replies in special issues of *Current Anthropology* 43, no. 4 [2002]; *Sociological Research Online* 4, no. 3 [1999], www.socresonline.org.uk/4/3/gmfood.html [accessed May 9, 2005]; and *Medical Anthropology Quarterly* 15, no. 1 [2001]).

15. Murcott, "Not Science but PR."

16. Emory Roe, *Narrative Policy Analysis: Theory and Practice* (Durham, N.C.: Duke University Press, 1994), 2.

17. Carol Cohn, "Sex and Death in the Rational World of Defense Intellectuals," *Signs* 12, no. 4 (1987): 687–718. Emily Martin, "Toward an Anthropology of Immunology: The Body as Nation-State," *Medical Anthropology Quarterly* 4, no. 4 (1990): 410–26; and Martin, "The Drama of the Egg and the Sperm: How Science has Constructed a Romance Based on Stereotypical Male-Female Roles," *Signs* 16, no. 3 (1991): 485–501.

18. On the importance of metaphors and narratives in policy debates, see George Lakoff and Mark Johnson, *Metaphors We Live By* (Chicago: University of Chicago Press, 1980), and Lakoff, *Don't Think of an Elephant: Know Your Values and Frame the Debate* (White River Junction, Vt.: Chelsea Green, 2004). See also, Louise Wells Bedsworth, Micah Lowenthal, and William Kastenberg, "Uncertainty and Regulation: The Rhetoric of Risk in the California Low-Level Radioactive Waste Debate," *Science, Technology, and Human Values* 29, no. 3 (2004): 406–27; Hugh Gusterson, "Endless Escalation: The Cold War as Postmodern Narrative," *Tikkun* 6, no. 5 (1991): 45, 92; Gusterson, *Nuclear Rites: A Weapons Laboratory at the End of the Cold War* (Berkeley: University of California Press, 1996); Gusterson, "The Virtual Nuclear Weapons Laboratory in the New World Order," *American Ethnologist* 28, no. 1 (2001): 417–37;

Gusterson, *People of the Bomb: An Anthropologist Explores America's Nuclear Complex* (Minneapolis: University of Minnesota Press, 2004); and Alexandra Von Meier, Jennifer Lynn Miller, and Ann Keller, "The Disposition of Excess Weapons Plutonium: A Comparison of Three Narrative Contexts," *Nonproliferation Review* (Winter 1998): 20–31.

19. Martin Teitel, "Public Beliefs about GM Foods: Anne Murcott's Contribution," *Medical Anthropology Quarterly* 15, no. 1 (2001): 20–21.

20. Maria Margaronis, "The Politics of Food," *The Nation* 269, no. 22 (December 27, 1999): 11–16.

21. Quote from "The Next Endangered Species?" flyer put out by the Campaign to Label Genetically Engineered Foods.

22. Bay Area Resistance against Genetic Engineering (BayRAGE), "Value Your Family's Health" (flyer).

23. See Ulrike Felt, "On Rhetorics of Choice: Presenting GM Food to the Austrian Public" (paper presented at the conference of the Society for the Social Study of Science, Vienna, September 29, 2000); Les Gofton and Erica Haimes, "Necessary Evils? Offering up Closings in Sociology and Biotechnology," *Sociological Research Online* 4, no. 3 (1999), www.socresonline.org.uk/4/3/gofton.html (February 4, 2005); and Brian Wynne, "Discursive Construction of Ethical Issues on GMOs: Deleting Public Voices on Science" (paper presented at the conference of the Society for the Social Study of Science, Vienna, September 30, 2000). These authors offer interesting critiques of the movement for the labeling of GM foods. Felt argues that, in practice, it is hard to sustain the option for individual consumers to opt out of GM food consumption since, once the societal infrastructure for growing and distributing GM crops has been built, it commits the entire society and overwhelms individuals who may have to strive inordinately to live GM-free. Gofton and Haimes argue that most consumers do not have time to study labels and, in the absence of a concerted public debate on GM food, have difficulty knowing whether to purchase it anyway. "A belief in 'organic' or 'natural' products may be a response to this information overload by returning to the past: food's version of postmodern nostalgia," they argue. Wynne argues that the principal issue with regard to genetically modified organisms is not that of protecting the individual's right not to consume them but that of evaluating the risk they represent to an entire ecological system.

24. Grogran and Long, "Problem with Genetic Engineering"; and George Monbiot, "Just Say No to Biotech Business" (editorial), *Guardian*, March 2, 1999, 22.

25. Bay Area Resistance against Genetic Engineering (BayRAGE), "Fact Sheet on the Risks of Genetically Engineered Food."

26. Ronnie Cummins, "Length Matters: A Note on the GM Debate," *Anthropology Today* 16, no. 1 (2000): 8–11.

27. BayRAGE, "Value Your Family's Health." PCB (polychlorinated biphenyl) products were developed to be used as coolants and lubricants in electrical equipment. Carcinogenic in animals and neurotoxic for children, they have been banned in the United States since 1977, though they remain in the environment.

28. Eleanor Mills, "Slaying the GM Bogeyman," *Vancouver Sun*, March 31, 2000, 17A.

29. Warren Hoge, "Britons Skirmish over Genetically Modified Crops," *New York Times*, August 23, 1999, 3A.

30. *New York Times*, October 26, 1999, 15A.

31. The Marketplace, *Organics Today* (newsletter, Santa Fe, N.M., March 2000).

32. Grogan and Long, "Problem with Genetic Engineering"; Michael Pollan, "Desire: Control/Plant: The Potato," in *The Botany of Desire: A Plant's-Eye View of the World*, ed. Michael Pollan (New York: Random House, 2001), 181–238.

33. Council for Responsible Genetics, "Frequently Asked Questions about Genetically Engineered Food" (flyer, Cambridge, Mass., Summer 1999).

34. Grogan and Long, "Problem with Genetic Engineering."

35. BayRAGE, "Fact Sheet."

36. "What Many Farmers Have Found about Genetic Engineering," source unknown.

37. Phil Sutton, "Genetics and the Future of Nature Politics," *Sociological Research Online* 4, no. 3 (1999), www.socresonline.org.uk/4/3/sutton.html (accessed May 9, 2005).

38. Organic Consumers Association, "Consumer Warning" (flyer).

39. BayRAGE, "Fact Sheet."

40. James Meikle, "Duke Challenges Skeptics over GM Food," *The Guardian*, June 7, 2000, 7.

41. Philip Howard, "The Only Place Where There Were No GM Plants Was the Garden of Eden," *Times*, March 31, 2000, www.lexis-nexis.com.

42. Mills, "Slaying the GM Bogeyman," 17A. A number of pro-GM authors argue that genetic engineering may be safer than the techniques it supersedes because it is a more precisely targeted way of changing a plant's genome than repeated trial-and-error cross-breeding of different species, though questions have been raised about the possible disruption of gene regulation, as exogenous DNA is shot into the genome of a plant or animal. See Lewontin, "Genes in the Food!"

43. Nash, "Grains of Hope."

44. H. Sterling Burnett, "Destructive Precaution," *National Post*, November 20, 2000, 15C.

45. George McGovern, "The Wonder of Fighting Famine with Biotechnology," *Minneapolis Star Tribune*, November 6, 2000, 13A.

46. Hassan Adamu, "World's Starving People Need Food, Not Lectures," *Houston Chronicle*, September 27, 2000, 25A.

47. One flyer, for example, says that "'life sciences' corporations . . . [are] using us as unwilling test subjects and contaminating the planet, in the largest global research project since the first atomic bomb mushroomed its radioactive particles above our state." La Montanita Co-op, "Avoiding Genetically Engineered Food: A Consumer's Guide" (Albuquerque, N.M).

48. "Labeling GM Foods" (editorial), *Boston Globe*, March 28, 2000, 12A.

49. Paul Krugman, "Natural Born Killers," *New York Times*, March 22, 2000, 27A.

50. *Minneapolis Star Tribune*, "Biotech Foods: A Belated Effort to Reassure Consumers," May 7, 2000, 22A.

51. "Labeling GM Foods," 12A.

52. Mick Hume, untitled column, *Times*, February 28, 2000, www.lexis-nexis.com.

53. *Minneapolis Star Tribune*, "Biotech Protest: Under the Chanting, Some Worthy Points" (editorial), July 30, 2000, 24A.

54. Krugman, "Natural Born Killers," 27A.

55. Mills, "Slaying the GM Bogeyman," 17A.

56. Norman Borlaug, "We Need Biotech to Feed the World," *Wall Street Journal*, December 6, 2000.

57. Quoted in McGovern, "Wonder of Fighting Famine," 13A.

58. Debra Saunders, "A Golden Opportunity for Planet," *San Francisco Chronicle*, December 19, 2000, A31.

59. Douglas Powell, "Junk Science Week," *National Post*, June 24, 2000, 11D.

60. I am referring here in particular to the work of Losey et al., "Transgenic Pollen"; and Ewen and Pusztai, "Effects of Diets," 1353.

61. U.S. representative Hulshof (R-MO), *Congressional Record* (June 26, 2000).

62. Maria Margaronis, "The Politics of Food," *The Nation*, December 27, 1999, 11–16.

63. Hoge, "Britons Skirmish," *New York Times*.

64. Blunt, *Congressional Record*, June 26, 2000.

65. One of the key websites for the movement, for example, is www.pure foods.org.

66. Against this, Mark Harvey has argued, "As objects of transformation, plants . . . are subject to natural laws, and whatever modifications are made of them, the modifications are of organisms subject to those laws, rather than modifications of those laws. Thus, if genetic modification can be said to be historically the most radical form of cultivation, nonetheless it cannot produce non-natural entities." Harvey, "Cultivation and Comprehension: How Genetic Modification Irreversibly Alters the Human Engagement with Nature," *Sociological Research Online* 4, no. 3 (2000), www .socresonline.org.uk/4/3/harvey.html (accessed May 9, 2005).

67. On liminality, see especially Mary Douglas, *Purity and Danger: Analysis of the Concepts of Pollution and Taboo* (New York: Ark, 1984); Stanley Tambiah, "Animals Are Good to Think and Good to Prohibit," *Ethnology* 8, no. 4 (1969): 423–59; Sherry Turkle, *The Second Self: The Human Spirit in a Computer Culture* (New York: Simon and Schuster, 1984); Victor Turner, *The Ritual Process: Structure and Anti-structure* (Chicago: Aldine, 1969); and Turner, *Dramas, Fields, and Metaphors: Symbolic Action in Human Society* (Ithaca, N.Y.: Cornell University Press, 1974).

68. Douglas, *Purity and Danger*, 4.

69. Douglas, *Purity and Danger*, 35.

70. Crook, "Biotechnology," 135.

71. Donna Haraway, *Simians, Cyborgs, and Women: The Reinvention of Nature* (New York: Routledge, 1991); and Haraway, *Modest_Witness@Second_Millennium .FemaleMan_Meets_OncoMouse: Feminism and Technoscience* (New York: Routledge, 1997).

72. Haraway, *Modest_Witness*, 88.

73. Myerson, *Donna Haraway and GM Foods*, 32.

74. Myerson, *Donna Haraway and GM Foods*, 21.

75. Haraway, *Modest_Witness*, 60–62.

76. Lewontin, "Genes in the Food!"

77. Henry I. Miller, "Biotech Food Labelling Is Regulatory Overkill," *Los Angeles Times*, October 27, 1996, 9B.

78. William Cronon, *Changes in the Land: Indians, Colonists, and the Ecology of New England* (New York: Hill and Wang, 2003).

79. Crook, "Biotechnology," 137.

80. Bruno Latour, *Science in Action: How to Follow Scientists and Engineers through Society* (Cambridge, Mass.: Harvard University Press, 1987).

81. Harry Collins and Trevor Pinch, *The Golem* (Cambridge: Cambridge University Press, 1998).

82. Burcke, quoted in Myerson, *Donna Haraway and GM Foods*, 43.

83. See Gusterson, *People of the Bomb* chapter 9.

84. Myerson, *Donna Haraway and GM Foods*, 49.

85. For example, Peter Riley of the Friends of the Earth says, "The public will not be hoodwinked into accepting so-called independent advice from scientists who are being paid by the industry to say GM foods are harmless." Quoted in Jeremy Watson, "Ministers Face GM Conference Protests," *The Scotsman*, February 27, 2000, 3.

86. John Hancox, "Scientist Should Not Be Blamed in Theory," *Glasgow Herald*, May 26 2000, 22, www.lexis-nexis.com.

87. Ulrich Beck, *The Risk Society: Towards a New Modernity* (Thousand Oaks, Calif.: Sage, 1992).

88. Jean-Francois Lyotard, *The Postmodern Condition: An Essay on Knowledge* (Minneapolis: University of Minnesota Press, 1984).

6

The Aliens Have Landed!
Reflections on the
Rhetoric of Biological Invasions

Banu Subramaniam

Two years ago, in a special issue entitled *Biological Invaders* by the prestigious journal *Science*, an article begins as follows:

> One spring morning in 1995, ecologist Jayne Belnap walked into a dry grassland in Canyonlands National Park, Utah, an area that she has been studying for more than 15 years. "I literally stopped and went, 'Oh my God!'" she recalls. The natural grassland—with needle grass, Indian rice grass, saltbush, and the occasional pinyon-juniper tree—that Belnap had seen the year before no longer existed; it had become overgrown with 2-foot-high Eurasian cheatgrass. "I was stunned," says Belnap, "It was like the aliens had landed."[1]

One of the ironies in the world today is that in an era of globalization, there is a renewed call for the importance of the "local" and the protection of the indigenous. With the increased permeability of nations and their borders, and the increased consumption and celebration of our common natures and cultures, we begin to obsess about our different natures and cultures with a fervent nationalisma, stressing the need to close our borders to those "outsiders."[2] The anxieties around the free movement of capital, commodities, and entertainment and the copious consumption of natural and cultural products have reached fever pitch. In the realm of culture and the economy, nationalisms,[3] fundamentalisms,[4] World Trade Organization protests, and censorship of "foreign" influences, calls for the preservation of national cultures abound.[5] In the realm of nature, there is increasing attention to the destruction of forests, conservation, preservation of native forests and lands, the commodification of organisms, and concern over the invasion and destruction of native habitats through alien plant and animal invasions.[6]

"Development" is one area[7] in which both the natural and cultural worlds implode.[8] At the heart of the critiques is the fundamental question of what we mean by nature and culture. Who gets to define it? Are nature and culture static and unchanging entities? If nature and natural processes shift and change over time, as most biologists believe, how do we characterize and accommodate these evolutions?

Over the last two decades, feminist and postcolonial critics of science have elaborated the relationship between our conceptions of nature and their changing political, economic, and cultural contexts. Nature and culture, they argue, are co-constituted, simultaneously semiotic and material. Through Donna Haraway's "material-semiotic worlds"[9] can emerge a history of "naturecultures,"[10] tracing and elaborating the inextricable interconnections between natures and cultures.

Nowhere is this more apparent than in the growing panic about alien and exotic plants and animals. Newspaper articles, magazines, journals, and websites have all sprung up demanding urgent action to stem the rise of exotic flora and fauna. For anyone who is an immigrant or is familiar with the immigration process, the rhetoric is unmistakable. First consider the terminology: A species that enters the country for the first time is called an "alien" or an "exotic" species; after an unspecified passage of time, it is considered a resident; after a greater unspecified passage of time, it is considered a naturalized species.[11]

As Nancy Tomes argues, our anxieties about social incorporation (associated with expanding markets, increasingly permeable borders and boundaries, growing affordability of travel and mass immigration) have historically spilled into our conceptions of nature. For example, she documents how our panic about germs has historically coincided with periods of heavy immigration to the United States, of groups being perceived as "alien" and difficult to assimilate. She documents these germ panics in the early twentieth century in response to the new immigration from eastern and southern Europe and those in the late twentieth century to the new immigration from Asia, Africa, and Latin America. "Fear of racial impurities and suspicions of immigrant hygiene practices are common elements of both periods," she writes. "These fears heightened the germ panic by the greater ease and frequency with which immigrants travel back and forth between their old, presumably disease ridden countries and their new, germ obsessed American homeland."[12]

I argue in this chapter that the recent hyperbole about alien species is similar to the germ panics and is in response to changing racial, economic, and gender norms in the country. The globalization of markets and the real and perceived lack of local control feed nationalist discourse.[13] Despite the supposed low unemployment rates and a great economy, the search of companies for cheap labor abroad and the easing of immigration into the country have increasingly been perceived as threats to local employment. These shifts continue to be interpreted by some elements of both the Right and the Left as a problem of immigration. Immigrants and foreigners, the product of the "global," are perceived to be one of the reasons for the problems in the "local." These shifts and trends are evident in the national rhetoric surrounding alien and exotic plants and animals.

THEY CAME, THEY BRED, THEY CONQUERED[14]

Newspapers and magazines introduce the topic of biological invasions with the sound of alarm. Consider some of the titles:

Alien Invasion: They're Green, They're Mean, and They May Be Taking Over a Park or Preserve Near You[15]
Aliens Reeking Havoc; the Invasion of the Woodland Soil Snatchers[16]
Native Species Invaded[17]
Bio-invasions Spark Concerns[18]
It's a Cancer[19]
Creepy Strangler Climbs Oregon's Least-Wanted List[20]
Biological Invaders Threaten U. S. Ecology[21]
U. S. Can't Handle Today's Tide of Immigrants[22]
Alien Threat[23]
Biological Invaders Sweep In[24]
Stemming the Tide of Invading Species[25]
Congress Threatens Wild Immigrants[26]
Invasive Species: Pathogens of Globalization[27]

The majority of these titles do not specify that the article is about plants and animals but rather present a more generalized classic fear of the outsider, the alien that is here to take over the country. An opening line of an article reads, "The survey is not even halfway done, yet it has already revealed a disturbing trend: immigrants are forcing old-timers out of their homes."[28] Invaders are reported to be "racing out of control" causing "an explosion in slow motion."[29] Aliens, they claim, are redrawing the global landscape in ways no one imagined. Exotic plants, they argue, are irreversibly altering waterways and farmlands. The "irreversibility" is highlighted as a way to stress the sharp departure from the past—a vision of how we are moving from a peaceful, coevolved nature in perfect harmony and balance to an uncertain future with alien and exotic plants and animals. They argue that we cannot recapture the glorious past, our nostalgia for a pure and uncontaminated nature in harmony and balance, if we do not act *now* to stem the tide of outsiders.

The parallels in the rhetoric surrounding foreign plants and that of foreign peoples are striking. Like the earlier germ panic surrounding immigration and immigrants, questions of hygiene and disease haunt exotic plants and animals. Similar to the unhygienic immigrants, alien plants are accused of "crowd(ing) out native plants and animals, spread(ing) disease, damag(ing) crops, and threaten(ing) drinking water supplies."[30] The xenophobic rhetoric that surrounds immigrants is extended to plants and animals.

The first parallel is that aliens are "other." One *Wall Street Journal* article quotes a biologist's first encounter with an Asian eel: "The minute I saw it, I knew it wasn't from here," he said.[31] Second is the idea that aliens and exotic plants are everywhere, taking over everything: "They're in national parks and monuments. In wildlife refuges and coastal marine sanctuaries. In wilderness areas that were intended to remain living dioramas of our American paradise lost."[32] "Today, invasive aliens afflict almost every habitat in the country, from farms and pastures to forests and wetlands—and as every homeowner knows, gardens, flower beds and lawns."[33]

The third parallel is the suggestion that aliens and exotic plants are silently growing in strength and number. So even if you haven't noticed it, be warned about the alien invasion. And if you haven't heard about biological invasions, the reason is that the "invasion of alien plants into natural areas has been stealthy and silent, and thus largely ignored." E. O. Wilson states, "Alien species are the stealth destroyers of the American environment."[34] Articles remind us that alien plants are "evil beauties"—that while they may appear to look harmless and even beautiful, they are evil because they destroy native plants and habitats.[35] The fourth parallel is that aliens are difficult to destroy and will persist because they can withstand extreme situations. In an article on the invasion of the Asian eel in Florida,

> The eel's most alarming trait, though, is its uncanny ability to survive extreme conditions. In one study by a Harvard zoologist, an Asian swamp eel lived seven months in a damp towel without food or water. The olive-brown creature prefers tropical waters, yet it can flourish in subzero temperatures. It prefers fresh water but can tolerate high salinity. It breathes under water like a fish, but can slither across dry land, sometimes in packs of 50 or more, sucking air through a two-holed snout. . . . Even more of a riddle is how to kill the eel: It thus far appears almost immune to poisons and dynamite.[36]

The fifth parallel is that aliens are "aggressive predators and pests and are prolific in nature, reproducing rapidly."[37] This rhetoric of uncontrollable fertility and reproduction is another hallmark of human immigrants. Repeatedly, alien plants are characterized as being aggressive, uncontrollable, prolific, invasive, and expanding. One article summarizes it as "They Came, They Bred, They Conquered."[38]Alien species are characterized as destroyers of everything around. A park warden is quoted as saying, "To me, the nutria [a swamp rat] are no different than somebody taking a bulldozer to the marsh."[39]

Sixth, once these plants gain a foothold, they never look back.[40] Singularly motivated to take over native land, the plants, the articles imply, have become disconnected to their homelands, will never return, and are therefore "here to stay." Finally, like that of human immigrants, the greatest focus is on the economic costs because it is believed that exotic plants consume resources and return nothing. "Exotic species are a parasite on the U.S. economy, sapping an estimated $138 billion annually, nearly twice the annual state budget of New York or a third more than Bill Gates' personal fortune."[41] Not only are aliens invading rural and natural habitats, but they are also endangering the cities. "Cities invaded," articles cry. From historical sites to urban hardwoods, alien bugs are reported to be causing millions of dollars worth of damage.[42]

> Just as human immigrants may find more opportunities in an already overcrowded city than in a small town, invasive plants take advantage of the constant turnover and jockeying for position that characterizes species-rich ecological communities. The classical dictum that "diversity begets stability," Stohlgren says, is simply not true in some ecosystems. Communities with high diversity tend to be in constant flux, creating openings for invasives. . . . From a conservation perspective, the results of these multi-site, multi-scale studies are disturbing. The invasions may threaten some of the last strongholds of certain biologically rich habitats, such as tall-grass prairie, aspen woodlands, and moist riparian zones.[43]

THE OVERSEXED FEMALE

One of the classic metaphors surrounding immigrants is the oversexualized female. Foreign women are always associated with superfertility—reproduction gone amuck. Such a view suggests that the consumption of economic resources by invaders today will only multiply in future generations through rampant overbreeding and overpopulation. Consider this:

> Canada thistle is a classic invasive. One flowering stem can produce as many as 40,000 seeds, which can lie in the ground for as long as 20 years and still germinate. And once the plant starts to grow, it doesn't stop. Through an extensive system of horizontal roots, a thistle plant can expand as much as 20 feet in one season. Plowing up the weed is no help; indeed, it exacerbates the problem; even root fragments less than an inch long can produce new stems. . . . The challenge posed by thistle is heightened because, like other troublesome aliens, it has few enemies.[44]

Along with the superfertility of exotic and alien plants is the fear of miscegenation. There is much concern about the ability of exotic plants to cross-fertilize and cross-contaminate native plants and produce hybrids. Native females are, of course, in this story, passive helpless victims of the sexual proclivity of foreign and exotic males.

RESPONDING TO ALIEN SPECIES

Journalists and scientists borrow the images of illegal immigrants arriving in the country by means of difficult, sometimes stealthy journeys when they describe the entry of exotic plants and animals. Alien plant and animal movement are described with the same metaphors of illegal, unwelcome, and unlawful entry—for example, "Exotic species—from non-native fish to various plants, bugs and shellfish—have found their way into the country in numerous ways, such as *clinging* to ships, *burrowing* into *wooden shipping crates*, in food, *aboard aircraft* or *in water discharged* from foreign freighters" (italics mine).[45]

So how do we respond to these unlawful and stealthy entrants? Paralleling images of armed guards patrolling borders are images of the nation responding in kind to plants and animals.

"The alien species invasion—Interior Secretary Bruce Babbitt of the Clinton Administration calls it an 'explosion in slow motion'—is turning even staunch conservationists into stone killers."[46] Like our so-called solution to immigration and the drug problem, our answer to the problem of exotic and alien plants and animals is to "fight" and to wage wars against them. In 1999, President Clinton signed an executive order creating the national Invasive Species Management Plan, directing federal agencies to "mobilize the federal government to defend against these aggressive predators and pests."[47] Thus, the "Feds" were called on to "fight the invaders" and defend the nation against the "growing threat from non-native species."[48] It is implied that the situation is so dire and the number of invaders so great that even the most humane individuals (conservationists) cannot help but turn into killers in order to respond to the violations of alien species that are just not "welcome" into the country.[49]

One magazine published an article titled "When Ecologists Become Killers," allegedly transforming life lovers into "killer conservationists."[50] Like those of the human immigration problem, the resources are scant and the strategies often futile for the exotic species problem. "Two dozen federal agencies have stitched together a crazy quilt of detection and eradication efforts with state and local authorities. But much of the effort is aimed at ports, borders and threats to crops. There is little left over to combat emergencies."[51]

A recent review sponsored by the Ecological Society of America published in the *Issues of Ecology* concludes that the current strategy of denying entry only to species already proven noxious or detrimental should change.[52] Instead of "innocent until proven guilty," we should instead adopt "guilty until proven innocent." This strategy is further racialized when a biologist rephrases it by suggesting that we ought to replace our current system of "blacklisting" imported species (where a species must be proved to be harmful before it is banned) with a "whitelist" (where species has to proved to be safe before entry).[53] Thus, exotic and alien plants are marked as "guilty," foreigners, and black and therefore kept out purely by some notions of the virtue of their identity.

NATIVES

What is tragic in all this is, of course, the impact on the poor natives. "Native species invaded," "Paradise Lost," and "Keeping Paradise Safe for the Natives" are the repeated cries.[54] Native species are presented as hapless victims who are outcompeted and outmaneuvered by exotic plants. Very often, exotic plants are credited with (and by implication, native species are denied) basic physiological functions, such as reproduction and the capacity to adapt. For example, "When an exotic species establishes a beachhead, it can proliferate over time and spread to new areas. It can also adapt—it tends to get better and better at exploiting an area's resources, and at suppressing native species."[55] Invaders, interior secretary Bruce Babbitt says, "are racing out of control as the nonnative species in many cases overpower native species and alter regional ecosystems."[56] Experts warn of the growing invasion of foreigners into the nation's aquatic systems, threatening native species, waterways, and ecology. Not only do they crowd out native plants and animals, but they also endanger food production through the spread of disease and damage to crops, and they affect humans through threatening drinking water supplies. Consider this:

> English ivy joins 99 plants on a state list of botanical miscreants that includes Himalayan blackberry, Scotch thistle and poison hemlock. With dark green leaves and an aristocratic heritage, however, it looks like anything but a menace.
> Don't be fooled.
> The creeper loves Oregon, where it has no natural enemies.
> It needs little sunlight. It loves mild, wet climates.
> Robust and inspired, English ivy jumps garden borders, spreading across forest floors, smothering and killing ferns, shrubs and other plants that support elaborate ecosystems and provide feeding opportunities for wildlife. Insatiable, English ivy then climbs and wraps trees, choking off light and air.[57]

Articles invariably end with a nostalgic lament to the destruction of native forests and the loss of nature when it was pure, untainted, and untouched by the onslaught of foreign invasions. At the end of one article, a resident deplores the dire situation: "I grew up on the blackwater," he declares, "and I'm watching it disappear, its really sad." And the article concludes, "Spoken like a true native."[58]

THE RHETORIC OF BIOLOGICAL INVASIONS

In this chapter, I have traced the striking similarities in the qualities ascribed to foreign plants and animals and foreign people. The xenophobic rhetoric is unmistakable. The point of my analysis is not to suggest that we are not losing native species nor that we should allow plants and animals to flow freely across habitats in the name of modernity or globalization. Instead, it is to suggest that we are living in a cultural moment where the anxieties of globalization are feeding nationalisms through xenophobia. The battle against exotic and alien plants is a symptom of a campaign that misplaces and displaces anxieties about economic, social, political, and cultural changes onto outsiders and foreigners.

In his article "Natives and Nativism," Jonah Paretti persuasively argues that the language of exotic and alien plant and animal "invasions" reflects a pervasive nativism in conservation biology that makes environmentalists biased against alien species.[59] Nativism strongly grounds most of the literature against biological invasions. For example, the final chapter of one of the many recent books on the topic is entitled "Going Local: Personal Actions for a Native Planet." Such rhetoric conjures up a vision where everything is in its "rightful" place in the world and where everyone is a "native."[60]

The "natives," however, are, of course, the white settlers who reached the Americas to displace the original natives, to become its new, true natives. In this chapter it is the white settlers that come to be the "local" and the "native." The chapter includes many suggestions for how ordinary citizens can help toward a quest for a native planet by eliminating the exotics—from drawing public attention to the issue of exotics by writing op-ed pieces on biological invasions to the local newspaper, pressuring local conservation groups to take up this important yet unpublicized issue, to planting native plants in one's garden.

I want to be clear that I am not without sympathy or concern about the destruction of habitats, which is alarming. Indeed, we need to publicize and spread awareness about the destruction of species and habitats. However, in their zeal to draw attention to the loss of habitats, such journalists and scientists feed on the xenophobia rampant in a changing world. They focus less on the degradation of habitats and more on alien and exotic plants and animals as the main and even sole problem. With humans, the politics of class and race are essential, thriving on the fear of not all immigrants but immigrants from particular places and of particular places and classes; however, the language of biological invasions renders *all* outsiders,[61] even the familiar albeit nonlocal outsiders, into the undesirable alien.[62] Conservation of habitats and our flora and fauna need not come at the expense of immigrants.

Instead, let us consider exotic and alien species in their diversities. Mark Sagoff points out that the broad generalizations of exotic and alien plants obscure the heterogeneity of the life histories, ecologies, and contributions of native and exotic plants.[63] For example, he points out that nearly all the U.S. crops are exotic plants while most of the insects that cause crop damage are native species. It seems to me the height of irony that alongside a national campaign in the United States to keep out all exotic and alien plants in order to preserve the purity and sanctity of native habitats, there is simultaneously another campaign that promotes the widespread use of technologically bred, genetically modified organisms for agricultural purposes.[64] In these cases, the ecological dangers of growing genetically modified crops in large fields are presented as being minimal. Concerns of cross-fertilization with native and wild plants for which there is little empirical evidence are dismissed as antiscience and antitechnology. Ultimately, it would seem that it is a matter of control, discipline, and capital. As long as exotic and alien plants know their rightful place as workers, laborers and providers, and controlled commodities, their positions manipulated and controlled by the natives, their presence is tolerated. Once they are accused of unruly practices that prevent them from staying in their subservient place, they threaten the natural order of things.[65]

What is most disturbing about displacing anxieties attending contemporary politics onto alien and exotic plants is that other potential loci of problems are obscured. For example, some scholars point to the fact that exotic and alien plants are most often found on disturbed sites.[66] Perhaps the increase in exotic and alien plants is less about their arrival and more about the shifts in the quality of natural habitats through the process of development that allow their establishment. When habitats are degraded by humans, the change causes a shift in the selection pressures on plants at those sites. A displacement of the problem on the intrinsic "qualities" of exotic and alien plants and not on their degraded habitats may produce misguided management policies. Rather than preserving land and checking development, we instead put resources into policing boundaries and borders and blaming foreign and alien plants for an ever-increasing problem. Unchecked development, weak environmental controls, and the free flow of plants and animals across nations all serve certain economic interests in contemporary globalization. Displacement of blame onto foreigners does not solve the problem of the extinction of species and the degradation of habitats.

More central to issues of native and exotic plants are questions of what gets to be called a "native" species. Given that the majority of U.S. Americans are immigrants themselves, the reinvention of the "native" as the white settlers and not the "Native Americans" is striking. The systematic marginalization and disenfranchisement of "Native Americans" makes the irony all the more poignant. In southern California, where my project is based, questions of what are deemed native and exotic are deeply fraught. How do we develop dynamic models of "nature," which do not need to be artificially managed to remain the same year after year? How do we understand the human species as part of nature, in all its shifts and evolutions? These important questions can guide biologists in the development of experimental research. Is it possible to characterize exotic and native plants? Do they all share common life-history parameters and ecological traits? How heterogeneous and diverse are the species within those categories? How static and coevolved are native communities? What is the relationship of plants and their soil communities, and what impact do exotic plants have on them? Do they destroy and degrade these communities? As ecologists, we can test these theories, intervene and participate in the national conversation not only on exotic plants but also on immigration and race relations.

As feminists, we must intervene in the global circulations of science. Feminist and postcolonial critics of science have shown us repeatedly how larger political, economic, and cultural factors inform and shape scientific questions, answers, practices, and rhetoric. While I have largely focused on science that has reached and been popularized in mainstream culture, the scientific community is much more heterogeneous.[67] There is a long tradition of dissent and alternative views in most scientific fields. Many ecologists and conservation biologists have developed alternate models and disagree sharply with the dominant framework of conservation biology.[68]Feminists in the humanities and social sciences can and must build alliances with progressive scientists in the natural and physical sciences. Further, women's studies programs must make it a goal to produce a scientifically and technologically proficient group of students and faculty who are not relegated only to the role of "critics" (important though this is) but are also members of the scientific enterprise, producing knowledge about the natural world, a world that is deeply embedded in its social and cultural histories. Studying "naturecultures" means being cognizant of how science is embedded in these cultural contexts. Just as science does not mirror nature, we must not reduce science to mirroring politics either—Right or Left. Living in naturecultures means developing a self-reflexivity, continually wrestling with the interconnections of natures and cultures, politics and science, the humanities and the sciences, and feminisms and science.

NOTES

An earlier version of this chapter was published in the journal *Meridians: feminism, race, transnationalism* 2, no. 1 (Bloomington: Indiana University Press, 2001): 26–40. My thanks to Indiana University Press for giving permission to reprint it here.

This work would not have been possible without my wonderful collaborators James Bever and Peggy Schultz. Most of the arguments in this piece have been developed in discussions with the two of them. I am deeply indebted to Kum-Kum Bhavnani and Geeta Patel for their encouragement to develop this piece for publication. I would like to thank Natalie Joseph for her painstaking research in unearthing many of the articles cited. Comments and advice of James Bever, S. Hariharan, Geeta Patel, and three anonymous reviewers have considerably strengthened the arguments and the text of this chapter.

1. Martin Enserink, "Biological Invaders Sweep In," *Science* 285, no. 5435 (September 17, 1999): 1834–36.

2. Connections between the body as fortress and nation as fortress, the body and nation in late capitalism, can be seen in Emily Martin, "The End of the Body?" in *The Gender Sexuality Reader*, ed. Roger N. Lancaster and Micaela di Leonardo (New York: Routledge, 1997), 543–59. For thinking about the persistence of national states in an age of globalization, see Jean Comaroff and John L. Comaroff, "Millennial Capitalism: First Thoughts on a Second Coming," *Public Culture* (Comaroff and Comaroff, guest eds.) 12, no. 2 (2000): 291–343.

3. For provocative thoughts about the production of ethnicity and civil society/ nation, botanical taxonomies, and immigration policies in the United States, see Minoo Moallem and Iain A. Boal, "Multicultural Nationalism and the Poetics of Inauguration," in *Between Women and Nation*, ed. Caren Kaplan, Norma Alarcón, and Minoo Moallem (Durham, N.C.: Duke University Press, 1999), 243–63.

4. For some recent work on ethnocentrism and nationalism produced as a certain politics, see Paola Bachetta's article on xenophobia and the Hindu right in India: Paola Bachetta, "When the (Hindu) Nation Exiles Its Queers," *Social Text* 17, no. 4 (Autumn 1999): 141–66.

5. For a study of cultures, including national cultures and cultural nationalism, see Marshall Sahlins, "'Sentimental Pessimism' and Ethnographic Experience: Or, Why Culture Is Not a Disappearing Object," in *Biographies of Scientific Objects*, ed. Lorraine Daston (Chicago: Chicago University Press, 2000), 158–202. For cultural nationalism and new modes of citizenship, see Aihwa Ong, *Flexible Citizenship: The Cultural Logis of Transnationality* (Durham, N.C.: Duke University Press, 1999).

6. For an excellent discussion of how environmentalists in governmental and nongovernmental organizations, corporations, and financial institutions have sought to fashion a new environmentalism based on markets, see *People, Plants, and Justice: The Politics of Nature Conservation*, ed. Charles Zerner (New York: Columbia University Press, 2000).

7. For discourses of development under current conditions of International Monetary Fund regulations and so forth, see the work of Arturo Escobar. In particular see Escobar, "Cultural Politics and Biological Diversity: State, Capital, and Social Movements in the Pacific Coast of Columbia," in *The Politics of Culture in the Shadow of Capital*, ed. Lisa Lowe and David Lloyd (Durham, N.C.: Duke University Press, 1997).

8. I use "implode" in Donna Haraway's sense of "heterogeneous and continual construction through historically located practice, where the actors are not all human." See Haraway, *Modest_Witness@Second_Millennium.FemaleMan_Meets_OncoMouse: Feminism and Technoscience* (New York: Routledge, 1997), 68.

9. See Haraway, *Modest Witness*, 68.

10. Thyrza Nichols Goodeve, *How like a Leaf: An Interview with Donna Haraway* (New York: Routledge, 2000).

11. Earthwatch, "The Aliens Have Landed," *Earthwatch: The Journal of Earthwatch Institute* 15, no. 6 (November/December 1996): 8.

12. Nancy Tomes, "The Making of a Germ Panic, Then and Now," *American Journal of Public Health* 90, no. 2 (February 2000): 191–99.

13. For standard discussions on globalization see works by David Harvey and Saskia Sassen. See Sassen, "Spatialities and Temporalities of the Global: Elements for a Theorization," *Public Culture* 12, no. 1 (2000): 215–32. An interesting reflection on nationalism and movement can be seen in Arjun Appadurai, "Sovereignty without Territoriality: Notes for a Postnational Geography," in *The Geography of Identity*, ed. Patricia Yeager (Ann Arbor: University of Michigan Press, 1996), 40–58.

14. Section title in Christopher Bright, "Invasive Species: Pathogens of Globalization," *Foreign Policy* 116, no. 51 (1999): 14.

15. Mark Cheater, "Alien Invasion: They're Green, They're Mean, and They May Be Taking Over a Park or Preserve Near You," *Nature Conservancy* 42, no. 5 (September/October 1992): 24–29.

16. Barbara Stewart, "The Invasion of the Woodland Soil Snatchers," *New York Times*, April 24, 2001, 1B.

17. United Press International, "Native Species Invaded," *ABC News*, March 16, 1998.

18. "Bio-invasions Spark Concerns," *CQ Researcher* 9, no. 37 (October 1, 2000): 856.

19. Quote by refuge biologist Keith Weaver in Joseph B. Verrengia, "When Ecologists Become Killers," *MSNBC News*, October 4, 1999, www.msnbc.com/news (accessed December 20, 2000).

20. Jonathan Brinckman, "Creepy Strangler Climbs Oregon's Least-Wanted List," *Oregonian*, February 28, 2001, 1A.

21. Kim A. McDonald, "Biological Invaders Threaten U. S. Ecology," *Chronicle of Higher Education* 45, no. 23 (February 12, 1999): A15.

22. Ling-Ling Yeh, "U.S. Can't Handle Today's Tide of Immigrants," *Christian Science Monitor* 87, no. 81 (March 23, 1995): 19.

23. Christopher Bright, "Alien Threat," *World Watch* 11, no. 6 (November/December 1998): 8.

24. Jocelyn Kaiser, "Stemming the Tide of Invading Species," *Science* 285, no. 5435 (September 17, 1999): 1836–40.

25. Kaiser, "Stemming the Tide."

26. H. Weiner, "Congress Threatens Wild Immigrants," *Earth Island Journal* 11, no. 4 (1996).

27. Bright, "Invasive Species."

28. Stewart, "Woodland Soil Snatchers."

29. Josef Hebert, "Feds to Fight Invaders," *ABC News*, February 3, 1998.

30. Verrengia, "When Ecologists Become Killers."

31. Mark Robichaux, "Alien Invasion: Plague of Asian Eels Highlights Damage from Foreign Species," *Wall Street Journal*, September 27, 2000, 12A.

32. Verrengia, "When Ecologists Become Killers."

33. Cheater, "Alien Invasion."

34. McDonald, "Biological Invaders," A15.

35. Cheater, "Alien Invasion."

36. Robichaux, "Alien Invasion," 12A.

37. Joseph B. Verrengia, "Some Species Aren't Welcome," *ABC News*, September 27, 1999, www.abcnews.go.com (accessed December 20, 2000).

38. Bright, "Invasive Species."

39. Verrengia, "Some Species Aren't Welcome."

40. Cheater, "Alien Invasion."

41. Verrengia, "When Ecologists Become Killers."

42. Verrengia, "When Ecologists Become Killers."

43. U.S. Geological Survey Midcontinent Ecological Science Center, "USGS Research Upsets Conventional Wisdom on Invasive Species Invasions" (news release, Fort Collins, Colo., May 13, 1999).

44. Cheater, "Alien Invasion."

45. Josef Hebert, "Feds to Fight Invaders," *ABC News*, February 3, 1998.

46. Verrengia, "When Ecologists Become Killers."

47. Hebert, "Feds to Fight Invaders."

48. Hebert, "Feds to Fight Invaders."

49. Verrengia, "Some Species Aren't Welcome."

50. Verrengia, "When Ecologists Become Killers."

51. Verrengia, "When Ecologists Become Killers."

52. Richard N. Mack et al., "Biotic Invasions: Causes, Epidemiology, Global Consequences and Control," *Issues in Ecology* 15, no. 5 (Spring 2000): 12.

53. Daniel Simberloff, quoted in Kim Todd, *Tinkering with Eden: A Natural History of Exotics in America* (New York: W. W. Norton, 2001), 253.

54. Respectively, United Press International, "Native Species Invaded"; Verrengia, "Some Species Aren't Welcome"; and Richard Stone, "Keeping Paradise Safe for the Natives," Science 285, no. 5435 (17 September 1999): 1837.

55. Stone, "Keeping Paradise Safe," 1837.

56. Josef Hebert, "Feds to Fight Invaders," *ABC News*, February 3, 1998.

57. Jonathan Brinckman, "Creepy Strangler Climbs Oregon's Least-Wanted List," *Oregonian*, February 28, 2001, 1A.

58. Joseph B. Verrengia, "Some Species Aren't Welcome."

59. Jonah H. Paretti, "Nativism and Nature: Rethinking Biological Invasions." *Environmental Values* 7, no. 2: 183–92.

60. Jason Van Driesche and Roy Van Driesche, *Nature out of Place: Biological Invasions in the Global Age* (Washington, D.C.: Island Press, 2000).

61. Robert Devine, *Alien Invasion: America's Battle with Non-native Animals and Species* (Washington, D.C: National Geographic Society, 1999).

62. I am indebted to an anonymous reviewer for this insight.

63. Mark Sagoff, "Why Exotic Species Are Not as Bad as We Fear," *Chronicle of Higher Education* 46, no. 42 (June 23, 2000): B7.

64. The campaigns are, of course, not by the same groups. Many ecologists have expressed reservations about genetically modified food. My point however, is about the rhetoric that circulates in the mainstream United States.

65. Anna Lowenhaupt Tsing makes a similar point in her analysis of native and exotic bees. Tsing, "Empowering Nature, or Some Gleanings in Bee Culture," in *Natu-*

ralizing Power: Essays in Feminist Cultural Analysis, ed. Sylvia Yanagisako and Carol Delaney (New York: Routledge, 1994), 113–43.

66. Mack et al., "Biotic Invasions."

67. In this piece, I have largely focused on the popular press and those scholarly articles and scientists who have been publicized by the mainstream press. Scholarly articles, most often, do not share the sensationalism of the popular press. However, the same biologists employ different rhetoric in scientific and popular writings. The relationship of the popular and scholarly press is a complex one and beyond the scope of this chapter.

68. For example, see David R. Keller and Frank B. Golley, eds., *The Philosophy of Ecology: From Science to Synthesis* (Athens: University of Georgia Press, 2000).

Reflections

Impure Biology: The Deadly Synergy of Racialization and Geneticization

Alan Goodman

The two chapters in this part, Hugh Gusterson's on genetically modified foods and Banu Subramaniam's on the rhetoric of plant and animal invasions, highlight discourses on "impurity." As both chapters show, the history of the idea of race, the focus of this commentary, permeates discourses on impurity in the United States. Today, the deadly synergy of racism and geneticization offers to dominate how we think about human biologies and lends support to capital-driven institutions that control the production of knowledge about genes and bodies. Fears of impurity are predicated on ideas about the existences of pure races. And yet, what do we know about "race"? The following anecdote is a wonderful illustration of the fragility of the science of race.

On the morning of May 30, 1995, rescue workers made a final, melancholy sweep through the ruins of the Alfred P. Murrah Federal Building in Oklahoma City. The building was bombed by Timothy McVeigh, a white supremacist who was following the script of the *Turner Diaries*, a book promoting a race war. In the weeks after the bombing, the burned and dismembered bodies of 165 victims had been removed. Three more bodies had been located but were lodged in places too unstable to risk recovery. Workers marked the locations of these last bodies with Day-Glo orange paint before bringing the remaining building down with dynamite. Now they picked methodically through the rubble, searching for glimpses of orange.

Clyde Snow, a resident of Okalahoma and a forensic anthropologist with a long history of identifying victims of war and genocide in Central and South America, was now stationed in his own state morgue listening to reports from the bomb site. "Everything was going swimmingly," he later recalled. "When they got down to level zero, people could hear them talk-ing on their mobile phones: 'Okay, we have one, two, three bodies. . . . Fine, wrap it up, we can all go home.'" The rescue team, events soon showed, was jumping the gun. Two or three minutes after the third body had been found, a voice suddenly broke back over the airwaves: "Hey wait a minute! We've got a leg down here. A left leg."

During the explosion and its aftermath, about twenty-five of the victims had been dismembered. Snow assumed, at first, that the leg must belong to one of those individuals. "In all the confusion, with bodies going back and forth for X-rays, I thought somebody just overlooked that one body had a left leg missing," he said. "So, we'll just have to match it up." But one recount af-ter another yielded the same number: 168 right legs, 168 left legs; none of the survivors was missing a leg. "We went through autopsy records, pathology reports, body diagrams, and photographs. I did it twice, the pathologist did it twice," Snow said. "It was just a mathematical paradox."

Baffled, Snow took a closer look at the leg itself. Sheared off just above the knee, the leg revealed the remains of a black military-style boot, two socks, and an olive-drab blousing strap still adorning the body part. The skin, Snow said, suggested "a darkly complected Caucasoid." By measuring the lower leg and plugging the numbers into a computer program that characterizes bones by race and sex, Snow confirmed his hunch: the leg probably came from a white male. An attorney for the then-suspect, now convicted Timothy J. McVeigh pounced on the news, suggesting that the leg belonged to the "real bomber." Rumors turned to news reports that the bombing was the re-sult of Arab terrorists. Snow himself wondered if the leg might have be-longed to one of the transients who hung out on the first floor of the build-ing. Fred B. Jordan, the chief medical examiner for the state of Oklahoma, guessed that the leg belonged to a person walking alongside the truck car-rying the explosives.

As it turned out, the leg belonged to none of the above. Its owner was one Lekesha R. Levy of New Orleans, an airman first class, stationed at Tinker Air Force Base in Midwest City, Oklahoma. On April 19, Levy had gone to the Murrah building to get a Social Security card and was caught near the epi-center of the blast. Levy was five feet, five inches tall, twenty-one years old, and female. She was also, in the words of one forensic expert, "obviously black." With that disclosure, McVeigh's attorney declared, "No one can have confidence in any of the forensic work in this case."

Just a few weeks before the leg was found, Dr. Snow repeated a factoid that had been left unchallenged in articles and textbooks in forensic anthro-pology and in popular articles, books, and television shows for about thirty years. Race, he said, could be accurately discerned from a victim's skull 90 percent of the time.[1] True, the size and shape of a skull provides more clues to its owner's identity that a leg does. But in the case of Levy's leg, it was covered in skin only partly decomposed, and skin is the most common indicator of "race."

In fact, numerous examples suggest that mistakes like the one in Oklahoma City are common. I have shown that the percentage of correct identification of "race" from skull shape is closer to what one could guess at random than what Snow had imagined.[2] The point is that mistakes are common not because forensic experts do shoddy work—they don't. McVeigh's lawyer was wrong to extrapolate from a mistake in the forensic identification of Levy's race and sex to other parts of the investigation of the bombing site. No, errors in identification are a lot more common than Snow or others realized because they are based on a deeply flawed premise. As long as race is used as a shorthand to describe human biological variations—variations that blur from one so-called race into the next and are greater within these imagined biological races than they are among them—misidentifications are inevitable. Whether it is used in police work, medical treatment, or countless everyday situations where people are grouped biologically, race science is bad science.

In this commentary, I use six propositions to explain why race should not be used as a proxy for genetic or biological variation—that is, why race science is bad science. I then illustrate the two unfounded assumptions, what I call *racialization* and *geneticization*, that are needed to posit that racial differences in disease—or, for that matter, any other characteristics—are due to genetic differences among races. I end by reflecting on the reason that the typological and hierarchical notion of race as biology holds on and some of the relationships between race as biology and fears of Otherness.

RACE AS BIOLOGY IS A MYTH

The first of six reasons that race is a poor and even harmful way to think about human biological differences is based on the history and theoretical underpinnings of the idea of race. The next three all have to do with the structure of human biological variation. The last two pertain to the use of race in practice.

Race is based on the idea of fixed, ideal, and unchanging types. Race was first a European folk idea, born in an era in which the world was seen as being fixed and unchanging. Such an idea, however, is completely incompatible with evolutionary theory.

In response, some who still use race might say that the concept, as now used in science, is dynamic, flexible, and even evolutionary. But the new race is the old race—typological and ideal. Like a chameleon changing its color to better hide in a chromatically different environment, race changed superficially to fit into a new intellectual environment.

Human variation is continuous. Allele frequencies tend to vary gradually. Therefore, there is no clear place to designate where one race begins and another ends. Skin color, for example, slowly changes from place to place. Alan R. Templeton has shown that most human variation is explained by geographic distance: individuals tend to be most like those who are close to them and least like those who are farthest away.[3] If you want a simple sound bite to replace race as an explanation for the pattern of biological diversity, try geography.

Human variation is nonconcordant. Traits tend to vary independent of other traits. Race classifications, therefore, vary by the traits used to classify. A classification based on sickle cell trait might include equatorial Africans, Greeks, and Turks, while another classification, based on lactase enzyme deficiency, might include eastern and southern Africans with southern Europeans, Japanese, and Native Americans. There is no possibility for consistency. As skin color is only correlated with a few other phenotypic traits, such as hair and eye color, it is true to say that "race is only skin deep."

Within a group, genetic variation is much greater than variation among "races." Starting with Richard Lewontin in 1972, studies have statistically apportioned variation in different genetic systems to different levels: among "races" and within "races" and smaller populations, such as the Hopi, the Ainu, and the Irish.[4] Lewontin collected data on blood group polymorphisms in different groups and races. He found that blood group variation among races statistically explains about 6 percent of the total variation.

The implication of his results is that if one is to adopt a racial paradigm, one must acknowledge that race will statistically explain only a small proportion of variation. Moreover, this small variation is better explained by geographic distance. It is not that even the small differences are racial, only that race is related to geographic distance.

There is no way to consistently classify by race. Race is impossible to define in a stable and universal way because race as biology varies with place and time, and the socially determined color line is even more dynamic.

Other continuous variables, such as head and foot size, are classified into hat sizes and shoe sizes, and these systems work. A problem with race in practice is that there is no agreed-upon "race scale," as there are hat and shoe size scales. Ideas about race are fluid and based on different phenotypic cues. The salient cues change over time, place, and circumstance. For instance, 37 percent of the babies classified as Native American on birth certificates have been classified as some other race on their death certificates.[5] If race changes so quickly in less than a year, one can only imagine the degree of misclassification over decades and across regions.

There is no clarity as to what race is and is not. The same may be true of other key methods of classification. For example, definitions of socioeconomic class vary widely. Although always imperfect, they begin to provide a glimpse at the underlying processes by which social and economic positions affect lived experience and health.

Where race critically differs is in the breadth of potential interpretations of the underlying processes. Some individuals view racial differences in disease as being due to genes, while others view race differences as the consequence of the lived experience of racing and racism or the totality of the countless everyday experiences of being considered different and less human. Obviously, this confusion has serious implications for theory and practice. One cannot do predictive science based on a changing and indefinable cause.

No single reason noted in the preceding may be sufficient to throw race onto the scrap heap of surpassed scientific ideas. But the combination clearly suggests that it is time to move beyond race. As we have moved beyond thinking that the sun revolves around the earth and that a fully formed little human lives in sperm, so too is it time to move beyond race.

THE DOUBLE ERROR INHERENT IN
GENETIC EXPLANATIONS FOR RACIAL DIFFERENCES

Two errors, two leaps of illogic, are necessary to accept the idea that racial differences in disease are due to genetic differences among races. The first leap is a form of geneticization, the belief that most biology and behavior are "in the genes." Genes, of course, are often a part of the complex web of disease causality, but despite the recent hype, they are almost always a minor, unstable, and insufficient cause. The presence of Gm allotype, for example, has been touted as a "cause" of the high rate of Native American diabetes. Gm allotype might correlate with increased rates of diabetes in Native Americans, but the causal link is unknown. Moreover, a focus on the allotype diverts attention from other correlates that are more likely to be causal, including the development of a reservation culture and economy that have lead to a reduction in exercise and increase in dietary fats and simple carbohydrates.

The second necessary leap of illogic is a form of scientific racialism, the belief that races are real and useful constructs. Importantly, this leap propels one from explaining disease variation as being due to genetic variation to explaining that racial differences in disease are due to genetic variation among races. To accept this logic, one needs to also accept that genetic variation occurs along racial divides—that is, most variation occurs between races. However, we know from Lewontin's work that this assumption is false for simple genetic systems. For a disease of complex etiology, genetics is an illogical explanation for racial differences.

RACE AS GENES FAILS IN PRACTICE

Scientific uses of race as biology divide into two groups: one, as a means of identification and classification and, two, as a means of explanation. The first is the territory of forensics. The second requires the first and, depending on what is to be explained, is the territory of many fields, including biological anthropology, exercise physiology, psychology, and public health.

Identification of humans from skeletal remains provides a clear example of the poor performance of a racial model of human variation. The most widely referenced method for identification of race from the skeleton is Giles and Elliot's discriminant function for racing cranial remains. In the original study of crania of individuals of known "race" and sex, Giles and Elliot were able to correctly classify about 85 percent of individuals as one of three races: Native American, white, or black.[6] This accuracy of correct racial classification is, as best as I can figure it, the basis for the often-cited 90 percent correct classification referred to by Snow and others. However, on four retests of the method's ability to correctly classify Native Americans, the percentage dropped to an average of around one-third correctly classified. In other words, the retest performance was about what one would expect by random assignment.[7] Failure to extend the method to other times and places illustrates the result of temporally and geographically changing color lines and biologies.

Explaining that racial differences in disease are due to genetic differences illustrates both logical flaws. For example, the rise in diabetes among some Native Americans is often thought to be due to a genetic variation that separates Native Americans from European Americans. Along with obesity, gallstones, and heart disease, type 2 diabetes is part of what has been called "New World syndrome." The designation of a panracial syndrome may fix in the mind the idea of homogeneity within race and that the syndrome is innate.

However, contemporary variation in diabetes rates among Native North American groups is tremendous, and the rise in diabetes rates is a relatively recent phenomenon. Other groups experiencing shifts from complex carbohydrates to colas, from fast-moving foods to fast foods, and from exercise to underemployment, have experienced very similar rises in the same diseases that are part of the "New World syndrome." Rather than resigning themselves to the fatalism that diabetes is "in their blood," as the Pima articulate, it might be more productive to locate diabetes in changeable lifestyles.

* * *

While the public in Oklahoma was looking for an alien to blame the bombing on, it turned out to be the work of a "white" boy. Timothy McVeigh learned his racism from sources such as the *Turner Diaries*, the book written by William Pierce. In the *Turner Diaries,* the bombing of a federal building is a key event in the launching of the "race war." Realizing that the country was going to shambles because of the nonwhites and racial mixing, whites fight to take back the country and make it for whites only. The fictional *Turner Diaries* supported and made further real his racist worldview, guiding him to take the lives of 168 citizens.

In contrast to works of fiction, science is alleged to be objective, and its theories can be tested. But as the preceding is meant to show, scientific racialism has been put to the test and has failed miserably. Yet, despite being shown to be false, the idea persists in works ranging from forensic anthropology to pharmacogenetics. Of particular concern is the rise in biotechnology and the ideology of geneticization.[8] Like proponents of the notion of race, they place the locus of causality away from relations of power to the naturalized world of human difference and genes. If one sees what one believes, then scientists and those in positions of power seem to share more with McVeigh than we might imagine.

Biotechnology is profitable, and it is easy to classify individuals by races. But race as genetics is a chimera, and genetic explanations are weightless. This union of scientific racialism and geneticization is "ideological iatrogenesis," harm and killing resulting from beliefs. A just alternative is to continually clarify how racialism affects individuals under the skin and to do something about it.

One of the questions we must ask concerns why we continue to focus upon simple genetic explanations for our differences and why we now exalt genetics as an explanation for our suffering. A starting point is to see what these ideologies do—that is, how they are productive in the real world.

NOTES

The introduction to this commentary is adapted from Alan Goodman, "Bred in the Bone?" *The Sciences* (March/April 1997): 20–25; and the middle portion of the paper from Alan Goodman, "Why Genes Don't Count (for Racial Differences in Health)," *American Journal of Public Health* 90, no. 11 (November 2001): 1699–1702.

1. Clyde Snow, "Murder Most Foul," *The Sciences* (May/June 1995): 16–20.
2. This section is adapted from Goodman, "Bred in the Bone?"
3. A. R. Templeton, "Human Races: A Genetic and Evolutionary Perspective," *American Anthropologist* 100, no. 3 (September 1998): 632–50.
4. M. A. Jobling, M. E. Hurles, and C. Tyler-Smith, *Human Evolutionary Genetics* (New York: Garland, 2004); R. C. Lewontin, "The Apportionment of Human Diversity," *Evolutionary Biology* 6 (1972): 381–98.

5. R. Hahn, J. Mulinare, and S. Teutsch, "Inconsistencies in Coding Race and Ethnicity between Birth and Death in US Infants," *Journal of the American Medical Association* 267, no. 2 (January 8, 1992): 259–63.

6. Eugene Giles and Orville Elliot, "Race Identification from Cranial Measurements," *Journal of Forensic Science* 7, no. 2 (1962): 147–56.

7. This section is adapted from Goodman, "Bred in the Bone?"

8. This section is adapted from Goodman, "Why Genes Don't Count."

IV

CIRCULATION

7

Emerging Cartographies of Environmental Danger: Africa, Ebola, and AIDS

Charles Zerner

Some geographical regions of the globe, in Western representations, have been branded with the mark of particular cultural imaginings and meanings.[1] This representational burden, although not fixed and certainly permitting historical variations in contour and emphasis, is also carried by the world's rain forests.[2] In Amazonia, for example, Candace Slater documents a variety of intertwined representations that she calls the Edenic Rainforest, distinguished by its vulnerability, fragility, and radiance, in addition to a sense of biological equilibrium within coherent ecosystem borders.[3]

Representations of African forests, like Africa itself, have also carried a heavy burden of meanings in the Western imagination. Containing in their recesses virulent pathogens, warrior tribes, and lurking predators, they possess a potential for violence, the capacity to explode or implode, and the possibility that their "endemic" virulence would seep across borders and saturate adjacent territories.

This chapter explores recent changes in rain forest representations in popular media in the United States, specifically representations of viral biodiversity in African equatorial forests. At the height of rain forest romanticism in the United States, a period that began roughly in the 1970s and lasted through the mid-1990s, a certain kind of rain forest imagery, associated particularly with Amazonia, and, to a lesser extent, Southeast Asia, prevailed. Whether described in popular magazines, in the literature of international environmental campaigns, or in a more scientific discourse as "biological diversity," this tropical rain forest was in danger and in need of protection. Like the unicorn encircled by the king's hunters, it was surrounded by threats on all sides. Images of encroachment and conversion, of intrusion, penetration, and invasion, by loggers, settlers, and a multitude of pernicious forms of re-source extraction were widespread.

The image of a fragile, bounded, ethereal Amazonian rain forest, of course, was only one of a multitude of representations of rain forests that cir-culated during the 1970s and 1980s. Among others were representations rain forests as targets for the modernization project, sites for clearance and de-velopment in the form of vast plantations or utopian urban settlements; rain forests as "nature's pharmacy," sites of salvation for the modern world; and rain forests as raw resources, sites made for massive extraction of timber as well as precious and strategic minerals.

I argue that, within the panoply of overlapping rain forest representations produced by conservation organizations during the mid- and late 1990s, a particular representation of African forests began to become prominent. Within this representation, the directionality and significance of forest pene-trations were reversed: the channels and processes that had been conceptu-alized by conservationists as penetrations into the heart of the rain forest—roads, timber trucks, agricultural conversion, and development—began to be described as exits from the forest to the world beyond. They became the first connections to the global highway of commerce and the spread of trop-ical diseases. I call this lethal aspect of representations of African equatorial forests "the viral forest."

The picture of the viral forest that is just coming into focus, however, is complicated by representations of globalizing forces and flows of media, commerce, capital, ideas, and technologies. When the African tropical forest is linked to regional and global circuits of movement and exchange by roads, jet transport, sexual congress, the trade in monkeys, blood transfusions and organ transplants, global tourism and local warfare, it becomes a traveling threat to humankind: the viral forest in motion.[4] Representations of a dan-gerous, outward-spiraling African viral forest emerging during the late 1990s appear to invert the image of the delicately balanced, benevolent Amazon-ian rain forest. What sense are we to make of the growing salience of this representation of the African rain forest as a "viral forest" and, more particu-larly, a representation of an outwardly spiraling "viral forest in motion"?

If the image of a lethal virus escaping from an African tropical rain forest and traveling across the globe, across national boundaries and bodily de-fenses, is the icon at the center of this chapter, the spectacle is the story of how this icon—Ebola virus on the loose—has been, and continues to be, in-serted into international networks in global health and national security; in movements against genomic experimentation; and in regional, national, and transnational networks mobilizing against globalization. How has Ebola been seized, rendered, and rearticulated as a figure conjuring up fears, anx-ieties, and meanings? How are we to make sense of the appearance, in 2001, of a *National Geographic* cover story entitled "The Green Abyss Megatransect," featuring an account of "choking vegetation, impassable swamps, and rumors that virulent Ebola virus has struck gorillas in Gabon"?[5] How have varied social and environmental movements deployed these figurations of Ebola in information flows and networks ramifying across the globe?

While rain forest representations may reflect realities that already exist as "facts on the ground," they are also cultural interventions in social life and thought, shaping the possibilities of the social imagination, policy, and everyday conduct. My principal concerns in this chapter are to investigate the character and implications of the image of a "viral forest in motion" through a detailed examination of Ebola on the move. I ask these questions through a close reading of a popular nonfiction book, *The Hot Zone*, and a Hollywood movie loosely based on the book, *Outbreak*. I am interested primarily in articulating how this representation is constructed. I am also concerned with understanding the range of social and political implications of this environmental representation for American perceptions of civil life within the United States, as well the potential for shaping American perceptions of, and policies toward, the tropical developing world, especially Africa.

THE CONSEQUENCES OF GLOBALIZATION IN OTHER DOMAINS

In *The Hot Zone*

In 1994, Richard Preston's book *The Hot Zone*, about the travels and depredations of a rain forest microorganism, was published and received with great enthusiasm by a general reading public. Beginning with an account of the death of a French engineer in Kenya in 1980, *The Hot Zone* provides accounts of previous Ebola outbreaks in southern Sudan and in Zaire. From those scattered villages and towns within or on the periphery of African rain forests, Preston tracks Ebola's movement into the world he knows the best, the West.

At the center of *The Hot Zone* is an account of a 1989 Ebola outbreak among a population of monkeys housed in the Reston Primate Quarantine Unit in Reston, Virginia. Many of the afflicted monkeys, captured in coastal rain forests of the southern Philippines and destined for use as laboratory animals in the United States, were decimated by a variety of the virus known as Ebola Zaire. Ebola Zaire was not fatal to human beings. Although four people associated with the Reston outbreak were infected, Ebola Zaire did not make them ill.

As Preston shapes the story of the Reston incident, the drama revolves around the horrors made possible by globalization and its ramifying networks—the possibilities opened by jet transport, webs of trade, and commerce in exotic primates—to carry these diseases across the globe and to penetrate national borders and the bodies of everyday American citizens. The pivotal question around which the Reston monkey house drama revolves is, will Ebola get out into the world? Will it create a fatal epidemic in "a prosperous community just 10 miles west of Washington, D.C.?"[6]

Within a year, *The Hot Zone* was offered at least four options for production as a film. *Outbreak*, a Hollywood-made bioterror movie about an African virus and the defense establishment, was loosely based on the book. Publication of *The Hot Zone* was also followed by an efflorescence of fictional and nonfictional accounts of frightening microorganisms, their destructive capacities, and their travels.[7] The commercial success of *The Hot Zone*, the number of similar nonfictional accounts of viruses and their dangers in a moment of globalization, and the popularity of a website called "Outbreak" suggest the American public's apparently boundless fascination with the potentials of viral travel, invasion, and infection.[8]

The Hot Zone was packaged as a "revenge of the rain forest" story, explicitly linked to the terror of AIDS and its spread across the planet:

> As the tropical wildernesses of the world are destroyed, previously unknown viruses that have lived undetected in the rain forest for eons are entering human populations. The appearance of AIDS is part of the pattern, and the *implications for the future of the human species are terrifying.*[9] [Emphasis added]

It is a given that these lethal viruses are frightening. Several questions piqued my curiosity after seeing Ebola images on full-page *New York Times* advertisements linked to protests concerning the World Trade Organization and the dangers of genetic engineering, as well as printed in red letters on Physicians for Social Responsibility fund-raising envelopes, trying to mobilize constituencies against global warming.[10] How and why has a rain forest virus from Africa become an icon? What range of meanings, fears, and anxieties does Ebola trigger in the late twentieth century? Because Preston's *The Hot Zone* is a key popular work in a proliferating genre of viral nonfiction and fiction, I wanted to know more about Preston's techniques for stimulating concern and fear.

Fear has a literary and social history. Americans and Europeans can no longer be seriously scared by stories about werewolves, for example. Particular ages produce figures of fear that resonate widely with different publics and specific historical concerns. But what kinds of fears did representations of Ebola and the viral forest in motion generate? If environmental representations of Ebola and the African viral forest are interventions, in what ways might they affect social attitudes and policy within and outside the borders of the United States? How might these recent representations suggest the shape of emerging cartographies of environmental danger?

How has Preston fashioned an anxiety-saturated environment through the skillful selection of facts, contexts, tone, and imagery? If rhetoric is the study of persuasive speech, then what are the means by which Preston conjures up fear and terror about African rain forests and their links to globalization?[11] If poetics can be defined as the study of how images are made, how do specific constructions resonate with particular social and historical contexts? How do particular representations constitute interventions in the social sphere? I conclude, in part, that Preston's language yokes Ebola to centuries of Western imagery about African environments, peoples, and disease and couples these fears with deep, less-accessed regions of primal bodily anxieties. Preston joins these representational legacies with a family of unsettling representations of circulation: "reverse flows" of microorganisms moving from the South and penetrating the global North.

Although Preston's arsenal of poetic technique is formidable, it is only part of the story. I argue that Preston's Ebola terror story is so successful because it amplifies widespread, intense anxieties about the spread of HIV, a virus believed to originate in Africa and to be genealogically related to primates inhabiting equatorial Africa; and a legacy of negative images of Africa as a primitive, chaotic, disease-ridden, and violent environment: the place of monkeys, the jungle, tribal excesses, and unexplained deaths.[12]

The Hot Zone also resonates with contemporary concerns about networked societies, their dangers, technological links, and unpredictable consequences. I speculate that a standard environmental narrative underlies widespread fears about the consequences of globalization: an exotic threat from a foreign location somehow becomes dislodged from its natural moorings and place of origin; travels in global circulation networks; crosses borders stealthily and undetected; and explodes and proliferates within the body national, the body somatic, and the body cultural.[13] This standard environmental narrative is easily nationalized. In America, arguably a center of economic globalization, fears are proliferating that our borders will no longer hold against alien movements—whether the aliens are tropical viruses, nonnative plants and animals, refugees, or illegal immigrants.

In *The Hot Zone*: Fashioning an African Rainforest

The Ebola virus, to be an effective trope, has to come from somewhere, a place that is itself suggestive of terror. Preston fashions an image of a dangerous rain forest and its viruses that is distinctively African. The story of Ebola in *The Hot Zone* begins with the journey of Charles Monet, an expatriate Frenchman tending the water supplies of the Nzoia Sugar Factory in western Kenya. We know from the first page that Monet, on an excursion to Mount Elgon and Kitum Cave, is going to be a victim of a "Biosafety Level 4 hot agent." But we do not know where or how he will contract the virus. As we follow Monet and his girlfriend up the slopes of Mount Elgon, Preston configures the landscape in which the Ebola virus reservoir is located. Mount Elgon is fashioned as an imposing power in the African landscape, its long shadow cast across national boundaries.

Preston selects Kitum Cave on Mount Elgon as a probable site of the Ebola reservoir, indulging heavily in what might be called the African Gothic in rendering images of the cave's interior. The interior of Kitum Cave suggests mythical journeys to the underworld and meetings with alien others, an ancient netherworld. Preston enlists a macabre cast of animals and animal organs ("hundreds of bats eyes, like red jewels") and Dracula-like acoustics ("echoed back and forth, a dry, squeaky sound, like many doors being opened on dry hinges") in the service of fashioning the cave as a site of the uncanny. The interior of the cave appears as an ancient ur–rain forest:

> Then they saw the most wonderful thing about Kitum Cave. The cave is a petrified rainforest. Mineralized logs stuck out of the walls and ceiling. They were trunks of rain forest trees turned to stone—teaks, podo trees, evergreens.[14]

Although Preston occasionally describes African forests as "rainforests," evoking soft-focus, romantic Amazonian imagery, the emphasis throughout *The Hot Zone* is on the African tropical forest as a jungle: a site of a violent, ancient, and threatening nature. In his description of Kitum Cave, the petrified rain forest becomes a representation of a lethal natural landscape, a cave of syringes:

> An eruption of Mount Elgon about seven million years ago had buried the rain forest in ash, and the logs had been transformed into opal and chert. The logs were surrounded by crystals, white needles of minerals that had grown out of the rock. The crystals were as sharp as hypodermic syringes, and they glittered in the beams of the flashlights.[15]

Beginning with his lurid account, Preston's preoccupation with the integrity of the surface of the human skin and the possibilities of rupture becomes obsessive. He muses on how Monet may have contracted the virus: "Did he run his hands over the stone trees and prick his finger on a crystal? . . . There were spiders hanging in webs among the logs. The spiders were eating moths and insects."[16] Did Monet touch these spiders? Did the spiders touch him without Monet knowing it?

The ecological web, object of countless rhapsodic paeans in popular and scientific literature, is transformed into a series of lethal connections as Preston evokes a palpable sense of terror at contact with any natural surface and every living thing. Every surface and creature is suspect—a potential site of viral reservoirs, hosts, and transmission. The weblike connections of tropical biodiversity become the object of an anxious gaze, as we are yoked into perpetually scanning and evaluating potential sources of the virus. Yet much of this evocation is fanciful, unrelated to actual sites and surfaces that virologists consider likely for human contact with Ebola virus.

Ebola, Africa, and AIDS

Ebola, Africa, and AIDS, each powerful enough as singular presences, are combined in Preston's story to augment anxiety and apprehension in a rapidly ascending spiral. As I began to track the way the tropical forest and Ebola virus were fashioned, I began to see that Preston's images of the virulent, African microbial world were stand-ins for the African rain forest—the jungle. With Tom Geisbart, a young microscopist attempting to identify a virus extracted from a monkey house in Reston, we take a safari through the lens of an electron microscope. We see what he sees in a cell:

> He could see forms and shapes that resembled rivers and streams and oxbow lakes, and he could see specks that might be towns, and he could see belts of forest. It was an aerial view of rain forest. The cell was a world down there, and *somewhere in that jungle* hid a virus.[17] [Emphasis added]

The Ebola virus, a malevolent presence, rules over African tropical nature. Images of the virus morph from buckets of rope, to worms, to snakes, until they become the Medusa, the face of nature herself:

> He saw virus particles shaped like snakes, in negative images. They were white cobras tangled among themselves, like the hair of Medusa, the obscene goddess revealed naked. This thing was breathtakingly beautiful. As he stared at it, he found himself being pulled out of the human world into a world where moral boundaries blur and finally dissolve completely. He was lost in wonder and admiration, even though he knew that he was the prey. Too bad he couldn't bring it down with a clean shot from a rifle.[18]

Preston fashions an infernal image of a "hot virus," moving from the human being's most intimate site of the self, the brain, to its surface, the skin. Preston's menagerie of African viruses—Ebola Zaire, Ebola Sudan, and their filovirus sibling, Marburg—are characterized by an astonishing array of constantly mutating metaphors and similes. These viruses are at one moment lethal, mechanical, and metallic—likened to "Exocet missiles." Then they are described as deadly as nuclear "radiation"; as magnificent and terrifying as predators ("sharks"); disguised as the Grim Reaper in viral drag (a "slate wiper"); animate; charged with "terrible beauty," predatory intentions, and primitive promiscuity.[19] Ebola and Marburg, in Preston's hands, call forth the power of something resembling the "Romantic sublime" and put it into play: they spellbind, ravish, terrify, and transfix their victims in a beguiling spectacle of beauty.[20]

Filoviruses are not just generic viruses; they are described as African viruses, ancient African viral predators:

> The more one contemplates the hot viruses, the less they look like parasites and the more they begin to look like predators. It is a characteristic of a predator to become invisible to its *prey* during the quiet and sometimes lengthy stalk that precedes an *explosive attack*. The *savanna* grass ripples on the plains, and the only sound in the air is the sound of *African* doves calling from acacia trees. . . . In the distance, in the *flickering heat*, in the immense distance, a herd of zebras graze. Suddenly from the grass comes a streak of movement, and a lion is among them and lands on a zebra's throat. . . . Some of the predators that feed on humans have lived on the earth for a long time, far longer than the human race, and their origins go back, it seems, almost to the formation of the planet.[21] [Emphasis added]

Ebola, and the ancient African nature it signifies, are vested with malevolent agency, charged with the sinuosity of animal movement: It "savaged patients and snaked like chained lightning out from the hospital through patients [visiting] families" and "jumped quickly through the hospital via the needles."[22] Ebola, like a wild African predator, retreats after a kill and prepares to strike again.

> [It] retreated to the heart of the bush, where undoubtedly it lives to this day, cycling and cycling in some unknown host, able to shift its shape, able to mutate and become a new thing, with the potential to enter the human species in a new form.[23]

Preston's impressive arsenal of poetic technique cannot fully explain how these images of African landscapes and viruses generate such intense anxieties. In part, these images intersect and resonate with a centuries-old legacy of European images of the African landscape as a dark, chaotic, pestilential, savage world, a distinctly threatening configuration of an African Other.[24] A key template for these images can be found in the inward spiral of Joseph Conrad's *Heart of Darkness*, where a heavy atmosphere of anxiety and foreboding permeates representations of the African rain forest:

> Going up that river was like traveling back to the earliest beginnings of the world, when vegetation rioted on the earth and big trees were kings. An empty stream, a great silence, and impenetrable forest. The air was warm, thick, heavy and sluggish. . . . And in this stillness of life did not in the least resemble a peace. It was the stillness of an implacable force brooding over an inscrutable intention. It looked at you with a vengeful aspect.[25]

Conradian images of the African forest seem to pervade Preston's representation of the Ebola virus itself: "It seemed to emerge out of the stillness of an implacable force brooding on an inscrutable intention."[26]

Conradian images of Africa are variations on a far older and more general theme. Chinua Achebe, the distinguished Nigerian novelist, writes in an acerbic passage,

> Conrad did not originate the image of Africa which we find in this book [*Heart of Darkness*]. . . . Africa is to Europe as the picture is to Dorian Gray—a carrier onto whom the master unloads his physical and moral deformities so that he may go forward, erect and immaculate.[27]

Although older, as well as more recent, representations of the African rain forest possess a sense of lurking threat, they differ in their direction of flow. In the *Heart of Darkness* and other older representations, the danger (especially to white Westerners) is one of being sucked into the forest and absorbed by it ("going native").[28] In the more recent representations, including Preston's, the danger resides more in the forest's capacity to spread rapidly outward, beyond its limits within the forest and into the world beyond. The trajectory of Conrad's narrative, and the cartography of danger he maps, is an inward-turning spiral, moving toward a center where a meltdown occurs. The trajectory of the African viral forest in motion at the beginning of the twenty-first century is, in contrast, that of a spiral moving out into the world from a lethal African center.

Underlying and reverberating below the narrative of *The Hot Zone* are dark fears of AIDS, the iconic plague of the late twentieth century, emanating out of Africa. Even the book jacket copy is structured to invoke these fears. Fears of AIDS are fused in *The Hot Zone*, which entangles stories about Ebola, Marburg, and other hemorrhagic viruses in ways suggesting common geographic origins, common modes of jet travel, and horrific outcomes. Fears of a new viral plague from Africa move and merge with currents of anxiety about a known virus, human immunodeficiency virus (HIV).

Preston is not alone in deploying negative images of African landscapes, peoples, and social institutions on the screen of contemporary policy analysis and prognostication. Preston's sense of horror about African viruses, for example, and the inevitability of their transmission to developed countries, resembles policy analyst Robert Kaplan's determinist views of the state and future of African peoples, environments, and polities.[29] But African environments are not the inevitably degraded, deforested sites of violence and social chaos evoked by Kaplan.[30] Indeed, Kaplan's dire views of African environments, driven by Malthusian visions of population and resource limits, have been soundly disputed by environmental and political analysts.[31] Preston's vision of a virulent rain forest coming here, and breaking out, in the suburbs of Washington, D.C., echoes Kaplanesque visions of Africa as a site of inevitable environmental degradation, disease, and social chaos.[32]

Emerging Cartographies of Danger

Preston stimulates anxiety through collapsing a sense of distance and time, a narrative technique that suggests the African rain forest's apparently growing capacity to relocate itself in sites and in networks formerly thought to be secure. I focus first on the ways in which formerly safe places—arrayed in a descending spatial scale, from nations and national borders to cities, affluent suburbs, laboratories and hospitals, and finally the living individual human body—are shown to be vulnerable to the entry of the African rain forest. I then show how Preston stimulates anxiety about the safety and viability of networks—transport, communications, air conditioning—on which middle- and upper-middle-class Americans increasingly depend.

An emerging cartography of danger is embodied in these travels. The African jungle, in the form of Ebola and other viruses, does not merely travel across the globe or across national boundaries in all directions. Preston focuses on a trajectory of viral travel from the South, the zone of poorer, developing countries, in the bodies of African green monkeys captured in equatorial forests, to the developed North. For example, the emergence of Marburg virus in a factory located in central Germany emphasizes the threat to northern European civilized life within an ancient European city. Preston fashions a contrast between the well-ordered, peaceful northern European landscape and its sedate city, "surrounded by forests and meadows, where factories nestle in green valleys," with the lurid, bloody havoc wrecked by Marburg, "an African organism with a German name."

It is not within old Europe, however, that the African jungle makes its most disturbing relocation but rather within the borders of the United States. Preston devotes more than half of *The Hot Zone* to describing and dramatizing the discovery and suppression of an Ebola virus infection among monkeys housed at the Reston Primate Quarantine Unit, located in Reston, Virginia, a few miles from Washington, D.C. Preston's descriptions of Ebola among monkeys housed at the primate unit suggest the transformation of a portion of suburbia ("one of the first planned suburbs in America, a visible symbol of the American belief in rational design and suburban prosperity . . . where disorder and chaos were given no sign of acknowledgement and no places to hide") into a wild jungle.[33] To provoke a heightened sense of anxiety, of things out of place in a newly dangerous neighborhood, Preston first conjures up Reston as a site of built and natural American order:[34]

> Reston was surrounded by farmland, and the town still contains meadows. In the spring, the meadows burst into galaxies of yellow-mustard flowers, and robins and thrashers sing in stands of tulip trees and white ash. The town offers handsome, expensive residential neighborhoods, good schools, parks, golf courses, excellent day care for children.[35]

Preston's account of pandemonium in the Reston monkey house begins with a description of "one hundred Philippine wild monkeys." He emphasizes presumably primitive, repulsive features of their primate bodies, food-eating preferences, and social behavior, establishing an atmosphere and a dramatis personae characterized by crudity and violence: the monkey's heads had a "protrusive, doglike snout with flaring nostrils and exceedingly sharp canine teeth, able to rip flesh as easily as a honed knife."[36] Their shrieking, aggressive, crab-eating habits are described in ways that suggest savagery: "A crab comes out of its hole, and the monkey snatches it out of the water. . . . He grabs the crab from behind as it emerges from its hole and rips off the claws and throws them away and then devours the rest of the crab."[37]

When the monkeys show symptoms of an Ebola infection, Preston creates a forest full of paranoid, depressed, and violent primates—an outbreak of African jungle in the midst of one of America's more placid suburban towns:

Seventy pairs of monkey eyes fixed on a pair of human eyes in a space suit—and the animals went nuts. They were hungry and hoping to be fed. They had trashed their room.[38]

As a military suppression of the outbreak proceeds, the primate unit resembles a cross between a wild African jungle and a madhouse "filled with hysterical, screaming, leaping, bar-rattling monkeys."[39]

Between the nation and the suburb lies the city. In the Reston incident, the nearby city happens to be the capital of the United States. Preston is clear about raising the anxiety level of the reading public and focusing it on the possibilities of the African equatorial jungle appearing in Washington, D.C. He stages his descriptions of the primate unit infection in ways that emphasize the proximity of Reston to the capital:

On a fall day, when a western wind clears the air, from the upper floors of the office buildings in Reston you can see the creamy spike of the Washington Monument, sitting in the middle of the Mall, and beyond it the Capitol Dome.[40]

Through Preston's Reston-centered optic, the reader sees and senses the possibility of the monkey-house horrors spreading just a few miles within the Beltway and infecting the bodies of our nations' political leaders: an epidemiological meltdown of the nation's capital, its political and symbolic center, and by extension, the nation itself.

The Forest in the Body

The human body presents astonishing possibilities for the stimulation of anxiety. Preston fully explores these possibilities in creating scenes of invasion and viral proliferation. Of all sites in *The Hot Zone*, Preston is often at his lurid best in fashioning somatic scenes that are bloody and disturbing. Rather than focus on the gore, I wish to emphasize the ways in which Preston's imagery of the living body is articulated in governmental, military, and architectonic metaphors:

> As Ebola sweeps through you, your immune system fails and you seem to lose your ability to respond to viral attack. Your body becomes a city under siege, with its *gates thrown open and hostile armies pouring in*, making camp in the public squares and setting everything on fire.[41] [Emphasis added]

Homologies between besieged cities and infected human bodies abound, reinforcing the central images of failing border defenses, the vulnerability of boundaries and openings, and the lack of a capacity to respond to an enemy attack. Preston has constructed a series of nested homologies: The African rain forest appears within national borders, upper-middle-class communities, and that most intimate of sites—the individual human body.

Failures in the WEB, Infestations of the Networks

In *The Hot Zone*, the viral African forest also appears within the networks and webs of communication, transport, and connectivity that are increasingly interpreted as the emerging technologies of globalization. Preston suggests the growing capacity of the African viral forest to invade and populate boundary-spanning networks on which the managerial and professional classes increasingly depend.[42] Preston suggests the potential horror of these connections:

> A hot virus from the rainforest lives within a twenty-four-hour plane flight from every city on earth. All of the earth's cities are connected by a web of airline routes. The web is a network. Once a virus hits the net, it can shoot anywhere in a day—Paris, Tokyo, New York, Los Angeles, wherever planes fly. Charles Monet and the life form inside of him had entered the net.[43]

Within the bodies of monkeys that are themselves within the bodies of jets, the viral forest is in a constant state of motion and relocation. Preston amplifies anxiety about the lethal potential of global transport networks and other forms of border-crossing connectivity.

Marburg virus is portrayed as a globe-hopper: "The Marburg virus was a traveler: it could jump species; it could break through the lines that separate one species from another, and when it jumped into another species, it could devastate the species. It did not know boundaries."[44]

Boundary-spanning forms of connectivity and their risks are not only large-scale phenomena such as jet flight paths, transcontinental highways, or interstate highways systems. Even air conditioning systems are potential paths for traveling viruses. African rain forest enemies, Preston asserts, are only hours away from us. Preston's story of Ebola depends on images of almost instantaneous travel, from the South to North, on a global scale.

Globalization processes themselves, especially jet travel, have indeed become the objects of intense anxiety about time and space compression. Legitimate concerns about the risks of disease spread are recognized by a large group of eminent virologists and public health specialists,[45] as well as medical journalists, including Laurie Garrett, the author of *The Coming Plague: Newly Emerging Diseases in a World Out of Balance.*[46] While accurately portraying the horrors of the kinds of symptomatology that Ebola produces in monkeys, as well as in humans, Preston's accounts of Ebola infection exaggerate the ease with which the virus can disseminate itself in space, the ease with which it can be transmitted to and among humans, and the likelihood that those strains that are transmitted across species barriers are fatal for human beings.[47]

Questions about the risk of jet transport spreading Ebola, and the possibilities of a major epidemic as a result, are far from settled. David Frazier, of the Epidemic Intelligence Service and Department of Microbiology and Molecular Genetics, Harvard Medical School, comments:[48]

> While rampant speculation on the dangers of Ebola aerosols is amusing in a manner similar to telling ghost stories around a campfire, such speculation has little grounding in truth. . . . The results [of a recent issue of *Morbidity and Mortality Weekly Report*, a Center for Disease Control publication of infectious disease outbreaks] suggest that while such transmission can occur, it is not likely, and appears to be limited to passengers seated in the immediate area surrounding the affected individual. . . . It seems unlikely that a non-airborne pathogen, such as Ebola, would be transmitted to other passengers on a commercial flight.[49]

Preston's fevered risk assessments of globally spread Ebola epidemics are parodied within the scientific community. Dr. Brian Hjelle, a researcher at the University of New Mexico, writes,

> In Preston-speak: Bricks of bad information and fear-mongering set up a highly-efficient, deadly cycle of hysteria replication in the populace. The public hemorrhages, spilling hysteria to the next unwitting victim. Fear gushes from every media orifice. No one is safe from the hype.[50]

Fighting the Forest, Enter the Military

The ubiquitous presence of the U.S. military in the biocontainment and clean-up operation at the primate unit is one of the more remarkable aspects of the staging of *The Hot Zone*. Preston fashions a narrative in which military control over the Reston incident seems natural. The branch of the federal government charged with jurisdiction over emerging diseases is the Centers for Disease Control. As the story of the Ebola infection in the primate unit unfolds, the question of whether the center or the United States Army Medical Research Institute of Infectious Diseases staff has legal and operational authority over the situation is treated in a brief, cavalier fashion. Despite the center's congressionally mandated authority, a military commander present at the scene opines that "this was a job for soldiers operating under a chain of command." At the time of the primate unit incident, the commander explains to his colleagues, "We [the military] are going to do the needful, and the lawyers are going to tell us why it's legal."[51]

Attempts are made to conceal the involvement of military personnel in the search-and-destroy operation at the Reston primate unit. Preston emphasizes military concern for minimizing public anxiety, rather than illegal usurpation of authority for a military operation in the civilian arena. The military teams wore civilian clothes because "no one wanted to attract attention" and "set off a panic" by creating a spectacle of "soldiers in uniforms and camouflage putting on space suits." Unmarked vans as well as unmarked military vehicles transported the troops and commanding officers to the unit. Perhaps the simplest, most revealing statement about the military's entry into civilian zones is Preston's comment on the occasion of Colonel Peters's invitation to visit and enter the private primate unit: "The Army was finally getting its foot in the door of the building."

EBOLA AT THE MOVIES: SCENES FROM OUTBREAK

In 1995, one year after *The Hot Zone* was published, the film *Outbreak* appeared in local movie theaters around the country, starring Dustin Hoffman as an army medical expert, Renee Russo as his physician wife, and Donald Sutherland as a military-biowarfare villain. One morning in the fall of 1995, as I rode the subway downtown to my job at the Rainforest Alliance office in Greenwich Village, I noticed wall-high posters in the subway-station entrance at West Fourth Street announcing *Outbreak*'s release. I recall Dustin Hoffman in a biocontainment space suit in the foreground, a glamorous Renee Russo near him, several nasty-looking monkeys, and a fringe of tropical forest. Palm trees may have waved in the distance.

Outbreak is the story of a fictional virus, Motaba, its discovery in the Congo in 1967, its reappearance in the 1990s in roughly the same area. The drama focuses on military attempts to contain the spread of the virus in a fictitious town, Cedar Creek, located somewhere in northern California, and efforts to keep knowledge of a Motaba-based bioweapon and its vaccine secret.

Like its portrayal in the posters, the jungle plays only a peripheral role in *Outbreak*. *Outbreak*, like *The Hot Zone*, is a morality tale about what a disrupted, invaded, ravished African nature has in store for the nations and peoples of the global North. *Outbreak* begins in equatorial Africa in 1967. A village ravaged by local warfare, surrounded by forest, and afflicted with Motaba virus is destroyed when American military personnel descend on the afflicted village. After drawing blood from a dying combatant, an American mercenary, the U.S. military firebombs the entire compound, presumably destroying every living organism, virus, and human being in a burst of orange flame. Secretly, samples of the virus are collected, carried back to the United States, and used to develop a secret biological weapon and its antidote, both based on Motaba. In the 1990s, another outbreak occurs. This time, the U.S. military sends Dustin Hoffman, the irreverent hero working for the medical division, back to the Congo to identify and gather samples of the virus for the U.S. military.

In *Outbreak*, a series of monkey scenes sets up the story line and show us how Motaba moves from central Africa to America. A young capuchin monkey is shown watching combat around the village that is eventually destroyed by U.S. military in 1967. Another monkey observes Hoffman and his colleagues fly away from a newly infected village in the 1990s. Yet another monkey is shown captured in a hunter's net. And a fourth monkey, later to be named Betsy, becomes a victim of the international trade in primates for scientific experimentation and pets. Betsy is an ambiguous symbol for Africa in the late twentieth century, the multivalent equatorial African rain forest, its viral dangers and its fate in an era of globalization, militarization, international trade in tropical animals, and the manipulations of biomolecular science in the service of the U.S. national security establishment.

We first watch Betsy in captivity on board a mysterious Korean vessel as she is shipped to the United States. On shore, Betsy is warehoused in an animal-holding facility in San Jose, California. She is stolen by an unscrupulous young worker who wants to sell her, as he has done with other tropical primates, to the private pet trade. Provoked by the man's disrespectful manner, Betsy squirts water from her mouth onto his face, thus beginning a chain of Motaba infection that then spreads via her bloody scratch on the arm of a northern Californian pet-store owner, followed by its transmission through a remarkably animated cough in a provincial movie theater in a small working-class town, and through a kiss planted firmly on the mouth of the thief's girlfriend. Prior to the thief's cross-country jet flight, he releases Betsy into the great and majestic silence of the Pacific Northwest forest, where she wanders as a disoriented, potentially lethal carrier of Motaba. As he flies east, Motaba swiftly and silently proliferates within Cedar Creek.

As in *The Hot Zone*, *Outbreak* generates and heightens fears of a viral forest in motion and its capacity to penetrate borders and formerly secure spaces. The placid working-class rural northern California town of Cedar Creek, a community nestled near the Pacific Ocean and flanked by the darkly majestic trees of a northern Californian forest, is reduced to a mass of people in panic, while others, weakened or dying, are laid on stretchers. Cedar Creek's probable closeness to San Francisco, as Reston's proximity to Washington, D.C. in *The Hot Zone*, suggests the possibility of an epidemic in a major metropolitan center.

Outbreak, like *The Hot Zone*, focuses on the potential of webs and net-works to facilitate the dispersion of infectious diseases. The virus is carried to American shores on an ocean freighter. It travels, via the U.S. interstate highway system, from a probable location in San Jose to sites along the road in northern California. Motaba is sucked up into the vortex of air condition-ing ducts in an improvised field hospital in Cedar Creek, only to be expelled into another room, where it finds new victims. From California to Boston, Motaba flies in a transcontinental jet.

Fears of disease dispersion in an era of jet travel are graphically displayed when Donald Sutherland, in an effort to convince the president and his ad-visors to permit the fire-bombing of Cedar Creek and its civilian population, presses a button to reveal a map of the entire United States. The map dis-plays relatively small clusters of red dots signifying the geographic distribu-tion of isolated Motaba cases. Within moments, the entire map is saturated with red. Using cartographic imagery as a spectacle and emotional prod, this scene makes the phenomenon of epidemic dispersion and its networked connections a bloody, red reality. And like *The Hot Zone*, *Outbreak* creates anxiety by obsessively focusing on the nodes and portals within webs: air-ports, shipping facilities, the air-lock doors of the temporary military-medical center of operations airlifted into Cedar Creek, the levels and locks of the biosafety labs.

Outbreak also emphasizes the militarization of public health interven-tions. The enormous, awesome, fear-inspiring resources of the American military and its technologies are deployed to mark and police the perime-ters of the afflicted Cedar Creek. Its disenfranchised citizens are herded from their homes to fenced-in containment areas, escorted by armed, in-timidating military personnel. Hovering over this working-class commu-nity are dragonflylike helicopters that fire their weapons against a few families attempting to escape the concentration camplike containment zone. Insulated physically from the normal citizenry and the air by their impressively sealed, high-tech biosafety operations center, these techno-science troops are as frightening as the Motaba virus. Exempt from the normal restraints and obligations of citizenship, these troops can kill civil-ians in the service of the state's proprietary interest in safeguarding the weapons of bioterror and national defense.

Unlike *The Hot Zone*—which seems to render reasonable the use of the American military force within spheres of civilian life, particularly in connection with public health operations—*Outbreak* appears to condemn the militarization of public health and everyday life. Sutherland, as the chief of the secret bioterror division, is an amoral figure. He wants to keep his stock of Motaba, collected during the 1967 initial outbreak, as a secret weapon of the American military. His decision to exterminate the remaining population of Cedar Creek is based on a desire to retain this American monopoly on a bioweapon and its remedy.

But *Outbreak* actually makes the interventions of a certain kind of military —the kind of military embodied by familiar antics of spunky, clever, and well-intentioned Dustin Hoffman—seem attractive and reasonable. By setting up a boldly drawn contrast between the appealing Hoffman and the gaunt, cold military-bioweapons commander Sutherland, *Outbreak* makes the decision easy. It is just a question of what kind of military we should welcome into our civic sphere, not whether there is a legitimate role for the armed forces in civilian life.

IMMIGRATION POLICIES AND INVASION RHETORICS

The jump from African rain forest viruses moving across American borders, viruses "jumping" across species boundaries, and talk about the movements of illegal immigrants moving across the southern border of the United States may appear startling. However, some striking, if partial, parallels exist between recent talk about the travels and threats of rain forest viruses and talk about the cross-border movements and character of illegal immigrants. How are we to account for the formal repetition of invasion analogies across several natural domains?[52] Why, at this historical moment, are the movements of rain forest microorganisms, nonindigenous plant and animal species, and immigrants apparently conceptualized in similar ways? Why does this rhetoric travel so easily across domains?

Anxieties about alien invasions, maintaining integrity in the face of border penetration and control, and racialized rhetorics of fear about exotic Others penetrating national boundaries and subverting American national identity are present in recent policy position papers and programs of the U.S. Immigration and Naturalization Service (INS). In 1993, the INS adopted and proceeded to implement an aggressive immigration-control campaign on the U.S.–Mexico border that seeks to develop "a host of new strategies and technologies designed to 'restore integrity and safety' to Southwestern borders."[53] This monumental effort at controlling the flow of illegal aliens across the Southwestern border, deploying a significant amount of capital and human resources, was implemented through four programs: Operation Gatekeeper, Operation Hold the Line, Operation Safeguard, Operation Rio Grande. These programs involve high-tech tracking-and-monitoring equipment deployed to restrict the flow of illegal aliens across a two-thousand-mile stretch of the U.S. Southwestern border.

In the words of Lisa Sanchez, a legal scholar currently investigating immigration rhetoric and policy in the United States,

> Through official reports, government testimony and publicized statements, the INS has established what Foucault would call an "authorized vocabulary" of border control. This vocabulary presents the border control effort as a strategy of safety and preservation, and it presents border control agents as righteous protectors of the common good. . . . The representation of undocumented border crossers as a racialized threat is accomplished through the discursive construction of three inter-related identity categories: undocumented immigrant as *criminal alien, undocumented immigrant as armed soldier, and undocumented immigrant as disease vector.*[54] [Emphasis added]

These ways of speaking, of course, have a deep history in the annals of public health, immigration, and labor. At least 120 years old, the vocabulary of disease, immigrants, and criminality is the rhetoric of Ellis Island–era politicians.

The alien-invasion narrative and all its constituent elements—fears of globalization; the dislocation of an alien, exotic Other entering the global web, passing the border zone/boundary, and proliferating—is present in *The Hot Zone* narrative as it is in INS border talk. Consider how undocumented workers and border crossers are regarded in INS documents outlining the control of the U.S.–Mexico border:

> Construed as armed soldiers and dangerous criminals in a war against American community and economy, they are as much represented as symbols of *disease*, seeping across the *fragile membrane* that separates "first" and "third" world, poised to infect the racial and cultural *integrity* of U.S. citizens.[55] [Emphasis added]

These narratives suggest a turn toward militancy at the border, even militarization, to the extent that they propose early warning systems, surveillance technologies, border interdiction strategies, and infrastructures for monitoring and control.

In attempting to safeguard "the last bastions of nature" and society at this moment in American history, is a militarized form of biosocial paranoia in gestation?[56]

EBOLA IN THE NEWSPAPERS: THE TURNING POINT PROJECT

Genetic Engineering Advertisements

In this section, I turn briefly to consider a recent series of newspaper advertisements that uses images of African Ebola virus to provoke fears of genetic recombinant research and xenotransplantation.[57] The newspaper series was sponsored by the Turning Point Project, an alliance of remarkably diverse social, environmental, and economic advocacy groups. It is useful to briefly look at the ways in which Ebola, African nature, and images of border-crossing in nature are used by the producers of these advertisements.

On November 1, 1999, the text of a full-page advertisement in the *New York Times*, in large boldfaced type, asked, "Where will the next plague come from?" The headline was located directly above a greatly enlarged photograph of an Ebola virus in the center of the page. The text below the headline answers by making a misleading analogy between the processes of disease transmission between primates and human beings in African forests and interspecies viral transmission resulting from laboratory-based genetic engineering and xenotransplantation practices in North America and elsewhere in the developed world:

> HIV and Ebola virus crossed from primates to humans. The 1918 influenza virus started in pigs. Now biotechnicians who shuffle live organs and genes between humans and animals could end up unleashing deadly new diseases without hope of a cure.[58]

In a section called "Crossover Diseases," the text shifts from fears of Ebola to anxieties about AIDS:

> The history of the twentieth century provides ample evidence of the catastrophes that can result when disease agents cross species boundaries. . . . A version of HIV, the retrovirus that leads to AIDS, *probably resided harmlessly in a wild forest primate before people invaded its habitat* and contracted it. Some forty million people worldwide will soon be carrying that deadly disease.[59] [Emphasis added]

In these intentionally disturbing advertisements, African viruses and their movements from equatorial forests are used as figures of fear. "From day one," a knowledgeable participant in the Turning Point Project comments, "the goal [of the ad series] was to articulate a description of a problem that would send you over the edge." Using the names of Ebola and AIDS and linking these terrifying viruses to contemporary experiments in genetic recombinance amounts to a form of word magic: the transfer, by means of analogy and association, of characteristics from one empirical domain to another. Coupling these names with photographs of the Ebola creates a wide spectrum of associations and anxieties: epidemics, uncontrolled dispersion, unholy border-crossing, and death. These ads use the movement of "African" viruses—AIDS and Ebola—across species boundaries and geographic space as metaphoric means of inciting anxiety about the risks of another domain, xenotransplantation. Among the key words in this series are species *barrier*, *integrity*, and *identity*. In language that refers to a science-fiction movie

about a mad scientist, *The Cabinet of Dr. Caligari*, the first Turning Point genetic engineering advertisement conjures up a monster-escape scenario that
echoes Preston's overwrought descriptions of Ebola on the loose: *These
things are alive. And they don't want to go back into their test tubes.*

By choosing to place ads in only the major print media of the Northeast,
the creators of the Turning Point ad series sought to provoke concern among
elite opinion- and policymakers in the Northeast corridor of the United
States.[60] In linking accounts of naturally occurring cross-species movements
of genetic material with scientifically generated genetic change, by linking
these processes to the feared AIDS and Ebola, and by conjuring up the representation of movement as a source of danger, the Turning Point genetic engineering ads create a vortex of invasion imagery and impending catastrophe across species, ecosystems, and national boundaries:

> Biotech creatures and microbes are unpredictable. They can reproduce, cross-
> pollinate, mutate and migrate. They can jump across species using virus vectors.
> They can hitch rides in cars, boats and planes or in your socks. They can show
> up in other ecosystems. Like the Gypsy Moth, Dutch elm disease, and Kudzu
> vines, "exotic organisms" can run amok and cause unparalleled environmental
> destruction.[61]

CONCLUSION

I have argued that in the late twentieth century, Edenic images of the Amazonian rain forest made popular during the 1970s and 1980s were rejoined
by earlier representations of the African forest as a lethal environmental
zone. The trajectory of danger, however, has been reversed. While earlier
European travel narratives to Africa followed a spiral inward and downward
to a fevered and chaotic center, the trajectory of African biodanger is now
represented as an outward movement, a spiral originating within the heart of
the equatorial forest, arcing across the globe, and penetrating the core nations of the North.

I have called this emerging representation "the viral forest in motion."
Once regarded as stable, coherent, bounded associations of endemic
species, representations of tropical African forests increasingly emerge in
popular media descriptions as ruptured ancient rain forests from which a
plaguelike explosion of multiple viruses is liberated, exiting on the same
rough roads that only recently forced an entry. Rather than experience an inward journey into the African forest, we are subject to the dangers of "reverse flows."[62]

I have argued that the image of a virus escaping from the forest and relo-
cating in the North, this icon, has come to represent the African forest and its

potential to travel, spread, and relocate within a variety of social spaces—nations, cities, small towns, and suburbs. It travels through boundary-spanning networks or webs formerly thought of as being safe and secure. This representation has coalesced at a moment of ramifying anxieties about the consequences of globalization and border-crossing flows and, possibly, an American military establishment in search of new missions and enemies.

These representations are instruments for the production of fear about security and survival within the North or developed world most broadly and within America and other European sites—nations, cities, suburban enclaves, middle- and upper-middle-class homes, and bodies—more specifically. The trajectory of this movement out of Africa, across oceans, and into the North suggests the outlines of an emerging cartography of environmental danger. This chapter has sought to provoke discussion about the possibility of an emerging environmental cartography of danger that crosses empirical and conceptual borders. Some striking if partial parallels exist between recent talk about the travels and threats of rain forest viruses, talk about the cross-border movements and character of exotic plants and animal species, and discourses on the movements of illegal immigrants into the United States. Many of these discourses focus on surveillance, capture, and control of the flow of aliens.

Is there a standard environmental narrative about endemic ecological and cultural systems whose vulnerable borders are to be fortified for protection from foreign threats? How are we to account for the formal repetition of invasion analogies across several natural domains?[63] Why, at this historical moment, are the movements of rain forest microorganisms, nonindigenous plant and animal species, and immigrants apparently conceptualized in similar ways?

What consequences might these representations have? If they are effective in stimulating the kinds of anxieties touched on throughout this chapter, then it is quite possible that they contain implications for social attitudes and practices, for policy, and for politics. In the most general terms, a heightened fear of alien organisms is one of the possible consequences of these representations. This diffuse fear or anxiety could embrace immigrants as well as microscopic viruses, nonnative plants, and exotic animals. The gamut of living creatures set in motion and moving from the global South to the global North might well become the objects of an increasingly anxious gaze.

It is also probable that these representations and the diffuse anxieties they engender could lead to increasing scrutiny and intensified surveillance around the borders of areas formerly considered safe and secure. These areas might include portals of entry and exit, ranging in scale from national borders and border-crossing areas to building security peripheries and entryways in institutional as well as domestic settings.

The emerging cartography of danger suggested in these pages could reinforce a generalized fortress mentality in which politics and policies of hardened borders, clarified boundaries, and strengthened barriers begin to be seen as desirable and justified. Is there a convergence of methods, models, and strategies leading toward a hardening of security and surveillance concerns in domains as disparate as domestic architectural design and urban planning, in conservation policy and planning, in border control and immigration policy in the American West, as well as in epidemiology and virology?

What are the potential social and political implications of this representation beyond American national borders? Both texts, as well as the Turning Point advertisements, revitalize and ratify a view of Africa, its environments in general, and its equatorial forests and biological diversity in particular as dangerous. They are environments and organisms, the representations seem to imply, that need to be stabilized, contained, and probably avoided. These conceptions, and the images that support them, dovetail neatly with older Eurocentric images of Africa as the dark continent. They also resonate and reinforce recently fashionable doctrines of inevitable African environmental, cultural, and economic decline. This new, old cartography of the African continent, as well as that of the African equatorial forest, portrays Africa as the site of catastrophic events including seemingly inevitable famine, plagues, and political terror. This simplified totalizing vision constitutes what might be termed a racist cartography, with the potential to become a self-fulfilling prophecy.

What implications might this representation have for the management and fate of the African equatorial rain forest? Given the volatile nature of this particular forest representation, its tendency to escape its bounds, to go traveling in places it doesn't belong, and to make mischief, perhaps the central tropical forest policy implication of these texts is, keep this forest in its place. A hard regime of strengthened borders, heightened surveillance, and military patrols may be imagined as the logical policy implication of this representation.

The virus has become one of the master metaphors of the early twenty-first century.[64] Tropical African nature and its plethora of microorganisms are being held hostage to the ravages of diffuse anxieties about border crossings, alien takeovers, and penetrations of and threats to the coherence of the self—individual, national, cultural, ecological, biological, and economic. The image of Ebola virus and the equatorial African rain forest—representing Ebola's natural origin and ruptured container—have become points of articulation within a remarkable variety of social, economic, and environmental movements. Ebola has been invoked as a symbol of nature's irrepressible instability and its virulence—its tendency to morph, jump species, move across boundaries, invade individuals, and penetrate Western civilization.[65]

The image of African Ebola, like a gladiator's shield emblazoned with a terrifying countenance, has become a symbol and a site—of articulation and linkage—through which a variety of movements speak on behalf of nature and humankind. Although the issues and anxieties animating these movements differ significantly—biomedical and epidemiological security, national defense, rain forest conservation, genetic recombinant research, xenotransplantation, world trade, and biological weapons development—they share common concerns with keeping endemic nature in its place, keeping the aliens outside, and policing the borders. Ebola, uncoupled and released from its rain forest origins in equatorial Africa, continues to flash its colors— as a template, a moving target, a chameleon-like living vessel for proliferating anxieties and environmental fears.

NOTES

An earlier version of this chapter, containing more extensive notes, was published as "The Viral Forest in Motion: Ebola, Africa, and Emerging Cartographies of Environmental Danger," in *In Search of the Rainforest* (Durham, N.C.: Duke University Press, 2003). This chapter is published with permission of Duke University Press. At Sarah Lawrence College, I am indebted to Claire Campbell, Ginger Hagan, and Alayna Baldanza, who provided capable research and editorial assistance.

1. Tropical forests and their representations have been regarded ambivalently by the West since the fifteenth century, alternately emphasizing paradisaical or darker, negative aspects. On the history of the idea of the tropics and tropicality, and variations in relative emphasis along this axis from paradise to green hell, see David Arnold, *The Problem of Nature: Environment, Culture, and European Expansion* (Oxford: Blackwell, 1996).

2. See Arjun Appadurai, *Modernity at Large: Cultural Dimensions of Globalization* (Minneapolis: University of Minnesota Press, 1996), for an earlier articulation of this notion of geographical branding. See also, Richard H. Grove, *Green Imperialism: Colonial Expansion, Tropical Island Edens, and the Origins of Environmentalism, 1600–1860* (Cambridge: Cambridge University Press, 1995), who describes the destruction of scrub and forests of Bengal as a means of improving the ventilation of miasmas.

3. See the publications of biologist E. O. Wilson for a recasting of the romantic sublime imagery of rain forests in terms of biological diversity. For an example of Wilson's rhapsodic, cosmologically benevolent image of biological diversity, see the opening chapter of *The Diversity of Life* (Cambridge, Mass.: Harvard University Press, 1992), 11–15. On Wilson's rapture with the wilderness idea, see Michael Lewis, *Inventing Global Ecology: Tracking the Biodiversity Ideal in India, 1945–1997* (Athens: Ohio University Press, 1985). See also, David Tackacs, *The Idea of Biodiversity: Philosophies of Paradise* (Baltimore: Johns Hopkins University Press, 1996).

4. The tropical forests of equatorial Africa always lay below the shadow of a darker, racist Western gaze, as demonstrated by Philip D. Curtin, *The Image of Africa: British Ideas and Action, 1780–1850* (Madison: University of Wisconsin Press, 1964);

and Christopher Miller, *Blank Darkness: Africanist Discourse in French* (Chicago: University of Chicago Press, 1985).

5. See David Quammen, "The Green Abyss Megatransect, Part II," *National Geographic* (March 2001): 8–37.

6. Richard Preston, *The Hot Zone* (New York: Random House, 1994), 107.

7. See, for example, Marc Lappe, *Breakout—the Evolving Threat of Drug-Resistant Disease* (San Francisco: Sierra Club Books, 1995); Richard Preston, *The Cobra Event* (New York: Random House, 1997); William Close, *Ebola—a Documentary Novel of Its First Explosion in Zaire* (New York: Ivy, 1995); Johan Marr and J. Baldwin, *The Eleventh Plague—a Novel of Medical Terror* (New York: Cliff Street Books, 1998); Joseph McCormick, Susan Fisher-Hoch, and Leslie Alan Horvitz, *Level 4 Virus Hunters of the CDC* (Atlanta, Ga.: Turner, 1996); Edward Regis, *Virus Ground Zero—Stalking the Killer Viruses with the Centers for Disease Control* (New York: Simon and Schuster, 1996); C. J. Peters, *Virus-Hunter—Thirty Years of Battling Hot Viruses around the World* (New York: Doubleday, 1997).

8. Pragmatica, *Outbreak*, April 26, 1998, www.outbreak.org/cgi-unreg/dynaserve.exe/index.html (accessed March 6, 2000).

9. Preston, *Hot Zone*, dust jacket.

10. The names of six "modern plagues," including Ebola, printed in red ink and large type, with the question "What terrifying Modern Plague will we face next?" were on the cover of an envelope I received in late April 2000 from the respected nongovernmental organization Physicians of Social Responsibility (PSR). The PSR letter read, in part, "Deadly new diseases are cropping up all over. Global climate change, commonly known as 'global warming,' is creating a breeding ground for diseases. And unless we take action now, more 'modern plagues' that sicken and kill people could be coming our way."

11. For recent analyses of environmental rhetoric, see Rom Harre et al., *Greenspeak: A Study of Environmental Discourse* (London: Sage, 1999); see also, Kevin Michael DeLuca, *Image Politics: The New Rhetoric of Environmental Activism* (New York: Guilford, 1999); and M. J. Killingsworth, *Ecospeak: Rhetoric and Environmental Politics in America* (Carbondale: Southern Illinois University Press, 1992).

12. See Susan Sontag's *AIDS and Its Metaphors* (New York: Farrar, Straus and Giroux, 1989), 52, on racist characterizations of AIDS and its links to cultural and environmental topographies.

13. The term *standard environmental narrative* was first used by Paul Greenough in analyzing scholarship on South Asian environmental history. I use the term to mean widespread narrative structures informing contemporary anxieties about aliens, cross-border flows, purity, and danger within a variety of bodies national, cultural, ecological, and somatic.

14. Preston, *Hot Zone*, 9.

15. Preston, *Hot Zone*, 9.

16. Preston, *Hot Zone*, 9.

17. Preston, *Hot Zone*, 135.

18. Preston, *Hot* Zone, 137.

19. See Preston, *Hot Zone*, describing African viruses as siblings (26) and comparing them to hair (26), a great flooding mess (26), worms (26), and snakes (26); and likening Ebola to nuclear radiation and the rabies virus (28), three filovirus sisters (2),

a virus queen (86), an exocet missile (32), a cobra (79), molecular sharks (59), a carnivore retreating to the heat of the bush (69), a slate wiper (27), and white snakes (137). Marburg virus, one of Ebola's viral "sisters," is described as being invasive, promiscuous, and obscene (93).

20. On the power of the romantic sublime to induce states of terror and awe, see William Cronon, "The Trouble with Wilderness; or, Getting Back to the Wrong Nature," in *Uncommon Ground: Toward Reinventing Nature*, ed. William Cronon (New York: W. W. Norton, 1995), 69–90.

21. Preston, *Hot Zone*, 93.

22. Preston, *Hot Zone*, 68.

23. Preston, *Hot Zone*, 69.

24. For an analysis of the historical interconnections between discourses on African climate, natural history, and the emerging science of biology, see Jean Comaroff and John Comaroff, "Africa Observed: Discourses of the Imperial Imagination," in *Perspectives on Africa*, ed. R. Grinker and C. Steiner (Oxford: Blackwell, 1997), 86–125.

25. Joseph Conrad, *The Heart of Darkness* (New York: Dover, 1990), 41–42.

26. Preston, *Hot Zone*, 69–70.

27. Chinua Achebe, "An Image of Africa," *Massachusetts Review* 18, no. 4 (Winter 1977): 782–94.

28. Roger Rouse, personal communication, April 6, 2001.

29. See Robert Kaplan, "The Coming Anarchy," *Atlantic Monthly* 273 (February 1994): 44–65. See also Jessica Tuchman Mathews's earliest formulation of the environment as a security domain, "Redefining Security," *Foreign Affairs* 68, no. 2 (Spring 1989): 162–77; and Thomas Homer-Dixon's analysis of the causal links between environmental scarcity and violent conflict, "Environmental Scarcities and Violent Conflict," *International Security* 19, no. 1 (Summer 1994): 5–40.

30. See Robin Mearns and Melissa Leach, *The Lie of the Land: Challenging Received Wisdom on the African Environment* (Oxford: International African Institute, 1996), and James Fairhead and Melissa Leach, *Misreading the African Landscape: Society and Ecology in a Forest Savannah Mosaic* (Cambridge: Cambridge University Press, 1996).

31. See Elizabeth Hartmann, "Population, Environment, and Security: A New Trinity," in *Dangerous Intersections: Feminist Perspectives on Population, Environment, and Development*, ed. Jael Silliman and Ynestra King (Cambridge, Mass.: South End Press, 1999), 1–23.

32. For powerful critiques of Kaplan's determinist scenario for Africa, see Elizabeth Hartmann, "Will the Circle Be Unbroken? A Critique of the Project on Environment, Population, and Security," in *Violent Environments*, ed. N. Peluso and M. Watts (Ithaca, N.Y.: Cornell University Press, 2001); Hartmann, "Population, Environment, and Security"; Eric Ross, *The Malthus Factor* (London: Zed Books, 1998); and Nancy Peluso and Michael Watts, "Violent Environments," in *Violent Environments*, ed. N. Peluso and M. Watts (Ithaca, N.Y.: Cornell University Press, 2001).

33. On the logic underlying how things out of place become dangerous, see Mary Douglas, *Purity and Danger: An Analysis of the Concepts of Pollution and Taboo* (London: Routledge, 1992).

34. Preston, *Hot Zone*, 119.

35. Preston, *Hot Zone*, 109.

36. Preston, *Hot Zone*, 122.

37. Preston, *Hot Zone*, 123.

38. Preston, *Hot Zone*, 243.

39. Preston, *Hot Zone*, 257.

40. Preston, *Hot Zone*, 122.

41. Preston, *Hot Zone*, 46.

42. Roger Rouse, personal communication, May 25, 2001.

43. Preston, *Hot Zone*, 12.

44. Preston, *Hot Zone*, 5.

45. See Stephen Morse, "Regulating Viral Traffic," *Issues in Science and Technology* 7 (1990): 81–84; Joshua Lederberg, "The New Global Security," on relationship between recent outbreaks of yellow fever and environmental disturbance by road building, in Richard Horton, "The Plagues Are Flying," *New York Review of Books* 48, no. 13 (August 9, 2001): 53–56.

46. Laurie Garrett, "The Return of Infectious Diseases," *Foreign Affairs* 74 (January 1996): 66–79, articulates the possibilities of jet transport speeding the movement of pathogens around the globe.

47. Roger Rouse, personal communication, May 25, 2001.

48. In response to a posting on virology.net asserting that "Ebola is the mightiest threat mankind has faced yet," Dr. Ed Rybicki—in his posting on the subject "The Ebola Virus—the End of the Civilized World," August 18, 1995, www.mcb.uct .ac.za/ebola/bothrea.html (accessed March 6, 2000)—offers the following assessment of Ebola risk, offered by Dr. Margaretha Isaacson, a senior virologist in South Africa: "Ebola . . . is of absolutely no danger to the world at large. It is a dangerous virus, but it's relatively rare and quite easily contained. . . . The media is scaring the world out of its wits, and movies like *Outbreak* are doing people a great disservice" (interview with Max Gebhardt, *Weekend Argus*, Cape Town, August 12–13, 1995).

49. Quoted at www.virology@net.bio.net.

50. See Brian Hjelle, "Re: The Ebola Virus: The End of the Civilized World," citing David Orenstein on August 24, 1995, at www.virology@net.bio.net.

51. Preston, *Hot Zone*, 159.

52. I am indebted to Michael McKeon for this formulation.

53. This section builds on Lisa Sanchez's research proposal "Millennial Borderscapes: Globalization, Recolonization, and the Southwestern Border" (unpublished manuscript, n.p.).

54. Sanchez, "Millennial Borderscapes."

55. Sanchez, "Millennial Borderscapes." On parallels between xenophobia and nativist anti-immigration discourse on the one hand and anti-immigration, endemic-species discourse in conservation biology on the other, see Mark Sagoff, "What's Wrong with Exotic Species?" www.puaf.umd.edu/IPPP/fall 1999/exotic_species.htm (accessed November 11, 2000).

56. The phrase "the last bastions of nature" is from John Terborgh, *Requiem for Nature* (Washington, D.C.: Island Press, 1999), who advocates a reinvigorated militarized approach to the protection of pristine areas of tropical nature.

57. Xenotransplantation is explained, in this advertisement, as "the transplantation of animal organs and tissues, including those which have been genetically engineered into humans."

58. Turning Point Project, "Where Will the Next Plague Come From?" *New York Times*, November 1, 1999, 9A.

59. Turning Point Project, "Where Will the Next Plague?"

60. At the time of this writing, the full-page Turning Point Series advertisements have appeared in only the *New York Times* and the *Washington Post*.

61. Turning Point Project, "Who Plays God in the 21st Century?" *New York Times*, October 11, 2001, 9A.

62. Roger Rouse, personal communication, May 25, 2001.

63. I am indebted to Michael McKeon for this formulation.

64. For post–September 11 discourse on the virus as master metaphor, see the announcement for a cross-disciplinary conference entitled "VIRUS!" circulated on the world wide web in early January 2002 at www.kah-bonn.de/fo/virus/Oe/htm (accessed January 15, 2002).

65. On international news coverage of Ebola outbreaks, the concept of a stable Western civilizational core, and a periphery in constant turmoil, see Aldo Benini and Janet Bradford's account "Ebola Strikes the Global Village: The Virus, the Media, the Organized Response" (October 1995), www.outbreak.org/cgi-reg/dynaserve.exe/Ebola/benini.htm (accessed October 10, 2001). Benini and Bradford emphasize the way in which the post–Cold War has accelerated a map whose imagery of core and chaotic periphery echoes an ideological formation articulated during Roman times: "The Roman world was one of strict, even physical division between the reign of its law versus the peoples who lived outside its fortified borders, the limes."

Reflections

Feeling Invasion

Emily Martin

A useful guide to the contradictory experiences of excitement, fear, and anxiety that surround invasion and flow is Cindy Patton's contrast between the different thought styles of tropical medicine and epidemiology.[1] She argues that in the thought style of tropical medicine, characteristic of the heyday of colonialism, tropical diseases are imagined to occur where there is not yet any civilization; the colonial subject is imagined as being infectious; and the colonizer is imagined as being susceptible to infection. Hygiene and vaccination are means of making the tropics safe for the colonizers and moving the tropics in the direction of civilization. Dangerous, uncivilized territories are cordoned off until experts can "improve" them so that they no longer represent a threat.

In the epidemiological thought style, the focus is not on the body, infectious or healthy, but on the infectious agent. Germs are everywhere; everyone is susceptible to them; and their movements are appropriately measured in terms of statistical risks. Global space is crosscut by a grid over which people, germs, and other substances flow. The experts' job is to measure the flow and warn of the degree of risk. Preventive and protective measures are applied in a highly anxious environment of continuous exposure to risk. The chapter in this part vividly illustrates the ways these different styles of thought and feeling about contagion can coexist in complex combinations. In particular, this chapter gives us insight into the range of emotions that people living in a global system intersected by webs of connections can experience: people can feel both exhilaration over the potential benefits of borders crossed by easy flows and fear over the potentially disastrous consequences of borders ruptured by tight global interconnections.

187

In Charles Zerner's analysis of representations of Ebola as an out-of-control alien force, we have a kind of limiting case that shows how fears of invading lethal organisms can multiply. Extending out from "a heightened fear of alien organisms," a "diffuse fear or anxiety could embrace immigrants as well as microscopic viruses, nonnative plants, and exotic animals. The gamut of living creatures set in motion and moving from the global South to the global North might well become the objects of an increasingly anxious gaze." In this case, the biological agent is so deadly and its effect so horrific that "these representations and the diffuse anxieties they engender could lead to increasing scrutiny and intensified surveillance around the borders of areas formerly considered safe and secure." Breaching of borders by Ebola has such lethality that the result can be "a generalized fortress mentality in which politics and policies of hardened borders, clarified boundaries, and strengthened barriers begin to be seen as desirable and justified." Ebola functions as a "template, a moving target, a chameleon-like living vessel for proliferating anxieties in an era of ramifying networks and intensified globalization." Instead of leading citizens and health workers to thoughts of the potentially protective effects of making interconnections across borders, fear leads people to shrink their horizons and withdraw into seemingly safe isolation.

FEELING MARKETS

While carrying out an ethnography of emotional states in late capitalism, I have found that people are similarly both entranced and horrified by the speed and power of global flows, particularly the flow of energy in markets. Journalist David Denby's book *American Sucker* begins with his experience of irrational exuberance, at a time when the most heady days of growth and profit taking of the 1990s were near at hand. The book extends to a more recent time, when his exuberance was in the past, replaced by anxiety and anger about the economy, and finally to a time when he "drifted in fear."[2]

Denby's transformation is in part a result of the experiences of fear and anxiety—fears of a general collapse—that struck Americans in new ways after the events of September 11. In the first weeks after the attacks, there were expressions of doubt that U.S. capitalism could continue in the same form: "It is hard to predict the effect a prolonged campaign against terrorism will have on a form of capitalism built around risk-taking, technological advances, lightning-fast reactions and a willingness to let goods, money and people move freely."[3] The nation was attacked in its "central nervous system," which is sure to remain "jittery, if not depressed." "The effect of the attack was felt more acutely precisely because of our economy's strength: technology has allowed businesses, investors, and consumers to spot change even as it is occurring and respond almost instantaneously. Such speed is usually a good thing. But sometimes, Mr. Greenspan has suggested, it blows our economic circuits."[4]

During this anxious time, I was conducting ethnographic fieldwork with people who have the medical label "manic" in connection with manic-depression (also known as bipolar disorder), and I was struck by their efforts to join hands across the divide between the mentally ill manic and the Wall Street manic. A newsletter for manic-depressive people describes how the terrorists know what we have found out through long experience: "our brains are fragile as glass, delicate as timepieces, and reliable as the operating systems on home computers. No one is immune. . . . Because we who suffer from depression or Bipolar are among the most vulnerable, we are effectively on the front lines in this new war on terrorism. . . . Over the years our brains have been through the equivalent of countless Omaha Beach landings. We're seasoned."[5] Other developments at about the same time, however, held the promise that exuberance could prevail over all obstacles. Immediately after September 11, there were tales of precedent-setting heroism in "carrying on regardless": "Bradley Jack, the head of Lehman Brothers' investment arm, was so keen to get back to work that he hired a bus to drive himself and his colleagues back to New York from a conference in San Francisco. The bus stopped for just one sit-down meal, at a steak house in Nebraska, and on his return Mr. Jack commandeered the entire Manhattan Sheraton hotel for use as temporary offices."[6]

A short while later, there were other signs that the hyperenergized fearlessness expressed by Denby would actually be intensified: advertisements with overt social Darwinist themes appeared in the winter after September 11 both for corporations and for institutions of higher education. And there were indirect expressions of Wall Street traders and financiers yearning to be back in close physical proximity with each other. "That's because Wall Street's product is ideas, and they come from bringing colleagues and competitors together in ways cyberconnections can't. . . . For many on The Street, you gotta be there, even if it feels a little dangerous right now."[7] As soon as a few weeks after September 11, market forecasters noted "bursts of cheer," "a babbling brook of glad tidings," and a "shamefully upbeat" Alan Greenspan.[8] We have entered, they say, a "post-mania mania in the stock market."[9] Those who continued to be pessimistic, let alone depressed, were found morally culpable and sometimes even unpatriotic. As in the tropical-medicine thought style, bad emotions threaten markets and need to be pushed away. In models that evoke the thought style of tropical medicine, powerful credence is being given to the possibility that emotions are "contagious": "bad" emotions, such as depression, can infect the workplace in damaging ways, and "good" emotions, such as exuberance, can infect it in productive ways. "Bad" emotions are also more and more being described as being endemic in groups defined by gender, race, and class—such as women enrolled in the program Temporary Aid to Needy Families. An intense spate of research and reporting on "emotional intelligence" and "emotional contagion" has appeared in trade books and the business press.[10] The initial claims were for "an incontrovertible link between an executive's emotional maturity . . . and his or her financial performance. Simply put, the research showed the 'good guys'—that is, emotionally intelligent men and women—finish first."[11] Subsequently, a more ambitious claim emerged:

> The leader's mood and behaviors drive the moods and behaviors of everyone else. . . . Emotional intelligence is carried through an organization like electricity through wires. To be more specific, the leader's mood is quite literally contagious, spreading quickly and inexorably throughout the business. . . . A leader's premier task—we would even say his primal task—is emotional leadership. A leader needs to make sure that not only is he regularly in an optimistic, authentic, high energy mood, but also that, through his chosen actions, his followers feel and act that way, too.[12]

Basic psychological research describes the elements that make emotions contagious.[13] Articles in magazines for parents detail how to prevent the worst moods from spreading between parents and children.[14] Books and articles directed to business managers warn that emotional contagion can directly affect business performance.[15]

Like Ebola, mental conditions such as depression can also be seen epidemiologically. In part because psychotropic drugs, which can be imagined to be tailor-made for genetically different subpopulations (by race or gender), are entering the planning phase of large pharmaceutical corporations, such differences are emphasized in new ways: depression becomes a risk factor found in all groups, to a greater or lesser extent, and public health publications exhort them to become visible to treatment. Here the equivalent of the "germ" is the genetically formed depressive "brain."

ANXIOUS MARKETS

Stepping back from these connections between the market and its emotional tone, we might wonder why emotions would have a place in relations to today's markets at all. Wouldn't an alienated, flat emotional void be more characteristic of advanced capitalist markets than the exuberance of mania? Many writers have described the splitting and fragmentation of advanced modernity and the flattening and deadening of the emotions in art, architecture, film, and daily life.[16] Others have laid modernity's pervasive emotional emptiness at the feet of the social forces of late capitalism, which require continuous growth under intense competition and ruthless entrepreneurialism for survival and have made catastrophic job loss a normal experience for an increasing segment of the population.[17] The psychological hallmark of these experiences has been said to be nameless agitation and anxiety rather than emotion. In fact, by the turn of the twentieth century in the United States, "nerve weakness" was a well-recognized set of symptoms for specifically modern anxieties. The symptoms of neurasthenia, "nervous dyspepsia, insomnia, hysteria, hypochondria, asthma, sick-headache, skin rashes, hay fever, premature baldness, inebriety, hot and cold flashes, nervous exhaustion, brain-collapse or forms of 'elementary insanity'" were thought to be brought on by "simple exposure to the hectic pace and excessive stimuli of modern life."[18] As a disorder, neurasthenia embodied a new anxious sensibility of the excitable subject as symptom, mirror, and source of worldly forces; suddenly, both the self and the surrounding world seemed at once diffuse, weightless, floating, and unreal; weighted down with symptoms; haunted, immobilized, and excessively sensory and concrete."[19] The neurasthenic's "paralysis of will, his sense that he was no longer able to plunge into 'the vital currents of life,' his feeling that life had become somehow 'unreal' amounted to a feeling of 'inner emptiness' that was nonetheless harnessed to an imperative to produce. The result was anxious busyness."[20]

Thinking about the role of anxiety and emotional flatness in late capitalism is puzzling, for on all sides we also experience the imperative to experience emotion. It has been a central tenet since Adam Smith that capitalist markets depend on consumers whose psychological mood rests on confidence and a degree of enthusiasm. Statistical measurement of consumer sentiment is a major industry and an important index for the stock market; many consulting firms attempt to read consumer mood so that advertisements and marketing can be designed to stimulate desire.[21] Advertisements are often intended to incite desire and hope to demand the engagement of strong feelings. Managers of employees, creators of brands, and ad campaigns learn detailed practical ways of arousing and harnessing emotion to increase productivity and market share. No less an economist than John Maynard Keynes wrote that the market itself depended on the arousal of our "animal spirits."[22] The puzzle is that capitalism both diminishes emotion, and the sociality that it depends on, and requires emotion for its markets to function. Many of the activities that capitalism demands divide, separate, flatten, and deaden feeling, producing anxious schizoid states; yet, to flourish, markets require strong emotions, exuberance, and vital animal spirits.

I find it striking that in this environment, U.S. government leaders seem actively to be encouraging states of anxiety. Under the current Bush administration, in tune with a style of government that George Lakoff terms "the strict father," many speeches and policies encourage a worldview that life is fundamentally dangerous.[23] Beginning several months before the 2004 election, direct accusations began to be made that Bush deliberately cultivated a "culture of fear" by continually raising the "red flag of terror," for example, in his State of the Union speech.[24] Some regard this as a bald effort to arouse anxiety and fear because "people kept in a state of constant stress will sacrifice their best instincts and even their real interests for the illusion of safety"—an illusion that a president posing as a strict father can foster.[25] Many are wondering whether the Bush administration's policies on spending, taxation, and unilateral invasion, isolated from our allies, will end by wrecking the U.S. economy. The effort to play up the anxiety and fear that global interconnections can, as we have seen, arouse, while dampening the exuberance and exhilaration that global flows can inspire (and require) may be a development we need to give much more recognition. Are the threats our government wants us to fear comparable to the utter lethality of Ebola? Threatened with deliberate encouragement to adopt a fearful style of thought, we would do well to remember what the chapter in this part shows us: almost all invasions have more than one potential emotional response, and fear is just one of them.

NOTES

1. Cindy Patton, *Globalizing AIDS* (Minneapolis: University of Minnesota Press, 2002), 33–43.

2. David Denby, *American Sucker* (Boston: Little, Brown & Company, 2004), 265.

3. Richard W. Stevenson, "Aftermath; the Prospect of a War without a Wartime Boom," *New York Times*, September 23, 2001, 4(1).

4. Stevenson, "Aftermath," 1.

5. John McManamy, *McMan's Depression and Bipolar Weekly*, September 18, 2001.

6. Andrew Clark, "On the Brink of War: Wall Street," *Guardian*, September 21, 2001, 26.

7. Neil Weinberg, "Rubbing Elbows," *Forbes* 168, no. 10 (October 15, 2001): 72.

8. Alan Abelson, "Bad News Bulls," *Barron's* 82, no. 10 (March 11, 2002): 1–2.

9. Abelson, "Bad News Bulls," 2.

10. Daniel Goleman, *Emotional Intelligence* (New York: Bantam Books, 1995).

11. Daniel Goleman, Richard Boyatzis, and Annie McKee, "Primal Leadership: The Hidden Driver of Great Performance," *Harvard Business Review* 79, no. 11 (December 2001): 42–51.

12. Goleman, Boyatzis, and McKee, "Primal Leadership," 44.

13. Elaine Hatfield, John T. Cacioppo, and Richard L. Rapson, *Emotional Contagion* (Cambridge: Cambridge University Press, 1994).

14. Noelle Fintushel, "Are Bad Moods Catching?" *Parents* 71 (April 1996): 106–8.

15. Peter Totterdell, *What Is Emotion Management?* (Sheffield, Eng.: Institute of Work Psychology, 2003), www.shef.ac.uk/esrccoi/pdf/whatis/emotion_management .pdf (accessed May 10, 2005).

16. Hanjo Berressem, "Emotions Flattened and Scattered: 'Borderline Syndromes' and 'Multiple Personality Disorders' in Contemporary American Fiction," in *Emotions in Postmodernism*, ed. G. Hoffman and A. Hornung (Heidelberg, Ger.: Universitatsverlag C. Winter, 1997), 271–308.

17. David Harvey, *The Condition of Postmodernity: An Enquiry into the Origins of Social Change* (Oxford: Basil Blackwell, 1986).

18. Tom Lutz, *American Nervousness, 1903* (Ithaca, N.Y.: Cornell University Press, 1991), 4–5.

19. Susan Harding and Kathleen Stewart, "Anxieties of Influence: Conspiracy Theory and Therapeutic Culture in Millennial America," in *Transparency and Conspiracy*, ed. H. G. West and T. Sanders (Durham, N.C.: Duke University Press, 2003), 258–86.

20. T. J. Lears, "From Salvation to Self-Realization: Advertising and the Therapeutic Roots of the Consumer Culture, 1880–1930," in *The Culture of Consumption: Critical Essays in American History, 1880–1980*, ed. R. W. Fox and T. J. Lears (New York: Pantheon Books, 1983), 1–38.

21. Roper Reports, "Stirred, Not Shaken: A Self-Reliant Nation Manages Stress," *Public Pulse*, December 5, 2001, www.roperasw.com (accessed December 15, 2001).

22. John Maynard Keynes, *The General Theory of Employment, Interest, and Money* (New York: Harcourt Brace and World, 1936), 161.

23. George Lakoff, *Moral Politics: What Conservatives Know That Liberals Don't* (Chicago: University of Chicago Press, 1996), 65.

24. *New York Times*, "The Democratic Candidates in Their Own Words," January 21, 2004, 19A.

25. Richard Goldstein, "Butching Up for Victory," *The Nation* 278, no. 3 (January 26, 2004).

V

TERROR

8

Inventing Bioterrorism: The Political Construction of Civilian Risk

Jeanne Guillemin

Bioterrorism is a new concept in the annals of war and crime. It emerged during the early 1990s in the United States in reference to terrorists' potential access to biological weapons and to the danger that this asymmetry, like terrorists' access to nuclear or chemical weapons, could cause American communities. Although little credible evidence existed that terrorists would or could resort to germ weapons, this newly perceived national security threat became the driving force behind domestic preparedness and biodefense programs of considerable institutional proportions.

Bioterrorism is rooted in state biological warfare (BW) programs of the twentieth century, within which the military vision and the technical means for germ weapons were secretly developed and tested.[1] French, Japanese, British, U.S., and Soviet programs, in that general order, used microbiology expressly to target enemy civilians with anthrax, tularemia, plague, and other infectious diseases. After the Cold War, high-level U.S. officials, including two presidents, vociferously broadcast the vulnerability of Americans to intentional epidemics. The dangerous threat did not materialize; instead, growing government secrecy in biodefense research and continued failures to promote international openness about potential programs have increased the risks that, by accident or intent, deadly microbes will endanger unsuspecting civilians.

BIOLOGICAL WEAPONS AND TOTAL WAR DOCTRINE

For at least seventy years prior to the perceived threat of bioterrorism, civilians worldwide had much to fear from large state-run BW programs, but most were completely unaware of the threat and powerless to protest. As early as the 1920s, the major military powers, while overtly against the use of chemical and biological weapons and lacking sure knowledge of any threat, nonetheless prepared aggressively for retaliation in kind and readied themselves for strategic air attacks with bombs and spray generators. The doctrine of total war in those years justified the indiscriminate targeting of enemy noncombatants, as in the aerial bombing of cities to destroy the infrastructure that supported troops. After World War I, the major states improved their weapons for destroying populations in enemy cities and industrial centers, with increased reliance on air power and scientific innovations in chemistry, physics, and biology. Unlike chemical weapons, used by all sides in World War I, and unlike nuclear bombs, used by the United States in World War II, biological weapons remained intensely secret. Even the unique instance in which a state resorted to their use was politically obscured in the West. Following World War II, the U.S. struck a bargain with Japanese military scientists to protect them from war crimes trials in return for information on their program's activities, which included using plague-infected fleas to attack Chinese cities and towns.[2] After guaranteeing Japanese program leaders full protection from war crimes prosecution, their American counterparts secretly pioneered airborne attacks that could well have caused disastrous pandemics in new enemy targets in the Soviet Union, North Korea, China, Southeast Asia, or elsewhere.

SECRET SIMULATIONS

The total war vision that drove the major programs was enacted in simulations of biological weapons attacks on test sites; ships at sea; and, using substitutes for dangerous disease agents, on their own cities. Following the invention of nuclear weapons, military advocates for biological weapons predicted that germ weapons could have equal or greater potential for indiscriminate killing of unprotected populations. Whether civilians could be effectively protected en masse from germ attacks was questionable. Theodor Rosebury, an eminent microbiologist who had worked in the U.S. wartime program, later described both atomic and biological weapons as "terror weapons applicable only to all-out war. Neither offers any encouraging prospects for defense."[3] The British agreed. Asked after World War II to embark on mass vaccination and other protective programs against germ weapons (in theory from Soviet attacks), U.K. public health officials dismissed the idea as posing an unwarranted burden on the existing health care system.[4] They added that the British public, unconvinced of the threat, would refuse cooperation.

Soldiers, in contrast, could be protected against germ attacks by vaccinations or antibiotics or, against chemicals, by special masks and suits. For this and other reasons, including the superiority of conventional arms, biological weapons were never used in battle or assimilated by any military. Some political leaders (including Adolph Hitler and Franklin Roosevelt) found them repulsive, or the military remained skeptical that germ weapons could ever be as predictable or reliable as explosives. Nor did biological weapons have the political clout of nuclear weapons, whose enormous destructive power, known to the world, could deter aggressors.

All the major programs depended on simulations of biological attacks on enemy populations. Thanks to the American tradition of openness, the history of the U.S. biological program, the world's largest effort for its time, is better known than others. Starting in the early Cold War years, its leaders rebuilt the wartime program that had been modeled on that of the United Kingdom. Shaky evidence that the Soviets might develop a BW capacity justified more than two decades of aerosol experiments designed to persuade the armed forces that germ weapons could be predictably effective in strategic attacks. In 1950, the United States secretly sprayed *Bacillus globigii* (BG; a bacteria similar to anthrax but relatively harmless) and, for tracking purposes, what was thought to be an innocuous bacteria (*Serratia marcescens*) over San Francisco from offshore ships. In 1953, under pressure from the Air Force, U.S. scientists organized the St Jo Munitions Expenditure Panel to simulate anthrax attacks on three North American targets chosen to approximate Soviet cities: St. Louis, Missouri; Minneapolis, Minnesota; and Winnipeg, Manitoba, in Canada, and produced the most rigorous calculations of massive casualties to date.[5]

From 1950 to 1954 alone, seventy-nine trials of BG were staged, including sea trials off the coasts of Virginia, California, and Florida. BG land trials were conducted at Dugway Proving Ground (Utah), Camp Detrick (Maryland), and six air force bases; furthermore, in 1955, two dispersion tests were conducted on major state highways in Pennsylvania. From 1951 to 1955, at Dugway, twenty-five open-air field trials were staged with pathogenic agents, including those for anthrax, plague, brucellosis, Q fever, and tularemia. Some of them, for example, a 1954 *Bacillus anthracis* trial, ran for months. In addition, wind-dispersal tests simulating BW attacks were conducted over Corpus Christi, Texas; the Mojave Desert; and, in 1956, the San Francisco Bay Area. In 1957 and 1958, trials were conducted in unspecified areas east of the Rocky Mountains. In 1959 and 1960, thirteen trials were conducted in unspecified locations in north central Texas. In 1957, as part of Operation LAC (Large Area Concept), the United States disseminated particles of zinc cadmium sulfide along a path from South Dakota to Minnesota. A repeat trial in February 1958 at Dugway Proving Ground showed a six-hundred-mile dispersal. In theory, millions of enemy civilians could be infected.

In the 1960s, the most important scenario innovation within the U.S. BW program was Project 112, a land-and-sea venture for testing chemical and biological weapons that grew to extravagant proportions as the Vietnam War escalated. Added to the industrial target (the Soviet Union) were populations in developing communist nations in Asia, which the United States also considered ideological threats. In 1962, the Army began using its new base, Deseret Test Center at Fort Douglas, Utah, to coordinate combined-services exercises for pilots, ground crews, and transport and technical personnel. From November 1962 to April 1967, Dugway Proving Ground in Utah was the near-constant site of field tests of agents for tularemia.

Public lands and cities were also test sites. Between June 1961 and November 1969, twenty-two fluorescent particle trials were staged in national forests in South Carolina and Minnesota, as well as in Fort Wayne, Indiana; Corpus Christi, Texas; and again, in 1968, San Francisco. St. Louis was retested three more times, from May to September 1963, from April to October 1964, and in March 1965.[6]

Ship Hazard and Defense (SHAD), the program name for Project 112 sea trials, involved thirteen warships, along with miscellaneous tugboats and with airplanes fitted with spray generators or, for biological weapons, bombs. One sea trial, named "Big Tom," was the epitome of what the army intended with Project 112. Held off the coast of Oahu, Hawaii, in May–June 1965, it brought together the Navy, Marines, and Air Force to "evaluate the feasibility of a biological attack against an island complex and to evaluate doctrine and tactics for delivery of such an attack."[7]

One goal was to develop offensive biological strategies for Vietnam, where guerrilla warfare mixed combatants and noncombatants; in this period of war, the U.S. program operated unfettered by either military review or congressional oversight and with the U.S. mainland safe from counterattack by the distant, weaker enemy. Thus, the trial "Yellow Leaf" tested competing Army and Navy BW weapons systems against targets in a jungle environment. Another trial, called "Magic Sword," was conducted to see if mosquitoes released in a tropical setting (Baker Island in the Pacific) might efficiently convey infectious diseases, such as dengue fever or yellow fever, into new areas. Within Project 112, the U.S. military trained hundreds of military personnel in their roles for mass killings in scenarios that verged on reality but posed no danger for them from infectious diseases.[8] The United Kingdom and Canada also cooperated in these trials.

In September and October of 1968, the final major biological trial (called DTC Test 68-50) took place, at the Eniwetok Atoll in the Marshall Islands. SEB (the incapacitating toxin produced by the bacterium *Staphylococcus aureus*) and BG were dispersed by a newly designed dissemination tank; the planes were F4 Phantom jets. The conclusion from these tests was that a single tank could disperse a pathogenic agent over nearly a thousand square miles, producing what the program leaders claimed would be a 30 percent casualty rate.

In 1969, with simulations at their height, President Richard Nixon terminated the U.S. BW program, leaving only a small part of it for vaccine and other defensive research. Unique among the major powers, the United States had never ratified the 1925 Geneva Protocol against the use of chemical and biological weapons, which gave its military dangerous latitude during the Vietnam War—for example, in using tear gas as a weapon. Part of Nixon's reasoning and that of his national security advisor Henry Kissinger was that nuclear weapons were a sufficient deterrent to any nation that might aggress against the United States. Both were strong on national defense but wanted to start initiatives to limit weapons of mass destruction. In 1972, the United States, the United Kingdom, and the Soviet Union formulated the terms of the Biological Weapons Convention (BWC), which complemented the 1925 Geneva Protocol by essentially banning germ and toxin warfare programs and the possession or transfer of biological weapons. In 1975, the United States ratified the Geneva Protocol. All but a few small nations have signed and ratified both treaties.[9]

For the next twenty years, little was heard about biological weapons. Rather, public anxieties grew about nuclear weapons aimed by the superpowers at each other, culminating in the nuclear freeze movement of the 1980s and then in accords between Soviet president Mikhail Gorbachev and U.S. president Ronald Reagan to decrease nuclear stockpiles. In a surprise turn, as the Cold War ended, defectors who had worked in the Soviet biological program began revealing the enormity of the Soviet's violation of the BWC. In 1975, in addition to having committed itself to modernizing its microbiology and genetics institutes, the Soviets secretly started a biological weapons program more than equal in production to that of the United States in the 1960s, marked by attempts to use advanced genetics to enhance the virulence of pathogens and equipped with long-range missiles.[10] The Soviet Union had taken full advantage of the lack of sanctions and verification that characterized the BWC to create a huge bureaucracy, with facilities placed in major cities and scattered throughout its eleven time zones, employing tens of thousands.

THE INVENTION OF BIOTERRORISM

In the 1990s, President Bill Clinton, Secretary of Defense William Cohen, Secretary of Navy Richard Danzig, and key members of Congress publicly emphasized the vulnerability of Americans to foreign bioterrorism.[11] In this unusual phase, no credible information existed that nation-states overtly hostile to the United States (such as Iraq, Iran, Libya, or Syria) had both the capability and the intention to support bioterrorist attacks on U.S. cities or that international terrorists groups agitating against the United States and its policies posed a serious germ-weapons threat.

The public, for the most part, was not initially impressed by talk of bioterrorism, but some terrorists were. In 2002, a memo from computer files discovered in Afghanistan revealed that Al Qaeda members, feeling limited only by a lack of skilled scientists, were considering anthrax spores and other biological agents. One memo read, "We only became aware of them when the enemy [the United States] drew our attention to them by repeatedly expressing concern that they could be produced simply."[12]

Four factors influenced the widely publicized top-down political perception that bioterrorism posed a serious threat to U.S. security: the U.S. emergence as the lone global superpower; anti-U.S. terrorism; revelations about secret biological weapons; and Washington bureaucratic and think-tank expansion in reaction to the identification of the new threat.

The United States as Lone Superpower

Between 1969 and 1989, the boundaries that separated the United States from the rest of the world and gave it a sense of advantage in war had been much weakened by efficient communication technology, more rapid air travel and trade, and its own growing population of non-Western immigrants and Hispanics. As the Soviet Union began to dissolve, the U.S. government defined its enemies—hostile small nations such as Iraq, North Korea, Sudan, Syria, and Libya—as "rogue states" that shared Soviet propensities to aggress against neighboring states; to oppose the spread of democracy; and to be guilty of violating, often in secret, international norms against nuclear and chemical proliferation.[13] The Clinton administration added biological weapons to the weapons of mass destruction (WMD) list that these small enemy states might acquire.[14] When the Soviet Union collapsed, the entire global framework of bipolar alliances, which provided stability and gave meaning to nuclear deterrence, broke down, leaving the United States as a giant Gulliver beset by antagonistic Lilliputian nations. In this context, infectious disease became a pervasive metaphor for American fears of political change.[15]

President Clinton supported a strengthening of the Biological Weapons Convention along the lines established by the 1993 Chemical Weapons Convention, which had an organization in The Hague dedicated to ensuring that signatory nations comply with the treaty's provisions. In 1994, though, conservative Republicans took control of Congress and, not for the first time in U.S. history, resisted international arms treaties as restraints on U.S. national sovereignty. Under the leadership of Senator Jesse Helms, they delayed U.S. ratification of the Chemical Weapons Convention and posed obstacles to a

BWC Protocol that would require compliance and transparency from the U.S. military and American pharmaceutical industry. Signatories to the treaty were obliged to declare their projects and facilities that might be suspected of offensive aims, but no legal means existed to require inspection or other verifications of the declarations. At the same time, Republicans and Democrats found common ground in fostering civil defense programs within the Department of Defense to protect Americans from terrorists using WMD.

International Terrorism

The number of terrorist attacks worldwide declined in the 1980s and 1990s, and international corporations were the main targets.[16] Yet, signs appeared during the latter decade that terrorists were targeting the United States and that the scale of attack was increasing. The 1995 Oklahoma City bombing, for example, which killed 168 and wounded 500, was the largest terrorist attack within the United States, perpetrated by a young American veteran of the Gulf War influenced by militia and the Christian identity movements. The American "lone actor" preoccupied U.S. intelligence agencies less than international terrorists hostile to the United States and its ally Israel. The long reach of such groups was evident in the 1992 Hezbollah bombing of the Israeli embassy in Buenos Aires and in 1994 of a synagogue there. These attacks, which killed 116 people, were conducted on short notice in retaliation for Israeli actions that had taken place thousands of miles away. The 1993 bombing of the World Trade Center, which resulted in six deaths and injured a thousand people, showed the power of a small terrorist cell to penetrate U.S. security. In keeping with this kind of assault, the August 1998 Al Qaeda attacks on two American embassies in Africa killed 213 and injured 4,500 in Nairobi and killed 10 and injured 77 in Dar es Salaam.

For some analysts, these attacks and the 1995 sarin gas attack on the Tokyo subway by the cult Aum Shinrikyo presaged a new age of terrorism motivated by transcendental goals as opposed to concrete political objectives. The Aum in particular, with their apocalyptic design to "destroy the world in order to save it," seemed to exemplify a move toward irrational attacks by groups not amenable to political negotiation or integration.[17] Although technically incompetent, the Aum had also apparently sought nuclear weapons, which led to conjectures that other terrorists would do the same.

Revelations about Secret Programs

Revelations about the enormous Soviet BW program prompted congressional concern that its former BW scientists would be lured to hostile states, such as Iran or Iraq, or that Russia would perpetuate the Soviet biological program. In addition, Russia became associated with the threat of smallpox. That the Soviet BW program had developed the smallpox virus as a weapon was particularly alarming. Following the global eradication of the disease in 1980, the Soviet Union and the United States were designated the two last repositories for smallpox strains. The poor security at the Siberian center where Russia housed some of the world's only smallpox agents created anxiety among some experts.[18]

In 1995, the United Nations special commission of experts (UNSCOM) investigating biological weapons in Iraq discovered another surprise, when it obtained information about Saddam Hussein's BW arsenal.[19] That same year, UNSCOM investigators had official testimony that the program had been demolished as early as 1991, just prior to their arrival. By 1998, when antagonism between Saddam and the United States forced them to leave, the investigators had found only a few remnants of Saddam's arsenal and had supervised the Iraqi destruction of the program's research and production facility.

During this same time, investigations revealed that the Aum Shinrikyo had tried and failed to conduct anthrax attacks in Japan.[20] Several U.S. militia members' attempts to acquire BW agents were also widely publicized in the media.[21]

Washington Bureaucratic and Program Expansion

The U.S. authorities' belief in the threat of bioterrorism led to legislation that funded federal, state, and local programs and gave the concept institutional niches throughout government. The most important civil defense legislation of this time was the bipartisan 1996 Defense Against Weapons of Mass Destruction Act (also known as the Nunn-Lugar-Domenici Act), whereby the Department of Defense funded domestic preparedness programs, including training exercises and equipment for local officials, police, firefighters, and emergency medical personnel, in 120 of the nation's most populous cities.

In response to President Clinton's 1998 directive to improve domestic preparedness, Congress increased funding to counter WMD terrorism, supporting at least forty federal offices or programs. During fiscal years 1998–2001, the Defense Department national security WMD budget went from $180 to $467 million. The Department of Energy, also with special WMD expertise, saw an increase from $276 to $364 million. Due to the increased importance of bioterrorism, the Department of Health and Human Services budget rose from $16 million to $265 million; the Department of Agriculture budget grew from $5 million to $40 million for the same reason. The Justice Department budget more than doubled, from $100 million to $255 million. The State Department budget more than tripled, from $23 million to $72 million.[22]

The total budget, around $1.5 billion, was small by federal standards but enough to attract political consultants and medical authorities with Washington connections in what became known as civilian biodefense. By the end of the decade, with new programs, institutes, conferences, and publications, the connection between terrorism and biological weapons was a given. The words of former Secretary of State George Shultz became a policy mantra: terrorist use of biological weapons "was not a matter of if but when."[23]

VISUALIZING BIOTERRORISM

Domestic preparedness relied on fictional scenarios of terrorist attacks involving WMD. Of all the WMD attack enactments, simulated chemical weapons attacks were easiest to stage. The effects of those agents were well known and usually quickly felt, and the 1995 Japanese subway attack provided a real-life example of police, firefighter, and medical response. Radiological ("dirty") bomb scenarios substituted for true nuclear attack (an incineration against which there is no civil defense), and these, too, could be enacted in real time.

Bioterrorism-attack scenarios were different. They tended (and still tend) to be played as board games, since (like real outbreaks) these scenarios could extend over weeks and involve many kinds of interventions, organizational complexities, and (with contagion) even the spread of disease to foreign countries. The biological scenarios that gained currency drew on aspects of industrial-age outbreaks. The 1972 smallpox outbreak in Yugoslavia, which resulted in thirty-five deaths among 175 cases nationwide, offered an example of a response by a highly centralized government that included enforced quarantines and of an unusually high rate of contagion. The primary example of an anthrax attack was drawn from research done on the 1979 Sverdlovsk anthrax outbreak, in which a plume of spores was accidentally released from a military facility over a working-class neighborhood, causing around seventy deaths.[24]

To be relevant for city governments, bioterrorism scenarios had to reach catastrophic proportions but stay within the realm of practical response; that is, they could not be like nuclear holocausts, or local preparedness would lose its purpose. The enemy was usually Middle Eastern or other foreign or faceless terrorists with the capacity to invisibly infect Americans and then escape. In this mode, a series of fictive bioterrorist scenarios was published by the Johns Hopkins Center for Civilian Biodefense. This think tank (later renamed the Center for Biosecurity and relocated to the University of Pittsburgh) was created in 1999 under the leadership of Dr. Donald A. Henderson, former dean of the Hopkins School of Public Health and a leader of the smallpox-eradication campaign sponsored by the World Health Organization in the 1970s. The Hopkins scenarios were invariably characterized by problems that government could readily address: insufficient supplies of drugs or vaccine, inadequate hospital resources, and an unruly and violent public in need of military control. Although creative and well intended, these scenarios were marred by technical mistakes and a disconcerting, almost totalitarian subtext: that *only* government authority could save these disorderly victims.[25]

In the center's anthrax scenario, for example, terrorists have secretly released an aerosol of lethal spores over a football stadium in a fictional city (modeled on Baltimore) and have infected twenty thousand people downwind of the release.[26] After five days, area hospitals become swamped with patients with symptoms. Six days later, sixty-three hundred people are estimated to have died, and the National Guard is called in to enforce law and order. Violence erupts among citizens because of a shortage of antibiotics; before the day is over, another nine hundred people are dead. After two more days, another twenty-four hundred people have died, and the city has come to a standstill. As its commercial area shuts down, looting commences, and again military control is warranted.

With little knowledge of aerodynamics, the authors of this scenario failed to realize that most of the released anthrax spores would float over the stadium. But their point, also made by others, about the need for antibiotic stockpiling was taken seriously by the Clinton administration.

In a similar scenario, concerning pneumonic plague, which is highly contagious, a slightly larger city is attacked. Again, thousands sicken and die because of inadequate antibiotics, and the military is brought in to quell public violence and disorderly resistance to enforced quarantine.[27] This scenario fails to point out that, as with all contagious diseases, an educated public can do much with simple hygiene to rapidly contain an outbreak. This and the anthrax scenario, in addition to similar ones from the federal government, gave local authorities scripts to rehearse and the basis for arguments for increased funding.

To test whether training was improving domestic response, in 1999 Congress asked the Justice Department (at the time, the new locus of the domestic preparedness program), the Federal Emergency Management Agency, and the National Security Council to stage a national exercise that would mobilize top officials—hence the name, TOPOFF. In May 2000, a private defense contractor organized the two staged events—a mustard gas attack in Portsmouth, New Hampshire, and a pneumonic plague attack in Denver—for $3 million. Originally a more ambitious plan involving three cities, the May 2000 TOPOFF still involved thousands of federal, state, and local personnel, along with the U.S. attorney general, the secretary of Health and Human Services, the FBI director, the director of the Federal Emergency Management Agency, and two state governors. Local officials and volunteers participated, and actors were hired to play some of the victim roles.

In the TOPOFF bioterrorism scenario, an aerosol of pneumonic plague was released at the Denver Performing Arts Center by unknown terrorists who quickly disappeared. By the fourth day, an estimated thirty-seven hundred cases were reported, with 950 dying amid chaos for lack of medicine and hospital beds, while virtual corpses piled up in makeshift mortuaries. The message returned to Congress was that more funding was needed for domestic preparedness and for drugs, and Congress responded with increased funding.

POLITICAL CONSEQUENCES: "DARK WINTER"

By 2000, the political consequences of the bioterrorism threat seemed minimal. Critics were documenting the disorganization in the domestic preparedness program at the local and federal levels and questioning their usefulness. From city to city, participation varied widely, and even comparable cities had radically different plans, some of dubious quality.[28] Other critics deplored the emphasis on a health threat that had not cost a single life, versus the erosion of health care for millions of Americans then experiencing the national shift to for-profit hospitals and managed care and for the quarter of the population underinsured or without health care coverage. Still, because the programs infused funds into local and state coffers and supported federal national security programs, legislators of both parties could claim that they were protecting their constituents.

Two events made the threat of bioterrorism consequential by exploiting its capacity to cause fear. One was the agenda of the administration of President George W. Bush to remove Saddam Hussein from power, which involved promoting Iraq's BW capability to the public, and the other was the 2001 anthrax postal attacks, which demonstrated the power of a disease weapon to unnerve the nation. In July 2001, the Bush administration used its influence to end a decade of international effort to create a Protocol for an effective organization and verification provisions for the BWC.[29] The U.S. argument was that the threat of Iraq and other lesser foes made secrecy imperative for its national security.

Secretary of State Colin Powell's February 2003 presentation to the United Nations Security Council made much of Iraq's presumed BW program, which later proved nonexistent.[30] Nearly two years before this, the American public had been primed for the threat of Saddam's bioterrorism. Early in the new Bush administration, the Johns Hopkins Center sought to convince Congress of the catastrophic potential of a smallpox pandemic and the need for vaccine stockpiles. Its campaign was centered on "Dark Winter," a tabletop exercise held July 22–23, 2001, at Andrews Air Force Base.[31] Unlike TOPOFF, this enactment posed no time or resource burden on any real city, and it tested only the highest levels of the central government's decision making. The dozen main participants were former and present officials who acted out their command post roles in reaction to unfolding events involving impending war in the Middle East and the spread of a deliberate smallpox epidemic in the United States. Senator Sam Nunn, a key sponsor of domestic preparedness legislation, played the American president; former White House advisor David Gergen played the national security advisor; Governor Frank Keating of Oklahoma played himself; Dr. Margaret Hamburg, former New York City health commissioner, played the head of the Department of Health and Human Services; and former FBI director William Sessions reenacted his role.

The simulated event condensed thirteen days of fictional catastrophe into two full working days. Iraq was the central villain in the drama, which began with a threatened invasion of Kuwait. Iraq was also the perpetrator of multiple covert smallpox attacks on the United States. The scenario called for rapid spread of the disease, which soon outstripped local resources and demanded emergency federal intervention, including deployment of the military. By the last day, over fifteen thousand cases were reported. Asked by Senator Nunn to extrapolate a worst-case scenario, the organizers conjectured an epidemic that extended worldwide to infect millions, but the Dark Winter exercise had only national security objectives.

Within a month, Dark Winter's organizers and influential participants testified at a congressional hearing on domestic response. Their main messages, that the United States needed smallpox vaccine and more funds for bioterrorism exercises, were well received. Dark Winter became the rationale for secret national stockpiles of smallpox vaccine for emergency use throughout the United States. The threat of smallpox attacks was also picked up by an uncritical media and exploited for its fright value. Over the next year, according to a national poll, many Americans became anxious about contracting smallpox and began considering seeking smallpox vaccination.[32]

The Dark Winter script drew harsh criticism from infectious disease experts for its exaggerated contagion rates and general hyperbole.[33] The scenario ignored the capacity of the public to respond rationally to preventive measures that had been used to stop smallpox for centuries, such as wearing simple masks, washing one's hands, and tending patients at home. Citizens were represented as being either passive or in violent panic. Even medical professionals could not cope. On day seven, for example, with nearly five hundred cases of smallpox cases occurring daily, the script described "scared and exhausted" doctors and nurses trapped in hospitals by frantic mobs clamoring for vaccines and drugs while crazed individuals began shooting at each other. Under these conditions, as in prior Hopkins scenarios, the U.S. military was called in to enforce vaccinations and quarantines.

In the fall of 2002, as his administration was making its case for the invasion of Iraq, President Bush signed legislation for a four-stage 2003 smallpox vaccination campaign intended for all Americans. The program would begin with the military, which was required to comply, and then extend to hundreds of thousands of civilians who as volunteers would be unable to hold the government or medical practitioners legally responsible for potentially serious side effects—for example, those with serious skin conditions or compromised immune systems. The campaign proved unsuccessful.[34] Among first responders, the first civilian group to whom the vaccine was made available, cardiac complications caused three fatal heart attacks and seven serious illnesses. These deaths and reported negative side effects among newly vaccinated young soldiers prompted eleven states and many hospitals to cease participation, a setback from which the program did not recover. By April, the smallpox vaccination campaign was displacing routine public health services—such as childhood immunizations, prenatal care, AIDS clinics, and tuberculosis surveillance—and putting populations that rely on public health services at medical risk. By the end of 2003, after Iraq had been invaded and no signs of an Iraqi biological program were found, the Centers for Disease Control and Prevention was still advocating the campaign, but urgent official promotion of the threat of smallpox attacks had evaporated.

THE 2001 ANTHRAX POSTAL ATTACKS

The 2001 anthrax letters, discovered within weeks of the September 11 attack, were unlike any scenario devised by government advisors or consultants.[35] The federal reaction, as cases emerged in Florida, New York, and especially in Washington, D.C., demonstrated the inability of different agencies (notably the Centers for Disease Control and Prevention, the FBI, the Defense Department, and the CIA) to communicate with each other and with local health providers and the public. The inflammatory messages sent with the spores were phrased as if written by a Middle Eastern Muslim extremist. But the FBI's conclusion was that a lone actor, a "disgruntled" microbiologist, perhaps an American, perpetrated the crime, which ultimately killed five people and sickened another seventeen and caused a national crisis. The anthrax letters figured in Secretary Powell's UN presentation when he held up a vial containing an anthrax substitute (BG) and reminded his audience of the crisis just a few grams had caused. What Powell left unsaid was the likelihood that an American scientist committed this crime and that most disruption nationally stemmed from the tens of thousands of copycat hoaxes that severely tested state public health laboratories, diverting them from disease surveillance.

Following the September 11, 2001, terrorist attacks on the United States and the postal anthrax attacks that followed soon after, the budget for counter-WMD reached $10 billion, such a rapid influx that the Defense Department had funds in programs with titles but no substance. Both startling events spurred the creation of the Department of Homeland Security, authorized just before the U.S. invasion of Iraq in March 2003 and slated to employ 180,000.

The 2001 anthrax postal attacks had a direct impact on the subsequent government initiative to fund large research programs for biomedical defense. Once a purely humane endeavor with universal benefits, in 2002 microbiology became redefined by the harm it could cause the nation—in the wrong hands—and by its utility in creating new pharmaceutical solutions to counter select agents—in the right hands. The National Institute for Allergies and Infectious Diseases received $1.6 billion for new basic research to protect Americans against anthrax, smallpox, plague, Ebola virus, and dozens of other diseases caused by "select agents." Additional funding went to ten major medical "Centers of Excellence" for the same national security goal. Not without controversy, plans proceeded for the building of six or more new biosafety level 4 laboratories to allow research on the most dangerous agents, under conditions of maximum security. The promise of dual use— that is, using biodefense research to discover medical interventions applicable to AIDS, malaria, or other widespread diseases—is associated with all these initiatives, although they relied on federal funding taken from basic research on just these diseases.

THE PROBLEM OF SECRECY

By one estimate, the civilian biodefense budget from 2001 to 2006 totaled $124 billion dollars.[36] Whether this level of funding will continue depends on the strength of interest groups supported by biodefense programs and on perceptions of the bioterrorism threat, whether based on imagination or real events. One wonders how long states and cities will stage the same WMD attack scenarios, now provided by the Department of Homeland Security,[37] while beset by real calamities, such as layoffs of police and firefighters and shortages of hospital staff, caused by economic downturns, federal and state budget shortfalls, and the costs of the war in Iraq. Except in illusory WMD scenarios, the federal government is increasingly uninterested in aiding citizens in distress. On the constructive side, states have been improving disease monitoring. Eventually emerging infectious diseases and serious epidemics not deliberately caused may take a more central place in biodefense projects. The routing of funds to emergency-oriented projects, though, still leaves American health care in general at a disadvantage.

The most troubling aspect of civilian biodefense is the pervasive secrecy characteristic of the involved federal agencies, a secrecy too similar to that which sustained the old BW programs. Strong provisions for secrecy were legislated for the Department of Homeland Security from its creation. It is protected from Freedom of Information Act requests and from the Federal Advisory Committee Act, which guarantees public access to government communication with consultants, who abound in the biodefense arena. The Department of Homeland Security's staging of another TOPOFF exercise, costing $16 million, was a multicity extravaganza for the benefit of Washington bureaucrats, with aspects of its results made classified. The Department of Health and Human Services, also charged with biodefense responsibilities, has claimed new secrecy prerogatives. In 2002, for example, the Centers for Disease Control and Prevention (within Health and Human Services), the nation's public health agency, for the first time acquired the right to classify its projects and documents. The U.S. military and intelligence communities also have a stake in biodefense, a glimpse of which was revealed in leaks to the press in 2001, before the anthrax letters lent credit to the bioterrorism threat.[38]

With basic research for biodefense has come a clampdown on openness: federal security checks on researchers, the licensing of facilities, and the designation of projects as "classified" or "sensitive," plus the distinct possibility that major journals will refuse articles that might aid bioterrorists, however that might be defined. Subject to visa delays and refusals, foreign students, a mainstay of American microbiology and medicine, are choosing European and other nations instead. Only a few scientists have questioned the narrow focus on technological solutions, the lack of credible threat assessment, or the risks engendered by giving thousands of microbiologists experience with developing and testing biological agents and increasing the national reserves of dangerous select agents that threaten laboratory workers and local communities with risks of exposure.[39]

When it comes to containing disease outbreaks, secrecy is a major problem. In reaction to early pressure to engage physicians in counterbioterrorism, Victor Sidel, a leading public health physician, argued that military and police intervention in health care and the secrecy already evident in federal policies were antithetical to physician–patient trust.[40] Taken to extremes, as in the Dark Winter scenario, these strategies also demean civilian autonomy. Studies of major disasters show that, far from reacting with panic, Americans confronting earthquakes, hurricanes, floods, and even terrorist attack overwhelmingly tend to organize their own collective defenses—a strength that an authoritarian government would deny.[41]

The lack of accurate information is the greatest obstacle to public safety. Similarly, withholding or distorting information about dangerous diseases increases the risks that individuals will, in ignorance, be unable to make the right choices to protect themselves.[42] China's early cover-up of the 2003 SARS epidemic is only a recent case of government secrecy concerning an unusual outbreak that can cause unnecessary deaths, illness, and fear. Secret military activities not only caused the 1979 Sverdlovsk anthrax epidemic; they delayed accurate diagnosis, and dozens of people died who might have been successfully treated. The 2001 anthrax letter attacks offer another example of the harmful effects of official secrecy. To preserve routine, government officials failed to alert Washington, D.C., postal workers of the hazards of building contamination or warn them to be alert for symptoms. They only belatedly made antibiotics available, after two workers died and three others became gravely ill.

The compelling lesson of the old U.S. and Soviet programs is that a secret, well-funded enterprise—even in the name of defense—can produce extravagant and dangerous innovations. Advanced industrialized nations, especially the United States and the Soviet Union, pioneered biological weapons at their own peril. The United States, at the forefront of basic science, might repeat its own history with new and riskier biotechnologies and also inadvertently encourage other nations to emulate its covert programs.

U.S. policies have yet to confront the inevitable transfer of new Western biotechnologies to developing nations whose militaries may see in them new possibilities for weapons, as American and other military scientists saw in microbiology in the last century. Even as biotechnology innovations spread and are of great interest to developing nations (from giants such as China, India, and Brazil to smaller states such as Taiwan and Indonesia), measures to promote compliance with the BWC lack both compelling incentives, such as technological cooperation, and effective legal sanctions.[43]

To pose a serious or sustained threat, any terrorist group interested in biological weapons would have to rely on state-level resources, including microbiologists and engineers; laboratories; production facilities; munitions factories; and personnel trained in weapons transport, testing, storage, deployment, and use. This kind of proliferation is preventable, with vigilant, international enforcement of transparency measures and collective pressure brought to bear on states that refuse cooperation.

In Weberian terms, many current counterbioterrorism policies encourage the self-perpetuating functions of federal bureaucracies and may therefore discount public well-being. They do this first by emphasizing authoritarian civil defense models based on poor threat assessment; second by enveloping biodefense research in secrecy; and third by ignoring the international political realm, where the better guarantees of safety lie. The question remains how long such flawed policies can be sustained before Americans become aware that U.S. civilian biodefense cannot effectively substitute for broader political defenses against biological weapons.

NOTES

1. Jeanne Guillemin, *Biological Weapons: From the Invention of State-Sponsored Programs to Contemporary Bioterrorism* (New York: Columbia University Press, 2005).

2. Sheldon H. Harris, *Factories of Death: Japanese Biological Warfare, 1932–1945, and the American Cover-Up* (London: Routledge, 1994). The Japanese used disease agents against the Soviets in the late 1930s as sabotage after losing a major battle. Although the 1984 Oregon salad bar poisonings by the Rajneeshee cult are sometimes called bioterrorist attacks, they appear more as biocrimes or sabotage and caused no deaths. See W. Seth Carus, "The Rajneeshees (1984)," in *Toxic Terror: Assessing Terrorist Use of Chemical and Biological Weapons,* ed. Jonathan B. Tucker (Cambridge, Mass.: MIT Press, 2000), 115–38.

3. Theodor Rosebury, *Peace or Pestilence? Biological Warfare and How to Avoid It* (New York: McGraw-Hill, 1949), 177.

4. Brian Balmer, *Britain and Biological Warfare: Expert Advice and Science Policy, 1930–1965* (London: Palgrave, 2001), 72–73.

5. Munition Expenditure Panel, *Preliminary Discussion of Methods for Calculating Munition Expenditure, with Special Reference to the St Jo Program* (Frederick, Md.: Camp Detrick, 1954).

6. Some tests—for example, those on Washington's National Airport, the New York subway system, and stockyards in the Midwest—had apparent defensive purposes. For the most part, however, the protection of civilians (or livestock or crops) was not an important part of the U.S. program.

7. U.S. government updates on SHAD are at www.projectshad.org.

8. See Erving Goffman, *Frame Analysis: An Essay on the Organization of Experience.* (Cambridge, Mass.: Harvard University Press, 1974), 59–62.

9. On signatories to the Geneva Protocol and BWC and also the Chemical Weapons Convention, see Nicholas A. Sims, "A Proposal for Putting the 26 March 2005 Anniversary to Best Use for the BWC," *CBW Conventions Bulletin* 62 (December 2003): 1–6.

10. During the Cold War, the United States tolerated other, smaller nations' having BW programs or turned a blind eye on their ventures. Apartheid South Africa's BW program developed in the late 1970s and was used against its own insurgents and those in neighboring countries where Marxist and socialists movements were in ascendance. Chandré Gould and Peter Folb, *Project Coast: Apartheid's Chemical and Biological Warfare Program* (Geneva: United Nations Institute for Disarmament Research, 2002), 11. When the United States was backing Saddam Hussein against Iran during the 1980s, Iraqi chemical weapons and early efforts to acquire anthrax were known but accepted. Israel has long been suspected of having an offensive BW program. Avner Cohen, "Israel and Chemical/Biological Weapons: History, Deterrence, and Arms Control," *Nonproliferation Review* (Fall/Winter 2001): 27–53, 27–28.

11. White House, Office of the Press Secretary, "Remarks by the President on Keeping America Secure for the 21st Century" (National Academy of Sciences, Washington, D.C., January 22, 1999).

12. Global Security Newswire, "Al-Qaeda: New Evidence of Chemical and Biological Weapons Pursuit" (Nuclear Threat Initiative posting, January 2, 2002), www.nti.org/d_newswire/issues/thisweek.

13. Michael Klare, *Rogue States and Nuclear Outlaws: America's Search for a New Foreign Policy* (New York: Hill and Wang, 1994), 26.

14. Klare, *Rogue States*, 30.

15. Nicholas Alexander King, "The Influence of Anxiety: September 11, Bioterrorism, and American Public Health," *Journal of Medical History and Allied Sciences* 58, no. 4 (October 2000): 433–41.

16. Anthony H. Cordesman, *Terrorism, Asymmetric Warfare, and Weapons of Mass Destruction* (Westport, Conn.: Praeger, 2002), 11–38.

17. Walter Laqueur, *The New Terrorism: Fanaticism and the Arms of Mass Destruction* (New York: Oxford University Press, 1999).

18. David Koplow, *Smallpox. The Fight to Eradicate a Global Scourge* (Berkeley: University of California Press, 2003), 193–204; Jonathan Tucker, *Scourge. The Once and Future Threat of Smallpox* (New York: Atlantic Monthly Press, 2001), 190–230. Donald A. Henderson believed in the threat ("Pathogen Proliferation: Threats from the Former Soviet Bioweapons Complex," *Politics and the Life Sciences* 19, no. 1 [March 2000]: 3–16). But the World Health Organization decided to oversee new smallpox research both in Russia and in the United States.

19. Graham S. Pearson, *The UNSCOM Saga: Chemical and Biological Weapons Non-proliferation* (New York: St. Martin's Press, 1999), 11. See also, Raymond S. Zilinskas, "Iraq's Biological Weapons Program: The Past as Future?" *Journal of the American Medical Association* 278, no. 5 (August 1997): 418–24.

20. See David E. Kaplan and Andrew Marshall, *The Cult at the End of the World* (New York: Crown, 1996).

21. See Jessica Eve Stern, "Larry Wayne Harris (1998)" in Tucker, *Toxic Terror*, 227–46.

22. Cordesman, *Terrorism*, 270.

23. George F. Shultz, "Introduction," in *The New Terror: Facing the Threat of Biological and Chemical Weapons*, ed. Sidney D. Drell, Abraham D. Sofaer, and George D. Wilson (Stanford, Calif.: Hoover Institution Press, 1999), xiii–xv.

24. Jeanne Guillemin, *Anthrax: The Investigation of a Deadly Outbreak* (Berkeley: University of California Press, 1999).

25. Suzanne E. Hatty and James Hatty, *The Disordered Body: Epidemic Disease and Cultural Transformation* (Albany: State University of New York Press, 1999): 242–43.

26. This scenario was presented at the Second National Symposium on Bioterrorism, Washington, D.C., November 28–29, 2000, as "Anthrax: A Possible Case History." The conference was sponsored by the Johns Hopkins Center for Civilian Biodefense Studies, Department of Health and Human Services, and the Infectious Diseases Society of America.

27. This scenario was also presented at the Second National Symposium on Bioterrorism, as "Decision Making in a Time of Plague."

28. Amy E. Smithson and Leslie-Anne Levy, *Ataxia: The Chemical and Biological Warfare Threat and the U.S. Response* (Washington, D.C.: Henry L. Stimson Center, 2000).

29. Susan Wright, "Introduction: In Search of a New Paradigm of Biological Disarmament," in *Biological Warfare and Disarmament: New Problems/New Perspectives*, ed. Susan Wright (Lanham, Md.: Rowman & Littlefield, 2002), 3–24.

30. See United Nations Monitoring, Verification, and Inspection Commission leader Hans Blix, *Disarming Iraq* (New York: Pantheon, 2004), 145–50, for his account of Iraq's threat and his briefing of Powell before the UN speech.

31. Cosponsors were the Center for Strategic and International Studies and the Memorial Institute for the Prevention of Terrorism. See the scenario's defense by Tara O'Toole, Michael Mair, and Thomas V. Inglesby, "Shining Light on 'Dark Winter,'" *Clinical Infectious Diseases* 34, no. 7 (April, 2002): 972–83.

32. R. J. Blendon et al., "The Public and the Smallpox Threat," *New England Journal of Medicine* 348, no. 5 (December 2002): 426–32.

33. Martin I. Meltzer et. al., "Modeling Potential Responses to Smallpox as a Bioterrorist Weapon," *Emerging Infectious Diseases* 7, no. 6 (November–December 2001): 959–69; and Thomas Mack, "A Different View of Smallpox and Vaccination," *New England Journal of Medicine* 348, no. 5 (January 2003): 460–63. For a critique by U.K. military defense scientists, see Raymond Ganl and Steve Leach, "Transmission Potential of Smallpox in Contemporary Populations," *Nature* 414, no. 13 (December 2001): 748–51.

34. H. W. Cohen, R. M. Gould, and V. W. Sidel, "The Pitfalls of Bioterrorism Preparedness: The Anthrax and Smallpox Experiences," *American Journal of Public Health* 94, no. 10 (October 2004): 1667–72.

35. For an overview, see Jeanne Guillemin, "Deliberate Release of Anthrax through the United States Postal System" in *Public Health Response to Biological and Chemical Weapons: WHO Guidance*, ed. Julian Perry Robinson (Geneva: World Health Organization, 2004), 98–108; P. S. Brachman, "The Public Health Response to the Anthrax Epidemic," in *Terrorism and Public Health: A Balanced Approach to Strengthening Systems and Protecting People*, ed. Barry S. Levy and Victor W. Sidel (New York: Oxford University Press, 2003), 101–17.

36. Ari Shuler, "Billions for Biodefense: Federal Agency Biodefense Funding, FY2001–FY2005," *Biosecurity and Bioterrorism: Biodefense Strategy, Practice, and Science* 2, no. 2 (June 2004): 86–89.

37. Department of Homeland Security, *Homeland Security Exercise and Evaluation Program*, vol. 1, *Overview and Doctrine*, NCJ199536 (Washington, D.C.: Department of Homeland Security, Office of Domestic Preparedness, 2003).

38. For an account of three recent intelligence/defense projects that veered toward BWC violations, see Judith Miller, Stephen Engelberg, and William Broad, *Germs: Biological Weapons and America's Secret War* (New York: Simon & Schuster 2001), 223–34.

39. Milton Leitenberg, *The Problem of Biological Weapons* (Stockholm: Swedish National Defence College, 2004).

40. Victor W. Sidel, "Defense against Biological Weapons. Can Immunization and Secondary Prevention Succeed?" in Wright, *Biological Warfare*, 77–101, 86.

41. Thomas A. Glass, "Understanding Public Responses to Disaster" (presented at the Second National Symposium on Medical and Public Health Response to Bioterrorism, Washington, D.C., November 28–29, 2000). Transcript available at www.upmcbiosecurity.org/pages/events/2nd_symposia/transcripts/trans_glas.html.

42. Jeanne Guillemin, "Bioterrorism and the Hazards of Secrecy: A History of Three Epidemic Cases," *Harvard Health Policy Review* 4, no. 1 (Spring 2003) : 36–50.

43. On the needed pursuit of reinforced legal sanctions, see Sims, "Proposal," 1–6; Matthew Meselson and Julian Perry Robinson, "Draft Convention to Prohibit Biological and Chemical Weapons Under International Criminal Law," in *Treaty Enforcement and International Cooperation in Criminal Matters*, ed. R. Yepes-Enríquez and L. Tabassi (The Hague: Organisation for the Prohibition of Chemical Weapons, 2002), 457–69; Angela Woodward, *Time to Lay Down the Law: National Legislation to Enforce the BWC* (London: VERTIC, 2003).

9

Pernicious Peasants and Angry Young Men: The Strategic Demography of Threats

Betsy Hartmann and Anne Hendrixson

In posing the question, "Will Israel survive?" I am thinking of something more long term than the current emergency, and in its way, even more elemental. I am thinking in terms of Israel's gradual but inexorable demographic eclipse over the next few decades. . . . The average Israeli woman bears two to three children, but the average Palestinian woman bears five to six. . . . What this means is that, by 2050, 8 million Jewish Israelis will be sitting cheek-by-jowl with 20 million Palestinians and a few million Israeli Arabs. . . . Already the suicide bombers have altered the casualty rates from about 15 Palestinians to 1 Israeli dead, to something closer to 3–1. If you put together the demographic projections and the narrowing killing rates, you have a truly awful prospect for Israel.

—Paul Kennedy

This is a particularly stark invocation of "strategic demography": the framing of national security threats in demographic terms.[1] In the case of Israel, strategic demography has very real effects. Uri Avnery argues that Israel is moving away from its official definition as a "Jewish Democratic State" to a "Jewish demographic state." This entails encouraging not only more Jewish births and more Jewish immigration but increased discrimination against Arab citizens of Israel.[2] Strategic demography is also linked to strategic geography, as the Israeli government literally fences off the Palestinian population.

Strategic demography employs not only demographic statistics in its calculus of threats but alarmist images, tropes, and narratives to identify, describe, and build fear of the enemy. In fact, there is a discursive synergy between the statistical legitimacy that demography confers on the construction

217

of threats and the more emotive imagery that infuses those statistics with meaning. Some images and narratives have remarkable staying power, persisting even as the statistics of population growth and distribution change over time. They become an integral part of a powerful worldview: through them, the world is both literally and figuratively understood. For example, many people in the United States still believe there is an uncontrolled population explosion in the Third World, when in reality population growth rates have declined significantly in most regions, with an almost universal reduction in fertility in the 1990s.[3]

In this chapter we examine two powerful narratives vital to today's strategic demography. The first is the "degradation narrative," the belief that population pressures in rural areas precipitate environmental degradation, migration, and violent conflict. The second is the "youth bulge" theory, which equates the presence of large male youth cohorts in countries of the global South with political unrest and violence, especially in urban areas. While both ideas predate the end of the Cold War, the chapter focuses primarily on their more recent impact. These two narratives are implicated not only in the identification of threats but ultimately in the production of violence.

It is difficult to understand the staying power of these two narratives without first recognizing the tremendous influence that neo-Malthusian ideas, images, and actors have had on foreign policy in the United States. The chapter thus begins with a short historical sketch of this impact.

POPULATION AND NATIONAL INSECURITY

Strategic demography has taken different forms over time. From the expansionist policies of ancient Rome, to sixteenth- and seventeenth-century European nation-state formation, to nineteenth-century geopolitics, national strength—territorial, economic, and military—was tied to increasing population size.[4] Even as late as 1967, political scientist Hans Morgenthau wrote in his classic *Politics among Nations*, "Though one is not justified in considering a country to be very powerful because its population is greater than that of most other countries, it is still true that no country can remain or become a first-rate power which does not belong to the more populous nations of the earth."[5] After World War II, however, strategic demography began to take a different turn, highlighting differential fertility rates between ethnic and religious groups or between nations and regions. The focus began to shift to rising populations in the Third World versus declining populations in the West. Coupled with Western "fears of being engulfed" by the Third World masses,[6] neo-Malthusian concerns about the negative social, economic, and political impacts of rapid population growth became a focus of strategic demography. In U.S. national security circles, these concerns mapped well onto the

Cold War. In the early 1950s, demographers began to argue that rapid population growth in poor countries was putting a serious brake on the modernization process, thereby weakening countries and making them more susceptible to communist influences.[7] There were two ways to fight the Cold War: military strength and modernization—and population control figured prominently as a strategy to accomplish the latter. Controlling population growth also figured in securing U.S. access to Third World raw materials and markets, since this access would ostensibly be imperiled by population-induced disorder.[8]

By the end of the 1960s, population control had become an essential element of U.S. foreign policy, with the U.S. Agency for International Development (USAID) becoming the largest single funder of family planning programs worldwide. This concern was not limited to government; on the contrary, during the same period, neo-Malthusianism seized the public imagination, becoming a veritable article of faith. There was intentionality to this process, as private foundations and individuals supported not only demographic research and family planning efforts[9] but also the diffusion of neo-Malthusian ideas and images through more popular channels.[10] John R. Wilmoth and Patrick Ball argue that the threatening coverage of population issues by popular magazines, newspapers, and other forms of media was central to building the popular consensus necessary to sustain massive and long-term U.S. investment in population control in the Third World.[11] Of particular importance were articles linking population growth to the destruction of the environment. Images such as that of the "population bomb" became a lens through which the public and policymakers alike came to view poor people in the Third World.

Neo-Malthusian mapped well onto the end of the Cold War too. With the loss of the Soviet enemy, discourses of danger began to focus more explicitly on the Third World,[12] and population pressure became an explanatory variable for all matter of perils, from the spread of deadly tropical diseases, to the invasion of immigrants, to the destruction of the rain forest, to growing water scarcity. In the 1990s a new strategic demography explicitly linked population-induced environmental threats to national security, using old causal logic based primarily on the degradation narrative. The power and persistence of this narrative are the subject of the next section.

DEGRADING THE POOR

"It is time to understand 'the environment' for what it is: *the* national security issue of the 20th century." So wrote Robert Kaplan in his infamous article "The Coming Anarchy," published in the *Atlantic Monthly*.[13] Much of the article dwells on West Africa, which Kaplan presents as a hopeless scene of overpopulation, squalor, environmental degradation, and violence, where young men are postmodern barbarians and children with swollen bellies swarm like ants. Using biblical allusions, Kaplan claims that Malthus is the region's prophet; and Thomas Homer-Dixon, chief architect of environmental conflict theory, an "unlikely Jeremiah."[14]

Both Kaplan and Homer-Dixon base their understanding of the relationship between environment and security primarily on the degradation narrative: the basic story line that population pressures and poverty precipitate environmental degradation, which in turn leads to migration and violent conflict. While Kaplan uses lurid, racially charged images to illustrate the narrative, Homer-Dixon employs the more respectable methodology of political science, formulating a model of environmental scarcity and conflict that spawned three major research projects and numerous publications after first finding its way into the pages of the prestigious journal, *International Security*.[15] Homer-Dixon maintains that

> population growth and unequal access to good land force huge numbers of people onto marginal lands. There, they cause environmental damage and become chronically poor. Eventually, they may be the source of persistent upheaval, or they may migrate yet again, helping to stimulate ethnic conflicts or urban unrest elsewhere.[16]

This conflict, in turn, can potentially disrupt international security as states fragment or become more authoritarian.

Together, these two approaches—Kaplan's sensationalism side by side with Homer-Dixon's academic treatment—created the kind of discursive synergy that makes certain strategic demographies so compelling to policymakers. In this case, the influence extended to the highest echelons of the U.S. government. A Canadian journalist writes,

> Until earlier this year, Homer-Dixon was known only in academic circles. . . . Enter journalist Robert Kaplan and his February cover story for the *Atlantic Monthly*. . . . The article struck a nerve and a media frenzy quickly followed. Homer-Dixon was deluged by interview requests from reporters fascinated with the more sensational aspects of his research and the idea of a coming apocalypse. But journalists weren't the only ones interested. Kaplan's article was sent to all U.S. embassies and soon became standard reading material in the Clinton administration. Homer-Dixon found himself briefing Al Gore and James Woolsey [then CIA director] on his stories.[17]

However, it was not only Homer-Dixon's and Kaplan's style of presentation that brought them influence but the fact that they were giving an old myth a new national security spin, a remake, as it were, of a trusted golden oldie. Degradation narratives have been around at least since colonial days, when they were used as a way to legitimize biases against native agricultural practices. In areas of European settler agriculture in eastern and southern Africa, for example, land expropriation policies were predicated on the perceived backwardness of African peasants and the superiority of Western knowledge.[18] The image of a backward and destructive peasantry carried over into post–World War II development thinking, with neo-Malthusian assumptions becoming increasingly prominent. The notion of a singular ahistorical peasantry is part of a larger process that Escobar terms "discursive homogenization," in which the poor are constituted as universal subjects, with little regard for differences outside of certain vague client categories, such as malnourished, small farmers, landless laborers, and so forth.[19] Despite important challenges from within the development field,[20] degradation narratives shaped the emerging concept of sustainable development in the 1980s.

It was the addition of migration, particularly from the countryside to the city, that gave the degradation narrative its security dimension. In the period leading up to the end of the Cold War, the degradation narrative became a common feature of articles and reports rethinking security in environmental terms. For example, international relations scholar Richard Ullman's influential article "Redefining Security" warned that Third World villagers, after cutting down the forests and denuding the land, would join "the worldwide migration from the countryside into the cities," which are "forcing grounds for criminality and violence."[21] In the mid-1980s these migrants became known as "environmental refugees," in a classic example of discursive homogenization. Along with exaggerated estimates of their numbering in the "millions" came exaggerated claims of their negative impact on regional stability.[22]

The stage was well set, then, for Kaplan's and Homer-Dixon's success. It was helped along by a variety of contextual factors. Vice president Al Gore was especially interested in the environment, and with the end of Cold War clientism, a series of "state failures" in the Third World, notably in Africa, were causing policymakers to seek new explanations and solutions for intrastate conflict. Certain segments of the population lobby in Washington were also looking for ways to build increased support for U.S. population assistance and participation in the 1994 UN Conference on Population and Development in Cairo among foreign policy and national security agencies.

The role of the population lobby in actively sponsoring Kaplan's and Homer-Dixon's work sheds light on the intentionality and human agency involved in promoting certain threat representations over others. In particular, it reveals the importance of "strategic philanthropy"—the active involvement of private foundations in the formulation and execution of public policy—in the production of strategic demography.[23] In the early 1990s, the Pew Charitable Trusts, whose wealth derives from the Sun Oil Company, became the largest environmental donor in the United States, as well as one of the most proactive.[24] Expanding its mandate, Pew began to look more closely at foreign policy issues related to the environment, and in 1993 it created the Pew Global Stewardship Initiative (PGSI) to address population and consumption issues in preparation for the Cairo population conference.

A central element of PGSI's plan was "to assist foreign policy specialists in framing the related concerns of population, environment, and sustainable development, and in identifying areas where demographic trends threaten regional or international stability."[25] At the same time it also aimed to influence the media and popular opinion. For example, the opinion researchers it hired recommended adding "an emotional component" and "targeted visual devices" such as pictures of traffic jams and degraded landscapes to population messages in order to create the necessary alarm.[26]

PGSI also hired the Future Strategies consulting firm to make recommendations on how to build a population-and-sustainable-development campaign in Washington policy circles. Although it is unclear whether PGSI followed all the consultants' advice, the Future Strategies report provides a fascinating window on the marketing of demographic fears. As part of a "grand strategy" to increase international family-planning assistance, the report notes that Americans will have to be convinced that "unchecked population growth and destruction of the environment are key national security concerns of the 21st century."[27]

The authors of the report consider a variety of arguments to sway the public and policymakers, including fears of migration. The authors write, "Unfortunately, the specter of 'environmental refugees' driven by scarcity of resources and flooding American borders may be necessary to build the public support necessary for required increases in funding for population and sustainable development."[28] Along with detailing such arguments, it recommends using visual tools, such as computerized mapping, which overlays information about "population growth, resource depletion, overt conflict and refugee movements,"[29]as well as adopting some of the campaign tools of the American Israel Political Action Committee.[30]

PGSI went on to fund two of Homer-Dixon's major research projects. The one with the most visibility was the Environment, Population, and Security Project, which produced a number of country case studies and a briefing book designed to persuade policymakers to take environmental conflict seriously. PGSI gave $300,000 to the project, including, at Homer-Dixon's urging, $30,000 for Robert Kaplan as a project consultant.[31] It also constituted an advisory committee on security with high-ranking officials from the National Security Council and the intelligence community, which met with Homer-Dixon in November 1994.[32] PGSI's support and connections propelled Homer-Dixon's environmental conflict model, and his particular rendering of the degradation narrative, into a number of foreign policy arenas. From about 1994 to 1997, some mention of environmentally induced conflict seems *de rigueur* in official speeches and reports on the environment, whether emanating from the administration, State Department, intelligence community, or Defense Department. In 1994 and 1995, even the administration's National Security Strategy, an important blueprint for foreign and defense policy, stated boldly in the preface, "Large-scale environmental degradation, exacerbated by rapid population growth, threatens to undermine political stability in many countries and regions."[33]

Homer-Dixon's ideas proved useful to a number of government institutions and initiatives during the Clinton administration. At the State Department, undersecretary for global affairs Timothy Wirth and USAID director Brian Atwood used them to build a broader constituency for the Cairo population conference and population assistance in general, while secretary of state Warren Christopher incorporated them into his 1996 environmental initiative. They figured in the Department of Defense's strategy of "preventive defense" as concerns about environmental security became an "engagement tool" to build bridges with military officials and civilian institutions in strategic areas such as the Middle East, Horn of Africa, and central Asia. In the intelligence community, they served multiple objectives: supporting the establishment of the CIA's environment center; justifying continuing expenditures on expensive satellite surveillance systems developed during the Cold War; facilitating engagement with nongovernmental organizations and academics; and providing an interface between environmental scientists and intelligence agencies in the design of early warning systems. Interestingly, many feminists in the population field were uncomfortable with these developments, believing that family planning assistance should be supported in the context of women's rights, not national security.[34]

Towards the end of the Clinton administration, Homer-Dixon's personal influence waned in Washington as international environmental issues diminished as a policy priority and Al Gore put his mind to other matters, such as running for president.[35] Yet the degradation narrative, which Homer-Dixon and Kaplan helped elevate into the "high politics" of national security, continues to survive and function discursively within the domains of strategic demography and geography. One of the main reasons for its continuing survival is its ability, like other Malthusian narratives (see Lohmann, this volume), to naturalize a wide range of complex social, economic, and political processes.

Writing more generally about ecological metaphors of security, Dalby notes, "If the social can be rendered natural then it is beyond political control. The realm of necessity is not the realm of freedom and political choice."[36] Naturalization also has the impact of obscuring very real political choices made by powerful actors. For example, top officials in the Clinton administration—including Al Gore and his wife, Tipper; secretary of state Warren Christopher; and undersecretary of state Timothy Wirth—used population pressures and the degradation narrative to help explain the genocide in Rwanda, in the process drawing attention away from the disastrous U.S. decision not to take any action to halt it.

While on the rhetorical level the degradation narrative naturalizes political violence, in the realm of practice it contributes to the increasing militarization of nature conservation. Coercive conservation measures are of course nothing new. From colonial times onward, wildlife conservation efforts have often involved the violent exclusion of local people from their land by game rangers drawn from the ranks of the police, military, and prison guards.[37] To legitimize this exclusion, government officials, international conservation agencies, conservation biologists, and aid donors have frequently invoked neo-Malthusian narratives of expanding local human populations destroying pristine park landscapes.[38] These narratives have survived even in the face of contrary evidence because of their congruence with "the embedded cultural systems of conservation, which emphasize militaristic and preservationist discourses predominantly expressed in law enforcement. These discourses thrive on defining an 'other' or 'external threat' in order to justify action."[39]

The addition of a national security claim further magnifies the supposed threat posed by local people. In 1988, concurrent with mounting interest in environmental security, a coalition of environmental groups led by the Worldwide Fund for Nature issued a report arguing that international conservationists should systematically approach national defense forces for protection of biological resources since many threats to national security are rooted in conflicts between people and resources.[40] This is a message that the U.S. military has apparently taken to heart. The U.S. Department of Defense now has biodiversity and conservation projects in fifteen African countries.[41] In Malawi, for example, it has facilitated the equipping of park guards with semiautomatic weapons. In Central America, the department and Southern Command are working to get national militaries involved in the development of a protected biological corridor; and in the Philippines, environmental aid is a component of the current antiterrorism effort.[42]

Linking national security to conservation not only legitimizes the direct participation of defense agencies in coercive conservation but also offers a rationale for the intensification of population-control programs at the local level. Joint population–environment projects undertaken by family planning, conservation, and development nongovernmental organizations, in fact, are becoming the new frontier of population control.[43] Despite a professed commitment to communities identifying their own health and environmental needs, the main priority of many such projects is to reduce population growth through increased uptake of contraception.[44] Ideologically, the projects also reinforce the message that it is the population growth and agricultural practices of the local people themselves that cause environmental degradation. This complements new "microdisciplinary" forms of coercive conservation where, through a combination of the carrot and the stick, villagers not only take on some of the policing functions of the state but they also, through a process of education and indoctrination, internalize "introduced ideologies" of conservation.[45]

It is not too difficult to imagine a scenario where coercive conservation, population control, and security objectives come together in one locale. Today, one of the most well-known cases of coercive conservation is the involvement of Conservation International (CI) in the Lacandon Forest in Chiapas, Mexico, where CI's local director has blamed deforestation on overpopulation.[46] With USAID assistance, CI is promoting a conservation campaign in the region, which uses aerial surveillance technologies to identify illegal settlements—often indigenous communities linked to the Zapatista movement—that are then forcibly removed. CI's close ties to bioprospecting corporations raise the question, for whom is the forest being preserved?[47]

These developments in Chiapas point to the possibility of an emerging population–environment–security complex, which uses state-sanctioned violence, sophisticated surveillance technologies, and more microdisciplinary forms of power to enforce its strategic demography and geography at the local level. Vital to this enterprise is the continuing deployment of the degradation narrative to construct local populations and their movements as threats.

The degradation narrative is linked to the current "war on terror" in a more indirect, though critical way. Relocated to urban areas, the destructive peasantry undergoes further discursive homogenization into a youth bulge of young men who are easily "mobilized for violent political action, like terrorism."[48] In the following section, we examine the concept of the youth bulge in more depth, from its ideological origins to its seminal role in the strategic demography of the "war on terror."

WHY WE HATE THEM

The current face of the youth bulge made the cover of *Newsweek* soon after the events of September 11.[49] Under the banner "Why They Hate Us" ran a picture of a five- or six-year-old Arab boy holding what appears to be an automatic weapon. In the section "Politics of Rage," the magazine portrays images of shouting young Arab men protesting and burning an effigy of Bush at an anti-U.S. demonstration. These images send a clear message of the "threat" to the United States in the "war against terror." *Newsweek* drives this message home with captions and commentary such as "Know Your Enemy."[50]

These popularized threatening youth bulge images have echoed through punditry and journalism ever since. In 2003, *Newsday* saw a "demographic time bomb ticking" behind familiar "images of war, revolution, insurgency and terrorism in the Middle East":

> Dangerous demographic trends typified by a massive youth "bulge"—an extraordinary high proportion of young people among the population—all but guarantee increased social instability that few regimes will be able to withstand.[51]

This forceful image of young men as terrorists not only sells magazines but also bolsters U.S. intellectuals' and military analysts' use of youth bulge theory as a rationale for military aggression. The youth bulge theory refers to the large proportion of the world's population aged twenty-seven years and younger, the majority of whom live in the global South.[52] Personified as alienated, angry young men, the youth bulge is characterized as an unpredictable, out-of-control force in the South generally, with Africa, the Middle East, and parts of Asia and Latin America all considered hot spots. Youth bulge conflicts, it is implied, are capable of spilling over into neighboring countries and even other areas of the world, including the United States, and are an immediate threat that must be stopped.

The concept is not entirely new. U.S. military analysts and academics have defined the growing number of young people in the South as a potential national security threat since the end of World War II, when the United States became increasingly aware of the need for access to Southern raw materials, to supply domestic industry, and for good relationships with Southern governments, while contending with anticolonial nationalism. Population growth, rather than centuries of colonial domination, was believed to fuel nationalist fires, with young people being the main instigators of social unrest.[53]

Two decades later, the National Security Council's 1974 "Implications of Worldwide Population Growth for U.S. Security and Overseas Interests" presented young people as a distinct threat to the United States owing to their presumed extreme, violent behaviors and susceptibility to "persuasion."

> Young people, who are in much higher proportions in many less developed countries, are likely to be more volatile, unstable, prone to extremes, alienation and violence than an older population. These young people can more readily be persuaded to attack the legal institutions of the government or real property of the "establishment," "imperialists," multinational corporations, or other—often foreign—influences blamed for their troubles.[54]

Buttressing such claims about the "volatility" of young people in general is scholarly work such as historian Herbert Moller's 1968 article "Youth as a Force in the Modern World," in *Comparative Studies in Society and History.* Moller, indeed, goes so far as to associate young people's presumed volatile behavior with psychopathology and asserts that "primitive tendencies and psychopathic behaviours can be expected to increase in any population commensurately with its youthfulness."[55]

This discourse of youth volatility in turn draws on a tradition of thought in the Western psychology of adolescence dating back to the early nineteenth century. At that time, many intellectuals depicted young people as primitive savages on the path to "civilized" adulthood, characterizing them as experiencing "storm and stress"; emotional changeableness; and, as savages, a proclivity for violence. People of color and women were often seen as being perpetually trapped in a "savage" stage of development, unable to obtain white men's level of civilization, reason, and maturity.[56]

Of course, much of the language used to describe young people has changed since then. However, many of the basic assumptions of this discourse of adolescent savagery remain—as does the colonialist language describing the savage young black Other. In this instance, they are used to create the angry young man of the youth bulge theory.

The counterpart to the image of the angry young man is that of a passive, veiled young woman, whose presence accentuates the implied male violence and menace. Volatile male youth in the South thus become a threat not only to U.S. national security but also to the women in their own countries. At this cue, the White House and the U.S. military step in as the saviors of these passive, veiled young victims in the name of "women's rights." In a November 2001 U.S. radio broadcast, First Lady Laura Bush credited the "war on terror" for liberating the women of Afghanistan, despite all evidence to the contrary. She added, "Yet the terrorists who helped rule that country now plot and plan in many countries. And they must be stopped. The fight against terrorism is also a fight for the rights and dignity of women."[57] The image is one that literary critic Gayatri Chakravorty Spivak identifies as a commonplace of the ideology of colonialism: "white men saving brown women from brown men."[58]

In line with the gender stereotyping of the veiled young woman, the young women of the youth bulge are seen mainly as potential mothers. This reinforces the notion that young Southern women's fertility is responsible for population growth—and, more specifically, for the rise in numbers of young male terrorists. For instance, U.S. public policy professor Jack Goldstone opens an article drawing links between demographic change and violent conflict by noting that the current number of young women in the global South ensures a rise in the number of young people there.[59] There is all the more reason, according to the youth bulge theory, for curtailing Southern birth rates immediately through population programs focusing on women.

The lobby group Population Action International, which works to strengthen political and financial support worldwide for population programs, proposes that the U.S. military team up with international aid agencies to further Southern women's education, family planning services, and economic opportunity to ensure both U.S. national security and the well-being of Southern countries themselves.[60]

U.S. ACCESS TO OIL

In line with the United States' post–World War II fears that a growing population of unruly young people could interfere with its resource flows, the youth bulge has also been seen, both before and after September 11, as a factor complicating strategic control of Middle Eastern oil exports. Anthony Cordesman, senior fellow in strategic assessment at the Center for Strategic and International Studies, opens his remarks on the youth bulge and other challenges to the U.S. military by noting that neither September 11 nor the "war on terror" changed the basic reasons for the U.S. military presence in the Middle East:

> We need to remember what our key strategic priorities are. The United States is ever more dependent on a globalized economy, and the global economy is becoming steadily more dependent on Middle Eastern energy exports.[61]

General Anthony C. Zinni, former commander in chief of U.S. Central Command, agrees. In testimony before the Armed Services Committee in March 2000, he asserts that primary among U.S. interests in Central Command's area of responsibility is "the promotion of regional stability and the insurance of uninterrupted, secure access to Arabian Gulf energy resources."[62] Youth bulge extremism, he continues, threatens that objective. Zinni also notes that population growth in the Arabian Gulf region is "increasing dramatically, putting pressure on natural resources, specifically water, and economic systems."

It is characteristic of talk about the youth bulge, as it is of population discourse more generally, that Zinni fails to mention forces other than that of population growth that might reduce the extent and availability of resources and divert much-needed funds from health, education, and job creation. Examples include seizure of resources by the rich, U.S. and other aid programs' erosion of basic food production, decay of public welfare institutions in the wake of neoliberal policies, and growing military expenditures.

As a source of terrorism, radicalism, and anti-Western violence, the youth bulge ranks in the minds of some alongside weapons of mass destruction as a major threat to U.S. security. Youth bulges have come under military surveillance in many countries and are an important object of military plans to fight terrorism in a whole range of Southern countries and regions where the United States has military and industrial interests.

Ex-CIA director George Tenet's suggestions for combating the threat of the youth bulge echo the tough-on-crime rhetoric common to policing in the United States. He pictures the U.S. military as a global cop, particularly in "stateless zones" and nations whose governments cannot contain their own youth bulges. "We're used to thinking of [the war against terrorism] as a sustained worldwide effort to get the perpetrators and would-be perpetrator off the street."[63]

Ironically, while military analysts warn of "extremist" groups recruiting new members from the youth bulge, the U.S. military itself is adopting the same tactic in a section of Africa stretching from the Horn to the Western Sahara's Atlantic Coast. In Mali and Mauritania, U.S. special operations forces are training and arming African soldiers as a "preventative" measure to guard against their recruitment by Al Qaeda and to "protect" the region. U.S. military training in the region is part of a larger, $7 million program, the Pan-Sahel Initiative, to "shore up border controls and deny sanctuary to suspected terrorists."[64]

HOMELAND INSECURITY

In policing suspected terrorists in the United States following the attack on the World Trade Center, the U.S. government has increasingly come to identify citizenship with race. In the words of American University law professor Leti Volpp,

> September 11 facilitated the consolidation of a new identity category that groups together persons who appear "Middle Eastern, Arab or Muslim." This consolidation reflects a racialization wherein members of this group are identified as terrorists, and are disidentified as citizens.[65]

One example of Volpp's "racialization" is the Department of Homeland Security's immigration enforcement, which uses racial profiling of Arab, Muslim, and South Asian men in the name of national security. In June 2003, federal efforts to predict and stop terrorist acts within the United States were pointedly exempted from a Justice Department ban on racial and ethnic profiling in law enforcement. Racial profiling is also now built into the "Special Call-In Registration System," which requires all immigrant men over the age of sixteen from a list of twenty-five Muslim and Middle Eastern countries and North Korea to register in person at immigration offices and to check in annually.[66]

The youth bulge image has helped put young male Arab and Muslim immigrants in special danger of deportation. In the wake of the government's post–September 11 detention campaign that swept through South Asian and

Arab communities in New York and New Jersey, hundreds of detained immigrants were deported immediately, and, by 2003, more than thirteen thousand male registrants had been forced into deportation proceedings. As the proceedings unfold, predicts the National Network of Immigrant and Refugee Rights, "many more men will be deported or will opt for 'voluntary' departure, devastating families and harming communities."[67] In stark contrast to the "disidentification" of Arabs, Muslim, and South Asian men as U.S. citizens, U.S. soldiers—the global police force—have been allocated a level of "supercitizenship."[68] While those who appear "Middle Eastern, Arab, or Muslim" are experiencing an erosion of rights, U.S. soldiers can cross borders for the most part unhampered and in many cases are not held to international standards of conduct, as in the instance of U.S. soldiers' abuse of Iraqi prisoners at the Abu Ghraib prison, which came to light during 2004.

ANGRY YOUNG MEN VERSUS SUPERPREDATORS

A good place to begin assessing the dangers of policy responses to the youth bulge theory is with the "superpredator" theory that originated in the United States in the mid-1990s. The superpredator theory equated a rise in the proportion of young men in a given population with a rise in the numbers of criminal young men. It institutionalized the view that there is violence in numbers—specifically, numbers of young men of color in the United States. In the words of the Princeton professor John DiIulio (who has since served as the first director of the White House Office of Faith-Based and Community Initiatives, under George W. Bush), "more boys begets more bad boys."[69] DiIulio's influential article "The Coming of the Super-Predators" predicted that with the strength of numbers behind them, young male criminals, or superpredators, would tend to commit evermore serious crimes. DiIulio's assertion that "Americans are sitting atop a demographic crime bomb" resonated with policymakers and politicians alike. The theory had a tremendous impact on the way that the U.S. government dealt with young people, particularly young men of color, and contributed to the rise of a lethal image of a ruthless young male criminal, an image that caught and held public attention.

The superpredator image corresponds with another gendered, racialized, and age-based image, that of the teen-mother "welfare queen," which resembles in some ways the veiled young woman image of the youth bulge trope. If the superpredator image pictures young men of color in the inner city as potential criminals, the welfare queen image suggests that unmarried teenage mothers produce subsequent generations of menacing males.

In the pro-marriage U.S. environment, single mothers, particularly black mothers, have long been accused of raising their children inadequately and perpetuating generational cycles of poverty, addiction, and crime. As mothers of potential superpredators, they become even more of a problem. This could well be one reason that there were renewed government efforts in the 1990s to reduce teen birth rates through "family cap" measures that deny welfare recipients additional cash benefits for children born while their mothers are on welfare; through abstinence and contraception education initiatives; and through welfare-to-work measures. While the connection between the superpredator and the teen welfare queen was never made explicit in these initiatives, concern about teen motherhood accelerating U.S. population growth was obvious, with the President's Council on Sustainable Development expressing alarm about "another Connecticut" being added in population each year and "another California each decade."[70] The public fear resulting from promotion of the superpredator threat led to increased public support for punitive juvenile justice policies and encouraged alarmist news headlines, such as "Superpredators Arrive," on the January 22, 1996, cover of *Newsweek*. These fears proved so exaggerated that the government was ultimately forced to backtrack. In February 2000, the Department of Justice published a debunking report titled "Challenging the Myths."[71] The welfare queen image, however, although it is as exaggerated as the superpredator image, has yet to be retracted by the government, and both images live on in the public and media imagination. The United States continues to live with the punitive legacy of both theories, which perpetuate a public fear of young people as potential criminals and feed policies that increasingly police and criminalize young people in ways that affect their education, reproductive health, and likelihood of entering the adult criminal justice system.

The superpredator theory, for instance, is implicated in the rise in the number of young adults channeled into the criminal justice system. A 1998 report by the National Center for Juvenile Justice states that between 1992 and 1995, forty states and the District of Columbia passed laws making it easier for states to try juvenile offenders as adults.[72] Moreover, although levels of juvenile violent crime remained constant between the 1980s and 1990s, juvenile violent crime arrest rates went up, disproportionately affecting young people of color. African Americans make up more than half of youth admitted to prison but only 15 percent of the U.S. population.[73]

Zero tolerance policies that institute high levels of surveillance and policing have, meanwhile, changed public school environments radically. According to the Advancement Project, a democracy and justice action group, "the educational system is starting to look more like the criminal justice system."[74]

The devastating policy outcomes of the superpredator myth provide an instructive, although bleak, comparison of what we might expect from the youth bulge theory. Like the superpredator theory, its impact will likely continue even as it is discredited empirically. The greatest threat posed by the

youth bulge concept is its negative repercussions on the human rights of the
young men and women it targets, rather than the threat those young men ostensibly pose. Perhaps a more apt "bulge" concept might refer to a "military
bulge" that looks at how people in positions of power in the United States,
such as defense secretary Donald Rumsfeld and vice president Dick Cheney,
instigate violence and unrest.[75] This bulge might better define the "threat" in
the "war on terror."

TROPES AND CONSEQUENCES

Challenging the powerful neo-Malthusian narratives and tropes of strategic
demography is made all the more difficult by the fact that they have currency
in both popular and policy venues and often transcend ideological and political divisions between liberals and conservatives. It was Clinton-era policymakers, after all, who embraced the concept of environmental conflict. Yet
challenge them we must because these tropes can have real and violent consequences, especially when they guide the actions of law enforcement agencies at home and militaries abroad. Followed to their logical and lethal
conclusion, they can become a rationale for ethnic cleansing. A cautionary
case in point is Chechnya, where the International Helsinki Federation has
charged the Russian army of abducting and murdering young males in a deliberate process "of thinning out a population of young men."[76]

In other words, the stakes are extremely high.

NOTES

Paul Kennedy, "Birthrates: Distant Trouble for Jewish State," *Chicago Tribune*, April
7, 2002, www.chicagotribune.com/news/showcase/chi-020407maelstrom3.story (accessed September 10, 2003).

1. Frank Furedi, *Population and Development: A Critical Introduction* (New York:
St. Martin's Press, 1997).

2. Uri Avnery, "A Jewish Demographic State," October 12, 2002, www.gush-shalom
.org/archives/article215.html (accessed November 1, 2002). Ben Lynfield, "Marriage
Law Divides Israeli Arab Families," *Christian Science Monitor*, August 8, 2003, www
.csmonitor.com/2003/0808/p06s03-wome.html (accessed August 19, 2003).

3. UN Population Division, *Population Newsletter*, no. 77 (June 2004).

4. Deborah Anne Barrett, *Reproducing Persons as a Global Concern: The Making
of an Institution*, PhD thesis (Chapel Hill: Carolina Population Center, University of
North Carolina, 1995).

5. Hans J. Morgenthau, *Politics among Nations: The Struggle for Power and Peace*,
4th ed. (New York: Alfred A. Knopf, 1967), 118–19.

6. Amartya Sen, "Population: Delusion and Reality," *New York Review of Books* 22 (September 22, 1994): 62–71.

7. Dennis Hodgson, "Demography as Social Science and Policy Science," *Population and Development Review* 9, no. 1 (1983): 1–34. Simon Szreter, "The Idea of Demographic Transition and the Study of Fertility Change: A Critical Intellectual History," *Population and Development Review* 19, no. 4 (December 1993): 659–701.

8. Peter J. Donaldson, *Nature against Us: The United States and the World Population Crisis, 1965–1980* (Chapel Hill: University of North Carolina Press, 1990).

9. Betsy Hartmann, *Reproductive Rights and Wrongs: The Global Politics of Population Control* (Boston: South End Press, 1995).

10. Elizabeth Hartmann, *Strategic Scarcity: The Origins and Impact of Environmental Conflict Ideas*, PhD thesis (London: Development Studies Institute, London School of Economics and Political Science, 2003). John Sharpless, "Population Science, Private Foundations, and Development Aid: The Transformation of Demographic Knowledge in the United States, 1945–1965," in *International Development and the Social Sciences*, ed. Frederick Cooper and Randall Packard (Berkeley: University of California Press, 1997): 176–200.

11. John R. Wilmoth and Patrick Ball, "The Population Debate in American Popular Magazines," *Population and Development Review* 18, no. 4 (1992): 631–68.

12. David Campbell, *Writing Security: United States Foreign Policy and the Politics of Identity* (Minneapolis: University of Minnesota Press, 1998).

13. Robert D. Kaplan, "The Coming Anarchy," *Atlantic Monthly* (February 1994): 44–76 (see 58).

14. Kaplan, "Coming Anarchy," 56.

15. Thomas Homer-Dixon, "On the Threshold: Environmental Changes as Causes of Acute Conflict," *International Security* 16, no. 2 (Fall 1991): 76–116.

16. Thomas Homer-Dixon, *Environment, Scarcity, and Violence* (Princeton, N.J.: Princeton University Press, 1999), 155.

17. David Pugliese, "The World According to Tad: Canadian Scholar's Dark Vision Is Suddenly Being Studied in High Places," *Ottawa Citizen*, December 4, 1994, 1C.

18. Dianne E. Rocheleau, Philip E. Steinberg, and Patricia A. Benjamin, "Environment, Development, Crisis and Crusade: Ukambani, Kenya, 1890–1990," *World Development* 23, no. 6 (1995): 1037–51.

19. Arturo Escobar, *Encountering Development: The Making and Unmaking of the Third World* (Princeton, N.J.: Princeton University Press, 1995), 53.

20. Esther Boserup, *The Conditions of Agricultural Growth: The Economics of Agrarian Change Under Population Pressure* (Chicago: Aldine, 1965). Piers Blaikie and Harold Brookfield, *Land Degradation and Society* (London: Methuen, 1987).

21. Richard Ullman, "Redefining Security," *International Security* 8, no. 1 (1983): 129–53 (see 141).

22. Richard Black, *Refugees, Environment, and Development* (New York: Longman, 1998).

23. Ellen Condliffe Lagemann, *The Politics of Knowledge: The Carnegie Corporation, Philanthropy, and Public Policy* (Middletown, Conn.: Wesleyan University Press, 1989).

24. Mark Dowie, *American Foundations: An Investigative History* (Cambridge: MIT Press, 2001). Brian Tokar, *Earth for Sale: Reclaiming Ecology in the Age of Corporate Greenwash* (Boston: South End Press, 1997).

25. Pew Global Stewardship Initiative (PGSI), "PGSI White Paper" (Washington, D.C., July 1993), 13.

26. Pew Global Stewardship Initiative (PGSI), "Report of Findings from Focus Groups on Population, Consumption, and the Environment" (conducted for PGSI by R/S/M, Melman, Lazarus Lake and Beldon & Russonello; July 1993), 73–74.

27. Pew Global Stewardship Initiative (PGSI), "Building a Coordinated Campaign on Population and Sustainable Development Policy" (report submitted by Francis E. Smith and Pam Solo for Future Strategies to the PGSI, March 1994), 31.

28. PGSI, "Building a Coordinated Campaign," 33.

29. PGSI, "Building a Coordinated Campaign," 13.

30. PGSI, "Building a Coordinated Campaign," 33.

31. The second was the Environmental Scarcities, State Capacity, and Civil Violence Project, with roughly half of the $400,000 financing coming from PGSI, and the other half from the Rockefeller Foundation (Hartmann, *Strategic Scarcity*).

32. Pew Global Stewardship Initiative (PGSI), "Report of Stewardship and Security Steering Committee Meeting" (November 28, 1994). Information on PGSI funding to Homer-Dixon is from Hartmann, *Strategic Scarcity*.

33. From White House, "National Security Strategy of Engagement and Enlargement, July 1994 and February 1995," excerpted in *Environmental Change and Security Project Report* 1 (Spring 1995): 47–50 (see 47). See Hartmann, *Strategic Scarcity*, for a discussion of how environmental conflict is included in many official speeches and reports.

34. See Hartmann, *Strategic Scarcity*, for how Homer-Dixon's ideas circulated in Washington.

35. Stephen Hopgood, *American Foreign Environmental Policy and the Power of the State* (Oxford: Oxford University Press, 1998); and Richard Matthew, "The Environment as a National Security Issue," *Journal of Policy History* 12, no. 1 (2000): 101–22.

36. Simon Dalby, "Ecological Metaphors of Security: World Politics in the Biosphere," *Alternatives* 23 (1998): 291–319 (see 294).

37. Roderick P. Neumann, "Disciplining Peasants in Tanzania: From State Violence to Self-Surveillance in Wildlife Conservation," in *Violent Environments*, ed. Nancy Lee Peluso and Michael Watts (Ithaca, N.Y.: Cornell University Press, 2001), 305–27.

38. Lee Alexander Risby et al., "Environmental Narratives in Protected Area Planning —the Case of Queen Elizabeth National Park, Uganda," *Policy Matters* (International Union for the Conservation of Nature and Natural Resources / Commission on Environmental, Economic, and Social Policy) 10 (August 2002): 40–49. Ramachandra Guha, "The Authoritarian Biologist and the Arrogance of Anti-Humanism: Wildlife Conservation in the Third World," *Ecologist* 27, no. 1 (1997): 14–20.

39. Risby et al., "Environmental Narratives," 47.

40. Nancy Lee Peluso, "Coercing Conservation: The Politics of State Resource Control," in *The State and Social Power in Global Environmental Politics*, ed. Ronnie D. Lipschutz and Ken Conca (New York: Columbia University Press, 1993).

41. U.S. Army War College, "Environmental Security Briefing" (PowerPoint presentation, Carlisle, Pa., 2000).

42. Phone interview by Betsy Hartmann of Kent Butts, director, National Security Issues Branch, Center for Strategic Leadership, U.S. Army War College, Carlisle, Pa., June 19, 2002.

43. United Nations Fund for Population Activities, *The State of World Population 2001* (New York: United Nations Fund for Population Activities, 2001).

44. Denise Caudhill, "Exploring Capacity for Integration: University of Michigan Population-Environment Fellows Program's Impact Assessment Project," *Environmental Change and Security Project Report* 6 (Summer 2000): 66–76.

45. Neumann, "Disciplining Peasants in Tanzania," 326.

46. Dudley Althaus, "The Fated Forest," *Houston Chronicle* (2002), 2, www.chron.com/content/chronicle/special/01/forest/index.html (accessed August 1, 2002).

47. Matthew MacLean, "Mexico's Government Wants to Relocate Illegal Squatters, but Some Threaten Violence," *Christian Science Monitor*, July 16, 2003, www.csmonitor.com/2003/0716/p08s01-woam.html (accessed September 4, 2003).

48. Thomas Homer-Dixon, "Standing Room Only," *Globe and Mail* (Toronto), March 6, 2002, www.homerdixon.com/download/why_population_growth.pdf as "Why Population Growth Still Matters" (accessed May 10, 2005). R. Cincotta, R. Engelman, and D. Anastasion, *The Security Demographic: Population and Civil Conflict after the Cold War* (Washington, D.C.: Population Action International, 2003).

49. A version of this section appears in the Corner House's "Angry Young Men, Veiled Young Women: Constructing a New Population Threat" (briefing 34), www.thecornerhouse.org.uk/item.shtml?x=85999 (accessed May 10, 2005).

50. Fareed Zakaria, "Why They Hate Us: The Roots of Islamic Rage—and What We Can Do about It," *Newsweek*, October 15, 2001, 22–40.

51. Graham Fuller, "Demographics = Mideast Turmoil," *Newsday*, September 29, 2003, 21A.

52. Gary Fuller, "The CIA on Youth Deficits," *Population and Development Review* 16, no. 4 (1990): 801–7.

53. Hartmann, *Reproductive Rights and Wrongs*, 102.

54. National Security Council, "Implications of Worldwide Population Growth for U.S. Security and Overseas Interests," National Security Study Memorandum 200 (Washington, D.C., 1974), www.africa2000.com/INDX/nssm200all.html (accessed November 2004).

55. Herbert Moller, "Youth as a Force in the Modern World," *Comparative Studies in Society and History* 10, no. 3 (April 1968): 237–60.

56. G. S. Hall, *Adolescence*, vols. 1–2 (New York: D. Appleton, 1904).

57. White House, "Radio Address by Mrs. Bush" (November 17, 2001), www.whitehouse.gov/news/releases/2001/11/20011117.html (accessed August 2004).

58. G. C. Spivak, "Can the Subaltern Speak?" in *Marxism and the Interpretation of Culture*, ed. C. Nelson and L. Grossberg (Urbana: University of Illinois Press, 1988).

59. Jack A. Goldstone, "Population and Security: How Demographic Change Can Lead to Violent Conflict," *Journal of International Affairs* 56, no. 1 (Fall 2002): 3.

60. Cincotta, Engelman, and Anastasion, *Security Demographic*, 15.

61. Anthony H. Cordesman, "The U.S. Military and the Evolving Challenges in the Middle East" (2002), www.nwc.navy.mil/press/Review/2002/summer/art3-su2.htm (accessed September 2002).

62. Anthony Zinni, "Prepared Testimony of General Anthony C. Zinni, Commander in Chief U.S Central Command," Federal News Services, March 15, 2000.

63. George Tenet, "The Worldwide Threat 2004: Challenges in the Changing Global Context" (2004), www.odci.gov./cia/public_affairs/speeches/2004/tenet_testimony_ 03092004.html (accessed August 2004).

64. Craig Smith, "U.S. Training North Africans to Uproot Terrorists," *New York Times*, May 11, 2004, 1A.

65. Leti Volpp, "The Citizen and the Terrorist," *UCLA Law Review* 49 (2002): 1575–1600 (see 1575).

66. N. Murray, "Profiled: Arabs, Muslims, and the Post 9/11 Hunt for the 'Enemy Within,'" in *Civil Rights in Peril: The Targeting of Arabs and Muslims*, ed. Elaine C. Hagopian (Chicago: Haymarket Books, 2004).

67. Heba Nimr, Catherine Tactaquin, and Arnold Garcia, "Human Rights and Human Security at Risk: The Consequences of Placing Immigration Enforcement and Services in the Department of Homeland Security" (prepared for the National Network for Immigrant and Refugee Rights, Oakland, Calif., 2003), 15.

68. Catherine Lutz, "Making War at Home in the United States: Militarization and the Current Crisis," *American Anthropologist* 104, no. 3 (September 2002): 723–35 (see 731).

69. John J. DiIulio, "The Coming of the Super-Predators," *Weekly Standard* 1, no. 11 (1996): 23.

70. White House, "President's Council on Sustainable Development: Population and Consumption" (1996), www.whitehouse.gov/PSCD/Publications/TF_Reports/ pop-chap-1.html (accessed October 2000).

71. U.S. Department of Justice, "Challenging the Myths," in *1999 National Report Series: Juvenile Justice Bulletin* (Washington, D.C.: Office of Juvenile Justice and Delinquency Prevention, 2000).

72. U.S. Department of Justice, *Trying Juveniles as Adults in Criminal Court: An Analysis of State Transfer Provisions* (Washington, D.C.: Office of Justice Programs, 1998).

73. The Center on Juvenile and Criminal Justice. "Disproportionate Minority Confinement (DMC)" (2003), www.cjcj.org/jjic/race_jj.php (accessed August 2004).

74. Advancement Project, "Zero Tolerance Policies Put Thousands of Kids on Jailhouse Track," (press release, Washington, D.C., June 12–18, 2003).

75. Thanks to the participants in the Corner House's March 2003 Women, Population Control, Public Health, and Globalization Meeting for the idea of the "military bulge."

76. "Russia 'Thinning Out' Chechens" (July 23, 2002), *BBC News*, http://news.bbc .co.uk/2/low/world/europe/2146702.stm (accessed October 2002).

Reflections

Bioterrorism and National Security: Peripheral Threats, Core Vulnerabilities

Richard A. Matthew

A desperate disease requires a dangerous remedy.

—Guy Fawkes

Claims about the threat of bioterrorism and neo-Malthusian arguments about scarcity-induced violence are elements of a new worldview being constructed to fill the gap left by the end of the Cold War. While the process relies in part on carefully collected data and rigorous analysis, it is also a political process in which, as Hartmann and Hendrixson write, "the stakes are extremely high."[1] This is true, albeit in different ways, for career-minded policymakers in Washington, for the defense industry, for the American public, and for many developing nations. Much depends on which threats are taken seriously, how they are framed, and how they are addressed. In consequence, facts mingle with conjecture; reason mixes with emotion; and persuasion is bolstered by bullying, as different constituencies jockey for position.

A serious concern raised in the chapters by Guillemin and Hartmann and Hendrixson is that the tragedy of September 11 and the subsequent anthrax scare could enable the consolidation and rise to dominance of a worldview that favors certain bureaucratic interests; overstates many threats; and advocates aggressive measures that, from the perspectives of national and human security, will do more harm than good.[2]

Should this happen, the blame will rest as much with academics seeking fame and activists seeking funds as with bureaucrats seeking power and businesses seeking defense contracts. The analysis of threats may be distorted or simplified by particular interests, but the public willingness to assign massive resources on the basis of such analysis reflects an attitude toward security that has roots in claims advanced by widely respected academic and activist communities. In particular, the perennial alarmism of a large and vocal wing of the environmental movement has had considerable success in convincing people that the world is an inherently dangerous place, perilously close to catastrophe and chaos. This sentiment has achieved its most systematic and elaborate formulation in the literature on environmental security, which has helped to create a platform for legitimizing, among others, the rhetoric of bioterrorism.

FROM ENVIRONMENTAL CHANGE TO SECURITY CRISIS

The fusion of environment and security throughout the 1990s contributed to a discursive landscape grounded in a widespread sense of impending—but hard to prove—disaster that could only be averted or mitigated through aggressive preventive policies.[3] Although some scholars raised doubts about alleged linkages between environmental conditions and violent conflict or other forms of societal crisis, many others made bold statements about these relationships and their trajectories that caught the attention of policymakers in the United States and abroad.[4] Peter Gleick envisioned wars over water and discussed the security implications of climate change.[5] E. O. Wilson predicted catastrophic social consequences of rapid biodiversity loss.[6] And Thomas Homer-Dixon argued that the "incidence of [civil] violence will probably increase as scarcities of cropland, freshwater, and forests worsen in many parts of the developing world."[7]

These writers extended a literature that had been pioneered by the authors of the new environmentalism that emerged in the 1960s and 1970s. The early repertoire of disaster scenarios included Paul Ehrlich's "population bomb," Garrett Hardin's "Tragedy of the Commons," Barry Commoner's arguments about the negative externalities of production technologies, and Donella Meadow's "limits to growth" thesis. Given the close connections between this new environmentalism and the peace movements of the same era, which focused on the threat of nuclear war and the possible end of humankind, the pervasive despair that is evident is scarcely surprising.[8]

Under such conditions, the obviously pressing question was, how could catastrophe be prevented? For many environmentalists, the appropriate approach to prevention was to adopt some version of the precautionary principle —avoid any behavior that seems like it could cause harm, even if causality has not been established scientifically.[9] From the conservation movement's emphasis on preserving ecosystems, through E. O. Wilson's biophilia, to the deep ecological concept of biocentrism, one sees many variations on the theme of the need for strong prevention measures in the face of impending disaster.[10]

Of course, environmentalists were not the sole source of the alarmist discourse of the twentieth century. Sociologists such as Ulrich Beck have written extensively about America's heightened sense of being encircled by life-threatening risks ranging from genetically modified foods to tropical diseases, from global mafias to soulless street gangs, from climate change to air pollution.[11] But while it may be impossible to weight the contribution of environmental discourse to the current political culture of fear, a sense of its importance can be had by considering the predominant arguments formulated in the process of rethinking security after the Cold War. They have come in large measure from the country's most senior scholars and power journalists—individuals who are not only prominent in the knowledge community but often serve as its conduits to the policy community. For example, in "The Coming Anarchy," Robert Kaplan writes,

> It is time to understand *the environment* for what it is: the national security issue of the early twenty-first century. The political and strategic impact of surging populations, spreading disease, deforestation and soil erosion, water depletion, air pollution, and, possibly, rising sea levels in critical, overcrowded regions like the Nile Delta and Bangladesh—developments that will prompt mass migrations and, in turn, incite group conflicts—will be the core foreign policy challenge from which most others will ultimately emanate.[12]

Matthew Connolly and Paul Kennedy pick up this line of argument in another widely read essay, "Must It Be the Rest against the West?"

> We are heading into the twenty-first century in a world consisting for the most part of a relatively small number of rich, satiated, demographically stagnant societies and a large number of poverty-stricken, resource-depleted nations whose populations are doubling every twenty-five years or less.[13]

In both scenarios, demographic and environmental variables figure prominently as factors contributing to conflict and insecurity. While not all of the influential predictions about the security challenges of the near future have emphasized environmental factors, many of them share Kaplan's and Connolly and Kennedy's sense of impending catastrophe.[14]

Presidents William J. Clinton and George W. Bush both agreed with the general sentiment of these scenarios, although they reached very different conclusions about the nature of the preventive policies needed to make the world less dangerous. Clinton advocated conservation, free trade, and democracy. Bush's focus has been on preemptive military strikes and democratization. Both presidents have clearly reflected the panicky anxiety of contemporary environmentalism and have used a familiar rhetoric of disaster and anarchy to persuade people that our world is a dangerous place to be, a place in which national and human security depend on extraordinary measures.[15]

Of course, the principal threat described by the Bush administration—transnational terrorists armed with biological and other weapons of mass destruction—may be a real and significant threat.[16] It may warrant billions of dollars of defense expenditures and an aggressive offensive strategy for disabling terrorist organizations as they emerge at home and abroad. But it is important that this threat be established, insofar as possible, on the basis of accurate data and rigorous analysis. Unfortunately, when citizens and policymakers have already been assured that the world is full of threat by experts in areas such as conservation biology, epidemiology, and demography, then similar assertions made by other "experts"—and the policies they demand—may be accepted without serious scrutiny. Perceptions are important in the security field. Misguided perceptions of offensive advantage were a key factor in triggering and sustaining World War I. Misguided perceptions about socialism contributed to aggressive—and flawed—American policies toward Vietnam, Nicaragua, and Cuba. In short, security-relevant perceptions that build on platforms that are themselves unstable and unproven surely need to be interrogated. We need to adapt the business principle of due diligence to the security realm. After all, due diligence does not put the brakes on business per se but only on bad business.

CONSTRUCTING A NEW POLICY OF PREEMPTION

On October 15, 2001, an envelope addressed to Senate majority leader Tom Daschle was delivered to his office in Washington, D.C. The envelope contained a gram of pure, weaponized Ames-strain anthrax, the distribution of which is strictly regulated by the U.S. Army Medical Research Institute of Infectious Diseases. It also contained a brief letter:

> 09-11-01
> YOU CAN NOT STOP US.
> WE HAVE THIS ANTHRAX.
> YOU DIE NOW.
> ARE YOU AFRAID?
> DEATH TO AMERICA.
> DEATH TO ISRAEL.
> ALLAH IS GREAT.

During September and October of that year, similar letters were mailed to several U.S. journalists and elected officials. Five people died. Following on the heels of the September 11 attacks, these letters seemed to provide further evidence that America was under siege from a shadowy, sophisticated, and dangerous web of terrorists. For the White House, and for many of the country's residents and citizens, the search for the dominant threat of the post–Cold War era ended that fall. The United States, they concluded, had joined a small group of countries—including Israel, Colombia, and Pakistan—plagued, and in some sense defined, by terrorist activity.

In the years preceding September 11 and the anthrax scare, some experts had warned that the "postmodern terrorists" targeting the United States and other countries had pioneered a radical new phase of political violence.[17] According to David Siegrist, "This reflects a shift in the goal of terrorists, from trying to make a political statement through violence to maximizing the number of casualties."[18] Postmodern terrorists do not have the clear political agendas of their ancestors, and they are not averse to causing mass casualties. Weapons of mass destruction are not off limits for them.[19]

In response to this fear, President Clinton introduced in 1998 "the first national effort to create a biological weapons defense for the United States."[20] At that time, White House spokesperson Richard A. Clarke noted that "some critics say that until we really know about a specific threat to use these weapons against the United States, we should not be raising the specter of horror. . . . [But] when we learn of a specific threat, it will be too late to do research and development, too late to procure medicines, too late to train local authorities."[21] The policy momentum of the late 1990s would be accelerated by the September 11 attacks, and the decisions of the Clinton years would be looked upon by many as being headed in the right direction but at far too slow a pace and with far too few resources.

On September 20, 2002, President George W. Bush issued the annual *National Security Strategy of the United States.*[22] Insofar as strategic doctrine is concerned, the most important innovation of the 2002 strategy might be its expansion of the concept of preemption in part V, "Prevent Our Enemies from Threatening Us, Our Allies, and Our Friends with Weapons of Mass Destruction." In a speech at West Point preparing the country for this innovation, the president stated, echoing the words of Richard Clarke, "Some have said we must not act until the threat is imminent. Since when have terrorists and tyrants announced their intentions, politely putting us on notice before they strike? If this threat is permitted to fully and suddenly emerge, all actions, all words and all recriminations would come too late."[23] In the 2002 strategy, this sentiment is reiterated and bolstered with assertions that "traditional concepts of deterrence will not work against a terrorist enemy" and that "we must adapt the concept of imminent threat to the capabilities and objectives of today's adversaries."[24]

In an analysis of the 2002 strategy, Michael E. O'Hanlon and colleagues write that "preemption, narrowly defined, has long been an important and widely accepted policy option for the United States. But the Bush administration argues that preemption must be extended to include 'preventive' attacks even in the absence of an imminent threat." The authors note that "prevention is a far less accepted concept in international law, even though the

United States has threatened or utilized it in previous eras as well, and even though it may be a necessary tool at times."[25]

FIRST USE

The first application of the new doctrine occurred the following year, against Iraq. Before the war, John Mearsheimer and Stephen Walt argued that the justifications being offered for a preemptive strike were weak and that such an attack was likely to be costly and counterproductive.[26] Their carefully honed realist analysis challenged claims about Saddam's aggressive and reckless past behavior, his willingness to use chemical weapons against Western countries, the state of his nuclear weapons program, and the likelihood that Iraq did or ever would support Al Qaeda or similar terrorist organizations. Mearsheimer and Walt concluded, "Saddam, though cruel and calculating, is eminently deterrable" at low cost.[27] Their thoughtful analysis, however, received little attention in early 2003, especially in comparison to the attention given to the bold assertions made by the president and by secretary of state Colin Powell regarding Iraq's alleged weapons of mass destruction programs, surge capacity, and support for global terrorism. Although evidence in support of these assertions has never been provided, perhaps because it does not exist, they nonetheless provided grounds for action that satisfied much of the American public and Congress: the preemptive attack took place between March and May. Some nine months after the war ended,

> Defense Secretary Donald H. Rumsfeld reaffirmed the administration's doctrine of preemptive military action . . . and offered an impassioned defense of the decision to invade Iraq, saying former president Saddam Hussein's defiance had forced the United States to act. . . .
>
> Rumsfeld argued forcefully for striking first, particularly in cases involving the potential use of a biological agent or other weapons that could cause thousands of deaths.
>
> "The greater the risk and the danger, the lower the threshold for action," he said, speaking at a conference on U.S. and European security issues here.[28]

Clearly, one of two things must be true. Either the hostile, threatening worldview advocated by the Bush administration, which incorporates explicit references to biological weapons as well as terrorism, is an accurate one—or it is not. In the first case, a generous doctrine of preemption may be warranted, although it would have to clear many moral, legal, and pragmatic hurdles before being palatable to much of the world. In the second case, it is hard to imagine how such a doctrine could ever be defended. Since so much is at stake, one might expect this worldview to be vigorously debated in a democracy—especially when considering that it cobbles together disparate phenomena such as the anthrax scare in the United States, the basement bioweapons programs of Saddam Hussein, and the ambitions of Al Qaeda to produce a terrifying but quite unsubstantiated image (here of a sophisticated global network of bioterrorism).[29] This has not happened. Perhaps it has not happened because during the latter half of the twentieth century Americans were flooded with doomsday scenarios and no longer need much evidence to accept strong claims about grave threats, looming crises, bold preventive actions, and firm responses. Many of these scenarios came from the environmental movement.

PERIPHERAL THREATS, CORE VULNERABILITIES

Claims about bioterrorism and neo-Malthusian arguments about scarcity and violence have been loudly endorsed by groups that hope to benefit if their assertions succeed in informing policy. These groups include civil servants and defense contactors, as well as some academics and activists. The public and policymakers accept these claims, even when they are not well supported, because they have been persuaded that the world is both a threatening and an interdependent place. Conceptually, the move from climate change to Al Qaeda is not that great. Unfortunately, the bold actions that follow may, from a security perspective, do more harm than good while lining the pockets of a few bureaucrats, contractors, and consultants. In consequence, the world does become a little more threatening, creating the conditions for a new round of alarming assertions. To exit this vicious cycle, we need, at the very least, to demand analysis that meets minimal standards for evidence and reason. The arguments against invading Iraq formulated by Mearsheimer and Walt provide an accessible model of such standards.

There is wide agreement that the security landscape has changed and that we now need to focus on global mafias, computer hackers, climate change, infectious disease, and transnational terrorists—all threats operating within networks that otherwise provide many desirable and even essential services. The policy outcome of this agreement has been a strategy that I call BAD: Bold Agile Defense. Put simply, we move military resources around the planet quickly and apply them generously in an effort to blast away the rotten parts of transnational networks.

Conceptually, BAD may not be a bad approach. We are facing a new generation of network-structured threats, and we do need to be bold and agile in countering them. For the most part, however, network threats are not well understood, and decisions to activate our Bold Agile Defense are often made on the basis of conjecture and assertion. We need to think carefully about whether it is worth spending thousands of lives and billions of dollars to neutralize a threat that has materialized from strident claims that domestic anthrax scares, Al Qaeda, and Iraq combine to produce global bioterrorism. Perhaps they do. But if they do not, then the only thing certain about what we are doing is that we are making a handful of Americans rich and powerful. Moreover, because both inside and outside our country some people will be disturbed by their perception that we are prepared to use force preemptively and on the basis of scant intelligence, we may also be undermining our security. Our actions place pressure on the Atlantic alliance we have carefully constructed and maintained over more than six decades and on the United Nations security systems we invented and established. They may also fuel the matrix of grievance that covers much of the world and gives terrorists and criminals a foothold on social acceptance, if not political legitimacy.

NOTES

1. Betsy Hartmann and Anne Hendrixson, "Pernicious Peasants and Angry Young Men: The Strategic Demography of Threats," in *Making Threats: Biofears and Environmental Anxieties*, ed. Betsy Hartmann, Banu Subramaniam, and Charles Zerner (Lanham, Md.: Rowman & Littlefield, 2005).

2. It seems equally possible, using the history of past empires as a measure, that the United States will underestimate threats to its position in world affairs and fail to take the strong actions necessary for its preservation.

3. As a longtime contributor to this literature, I want to emphasize that my concern is with some of the real-world consequences of the environmental movement's well-intended efforts to raise environmental issues on policy agendas and of its sincere convictions that the world's environment is in dire straits. Moreover, environmentalists have hardly been alone in contributing to the thickening of the American "risk society." From epidemiologists to economists, we have been bombarded by a steady stream of disaster warnings.

4. Skeptics include Daniel Deudney, "The Case against Linking Environmental Degradation and National Security," *Millennium* 19, no. 3 (Winter 1990): 461–76; Marc Levy, "Is the Environment a National Security Issue?" *International Security* 20, no. 2 (Fall 1995): 35–62; and Miriam Lowi, *Water and Power: The Politics of a Scarce Resource in the Jordan River Basin* (Cambridge: Cambridge University Press, 1993, upd. 1995).

5. Peter Gleick, "Water and Conflict: Fresh Water Resources and International Security," *International Security* 18, no. 1 (Summer 1993): 79–112; Gleick, "The Implications of Global Climate Changes for International Security," *Climate Change* 15, no. 1/2 (January 1989): 303–25.

6. E. O. Wilson, *Diversity of Life* (Cambridge, Mass.: Harvard University Press, 1992).

7. Thomas Homer-Dixon, *Environment, Scarcity, and Violence* (Princeton, N.J.: Princeton University Press, 1999): 177.

8. For a discussion of linkages between the peace and environmental movements, see Richard A. Matthew and Ted Gaulin, "The Ecology of Peace," *Peace Review* 14, no. 1 (Spring 2002): 33–39.

9. For a discussion of the precautionary principle, see Indur M. Goklany, *The Precautionary Principle: A Critical Appraisal of Environmental Risk Assessment* (Washington, D.C.: Cato Institute, 2001).

10. See Bill Devall and George Sessions, *Deep Ecology: Living As If Nature Mattered* (Salt Lake City, Utah: Gibbs Smith, 1985); E. O. Wilson, *Biophilia* (Cambridge, Mass.: Harvard University Press, 1984).

11. Ulrich Beck, *Risk Society*, trans. M. Ritter (London: Sage, 1992).

12. Robert Kaplan, "The Coming Anarchy: How Scarcity, Crime, Overpopulation, Tribalism, and Disease Are Rapidly Destroying the Social Fabric of Our Planet," *Atlantic Monthly* 274, no. 2 (February 1994): 44–76.

13. Matthew Connolly and Paul Kennedy, "Must It Be the Rest against the West?" *Atlantic Monthly* 274, no. 6 (December 1994): 61–84.

14. For a useful overview of the debate of the late 1990s, see John Mearsheimer, "Back to the Future: Instability in Europe after the Cold War," *International Security* 15, no. 4 (Summer 1990): 5–56; Samuel P. Huntington, "Clash of Civilizations?" *Foreign Affairs* 72, no. 3 (Summer 1993): 22–50; and one of the few well-known optimistic accounts of the near future, Francis Fukuyama, *The End of History and the Last Man* (New York: Free Press, 1992).

15. Concern about the alarmism of contemporary environmentalism receives a compelling treatment in Luc Ferry, *The New Ecological Order*, trans. Carol Volk (Chicago: University of Chicago Press, 1992).

16. This may be equally or even more true of climate change, biodiversity loss, and other forms of anthropogenic environmental change.

17. The term is borrowed from Walter Laqueur, "Postmodern Terrorism," *Foreign Affairs* 75, no. 5 (September/October 1996): 24–36.

18. David W. Siegrist, "The Threat of Biological Attack: Why Concern Now?" *Emerging Infectious Disease* 5, no. 4 (July/August 1999): 4, www.cdc.gov/ncidod/EID/vol5no4/siegrist.htm (accessed July 15, 2004).

19. See, for example, Jessica Stern, "The Prospect of Domestic Bioterrorism," *Emerging Infectious Disease* 5, no. 4 (July/August 1999), www.cdc.gov/ncidod/EID/vol5no4/stern.htm (accessed July 15, 2004); and D. A. Henderson, "Bioterrorism as a Public Threat," *Emerging Infectious Disease* 4, no. 3 (July/September 1998), www.cdc.gov/ncidod/EID/vol4no3/hendrsn.htm (accessed July 15, 2004).

20. Richard A. Clarke, "Finding the Right Balance against Bioterrorism," *Emerging Infectious Disease* 5, no. 4 (July/August 1999): 1, www.cdc.gov/ncidod/EID/vol5no4/clarke.htm (accessed July 15, 2004).

21. Clarke, "Bioterrorism," 1.

22. A copy of the strategy is available at www.whitehouse.gov/nsc/nss.html.

23. From a transcript of a speech entitled "Bush Calls West Point Graduates to Service in Anti-terror Fight," available at www.globalsecurity.org/military/library/news/2003/02/mil-030226-24187d9d.htm (accessed September 15, 2004).

24. U.S. Government, *The National Security Strategy of the United States* (September 2002), 9, www.whitehouse.gov/nsc/nss.html (accessed July 15, 2004).

25. Michael E. O'Hanlon, Susan E. Rice, and James B. Steinberg, "The New National Security Strategy and Preemption" (December 2002), www.brook.edu/comm/policybriefs/pb113.htm (accessed September 15, 2004).

26. John J. Mearsheimer and Stephen Walt, "An Unnecessary War," *Foreign Policy* 134 (January/February 2003): 51–62.

27. Mearsheimer and Walt, "Unnecessary War," 52.

28. Bradley Graham, "Rumsfeld Defends Preemption Doctrine," *Washington Post*, February 28, 2004, 21A, www.washingtonpost.com/wp-dyn/articles/A22155-2004Feb7 .html (accessed September 15, 2004).

29. It is interesting to note that this cobbling process might be said to reflect one of the most fundamental precepts of environmentalism—everything is connected to everything. Through this utterly unproven claim, Al Qaeda can be connected to Iraq and also to the anthrax scares in the U.S. in order to make claims about the imminent threat of large-scale bioterrorism.

10

Conclusion: Unraveling Fear

Betsy Hartmann, Banu Subramaniam,
and Charles Zerner

It isn't what we don't know that kills us, it's everything we do know that
ain't so.

—Mark Twain

In discussing the *Wizard of Oz*, Salman Rushdie rejects the conventional
view that the film represents a fantasy of escape from reality, ending with "a
comforting return to home, sweet home." Instead, he argues that the film
speaks to exile and shows that "imagination can become reality, that there is
no such place like home, or rather that the only home is the one we make
for ourselves."[1] In reflecting on the chapters in this volume, we reach a similar conclusion—that there is no easy return to a mythic peaceful past and
that any fantasy of a progressive future must begin with critical reflection,
understanding, and analysis of the present.

In discussing the fear and panic that consume our lives, the authors in this
volume argue that fears and threats are strategically "produced." While we
can be afraid of many things and perhaps should be afraid of yet others, we
are taught to be afraid of only certain phenomena. The fears that ultimately
consume us are neither random nor the most frightening. We are taught to
be afraid of "suspicious" looking people, white powdery substances, and
"strange" activities. The color codes of terror are elevated, and yet we are encouraged to move around as "usual" and continue to shop, watch movies,
and visit restaurants and bars. On the one hand, we are told to fear alien and
exotic plant and animal species because they destroy natural habitats, while
on the other hand the dangers of genetically modified food and their impact
on natural habitats are underplayed. Contradictions abound. But one thing is

clear—threat making is political, and what we are afraid of is the result of a complex web of ideology; politics; economics; and the social, cultural, and natural. The promise of safety and security is illusory.

What we set out to do in this volume was to interrogate biological and environmental fears and anxieties and to examine their role in the construction of threats. We have tried to isolate particular stagings of fear made by the government, corporations, environmental or other public interest groups, and policymakers, as well as by writers in books, magazines, and newspapers. This volume demonstrates through case studies and examples that there is no unitary analysis or explanation of fear. Rather, at various times, we can talk about fear being "produced," "manufactured," "amplified," "staged," "sustained," and "consumed." In focusing on certain sites, we explore how fears are put together, assembled, packaged (here we can think of a "product" analogy); how they are fashioned and disseminated (here, a gesture to the media and advertising); how they are staged, choreographed, and performed (here, a dramaturgical analogy); and how language and imagery on the one hand and dramaturgy and choreography on the other are some of the instruments of production. As many of the authors demonstrate, these stagings of fear can have profound material consequences, influencing the concrete actions of national and international security agencies and other political and economic actors.

WHERE TO FROM HERE?

So where do these analyses and revelations leave us? If fears and threats are "made," can they be "unmade"? If fears represent "masks," can they be "unmasked"? The authors remind us that "unmaking" and "unmasking" are too simplistic formulations. They are too simple for several reasons. First, drawing on the analogy in the *Wizard of Oz*, the problem is that we cannot tear off the Wizard's mask, because many of these articulations of fear and anxiety utilize referents that not only exist in the world but are legitimate sources of anxiety. For example, water is scarce in some parts of the world, and terrorism is a legitimate fear in others.

Second, there is no unitary explanation of how fear is produced or sustained. Through a variety of disciplinary lenses, the authors in this volume discover a myriad of ways to explain our current state of fear: some fears are displaced; others are exaggerated; some are new and heightened in our post–September 11 world, while others draw on pre–September 11 agendas of the national security state. And many fears yoke preexisting biases—racial prejudices, for example—to more recent preoccupations, including fears of immigrants and foreign germs and plants; they ride piggyback on already existing fears.

Third, we should not assume that the forms and representations of fear analyzed in this volume will be with us forever or even into the foreseeable future. The objects of fear change over time. We need contextual and evolving analyses of fear. The example of the bald eagle in the introduction is a good case in point: once feared and despised, it is now an icon of American survival, freedom, and imperial power.

Fourth, virtually all the authors in this volume document the complex processes by which fears are manufactured, sustained, and consumed. The project is in part cultural and literary—a story of metaphors and narratives—but, just as important, as Lipschutz and others suggest, it is also about the political economy of the national security state, as well as the more material economy of arms and biosafety level 3 and level 4 contracts awarded to universities. This is not at all a process of ummaking and unmasking: that is too simple an analogy for the complicated and various ways in which environmental fears have been produced.

What we have to offer then is not a simple solution of "taking off the mask." Instead, we offer a series of challenges to the production of specific biological and environmental fears by providing some very different kinds of analyses: performative, choreographic, literary, and imagaic, as well as material, political, economic, and historical. The authors in this volume show that it is not an easy task to expose empirically why certain fears are justified or unjustified; such a task involves unraveling a complicated network of history, politics, rhetoric, and ideology of the natural and the cultural. We do not offer the "true face" behind the mask at all. Rather, we offer some useful methodologies for examining and interrogating the production of specific biological and environmental fears in various policy arenas: population, public health, ecology, and national security.

Indeed, the authors in this volume suggest that we can never escape fear. Neither can we escape language, rhetoric, or performance. These are the currencies of life in the twenty-first century. Rather, our task is to fully understand the complexities of the production of biofears and environmental anxieties. We need to learn how to get up on stage, walk about the set, and look at how the costumes and puppets have been made, as well as understand how the illusions have been fashioned, how they fuse facts and fiction, how they articulate to work with both preexisting fears and newly emerging anxieties, and how they can be performed in ways that further the agendas of the national security state and corporate interests.

Ultimately, the authors in this volume suggest that understanding fear and anxieties is one of the pressing political projects of our time. To develop and enact a progressive political agenda, we must unravel the dense thicket of ideology, politics, and economies that are imbricated in the dramas of fears and threats. Fears and threats, and fear and threat making, are critical vehicles for political mobilization and policymaking. Progressive political activism cannot ignore the central role of fear and anxiety. We see this volume as a beginning to this political project and as a lesson in why this is a critical project for our times. The aim is not to do away with fear but rather to understand what we are afraid of and why. Unraveling fear is a difficult and complicated project because we have to face squarely the demons of our histories, politics, ideologies, and economies; but it is one we cannot afford to avoid. In the national security arena especially, fears and threats are intimately tied to the production of violence against real bodies and real environments. In these terror-filled times, the search for just and peaceful solutions depends on seeing through and beyond our fears to new moral choices and political possibilities.

NOTE

1. Salman Rushdie, *The Wizard of Oz* (London: British Film Institute, 1992).

Index

About the Editors and Contributors

Alan Goodman is professor of biological anthropology and the former dean of natural sciences at Hampshire College, Amherst, Massachusetts. Goodman is the editor of *Nutritional Anthropology: Biocultural Perspectives on Food and Nutrition* (with Darna Dufour and Gretel Pelto, 2000), *Building a New Biocultural Synthesis: Political-Economic Perspectives on Human Biology* (with Thomas Leatherman, 1998), and *Genetic Nature/Culture: Anthropology and Science beyond the Two Cultures* (with Susan Lindee and Deborah Heath, 2003). He is currently completing a book on the everyday racialization in the sciences. For this work with middle school students on this topic, he received the World of Difference Award from the Anti-Defamation League.

Jeanne Guillemin is professor of sociology at Boston College and senior advisor in the Security Studies Program at MIT. She has published extensively on high technology in medicine and is most recently the author of two books concerning biological weapons. One is *Anthrax: The Investigation of a Deadly Outbreak*, which describes the 1992 investigation of the Sverdlovsk anthrax epidemic in the Soviet Union. The other is *Biological Weapons: From the Invention of State-Sponsored Programs to Contemporary Bioterrorism*. Her work has been funded by the MacArthur Foundation, the Dibner Institute, the National Institutes of Health, and the Ford Foundation. Her current research is on the question of risk in the 2001 anthrax postal attacks.

Hugh Gusterson is associate professor of anthropology and science studies at MIT. He is the author of *Nuclear Rites: A Weapons Laboratory at the End of the Cold War* (1996) and *People of the Bomb: Portraits of America's*

Nuclear Complex (2004). He is also coeditor of the books *Cultures of Insecurity: States, Communities, and the Production of Danger* (1999) and *Why America's Top Pundits Are Wrong: Anthropologists Speak Back* (2005). His articles have been published in the *Bulletin of the Atomic Scientists; American Ethnologist; Cultural Anthropology; Science, Technology, and Human Values; Alternatives; Anthropological Quarterly; Interventions; Social Research;* and *Political and Legal Anthropology Review*. Lynn Cheney's American Council of Trustees and Alumni named him one of the most dangerous intellectuals in the United States in 2001.

Betsy Hartmann is the director of the Population and Development Program at Hampshire College. She is the author of the books *Reproductive Rights and Wrongs: The Global Politics of Population Control* (1995) and *The Truth about Fire* (2002), and coauthor with James Boyce of *A Quiet Violence: View from a Bangladesh Village* (1983). Her current research focuses on issues of gender, population, environment and security, and women's health and reproductive rights.

Anne Hendrixson has published several articles critiquing the "youth bulge" concept, including "Angry Young Men, Veiled Young Women: Constructing a New Population Threat" with the Corner House (2004) and "Superpredator Meets Teen Mom: Exploding the Myth of Out-of-Control Youth" in *Policing the National Body*, edited by Anannya Bhatacharjee and Jael Silliman (2002). She is a member of the Committee on Women, Population, and the Environment.

Ronnie D. Lipschutz is professor in the Department of Politics at the University of California, Santa Cruz. He is author of *Cold War Fantasies: Film Fiction and Foreign Policy* (2001), *Global Environmental Politics* (2003), and *Globalization, Governmentality, and Global Politics* (2005). He is also coauthor, with Mary Ann Tétreault, of *Global Politics As If People Mattered* (2005).

Larry Lohmann is based at the Corner House, United Kingdom. He is the author, with Ricardo Carrere, of *Pulping the South: Industrial Tree Plantations in the World Paper Economy* (1996) and articles and book chapters on land and forest conflicts, climate change, racism, Southeast Asian environmental politics, globalization, and the discourses of development and orthodox economics.

Emily Martin is professor of anthropology at New York University. She is the author of *The Woman in the Body: A Cultural Analysis of Reproduction* (1987) and *Flexible Bodies: Tracking Immunity in American Culture from the Days of Polio to the Age of AIDS* (1994).

Richard A. Matthew is associate professor of international and environmental politics in the Schools of Social Ecology and Social Science at the University of California at Irvine, and director of the Center for Unconventional Security Affairs (www.cusa.uci.edu) and the Global Environmental Change and Human Security Research Office (www.gechs.uci.edu), both at UCI. His research focuses on international relations in the developing world, especially South Asia, and he has published widely on transnational security threats, including environmental change, terrorism, and landmines. Recent books and coedited volumes include *Contested Grounds: Security and Conflict in the New Environmental Politics* (1999); *Dichotomy of Power: Nation versus State in World Politics* (2002); *Conserving the Peace: Resources, Livelihoods, and Security* (2002); *Reframing the Agenda: The Impact of NGO and Middle Power Cooperation in International Security Policy* (2003); and *Landmines and Human Security: International Relations and War's Hidden Legacy* (2004).

Jackie Orr is an associate professor of sociology at Syracuse University. She teaches and writes in the fields of cultural politics, contemporary theory, and feminist studies of technoscience and medicine. Her book *Panic Diaries: A Genealogy of Panic Disorder* (2005) chronicles the entanglement of bodies, pills, power, computers, capital, psyches, war, and (social) scientific discourses that have shaped and reshaped "panic" in the twentieth-century United States. She is also a performance theorist, using visual media and performative writing to encourage public memory.

Paul A. Passavant is associate professor of political science at Hobart and William Smith Colleges. He is the author of *No Escape: Freedom of Speech* (2002) and *The Paradox of Rights* (2002) and is the editor (with Jodi Dean) of *Empire's New Clothes: Reading Hardt and Negri* (2004).

Banu Subramaniam is associate professor of women's studies at the University of Massachusetts, Amherst. She is coeditor of *Feminist Science Studies: A New Generation*. Trained as a plant evolutionary biologist, she seeks to engage the social and cultural studies of science in the practice of science. Spanning the humanities, social sciences, and the biological sciences, her research is located at the intersections of biology, women's studies, and postcolonial studies. Her current work focuses on the xenophobia and nativism that accompany frameworks on invasive plant species, and the relationship of science and religious nationalism in India.

Heather Turcotte is a doctoral student in the Department of Politics at the University of California, Santa Cruz.

Michael Watts has taught at the University of California, Berkeley, for twenty-five years. He is a geographer by training, and his interests have encompassed the political economy of resources, the political history of food and famine, and agrarian transitions in Africa and elsewhere; more recently, he has been working on a book examining oil and petrolic violence in Nigeria. His books include *Silent Violence* (1983), *Reworking Modernity* (1992), and *Liberation Ecologies* (1996).

Charles Zerner is the Barbara B. and Bertram J. Cohn Professor of Environmental Studies at Sarah Lawrence College and codirector of the interdisciplinary colloquium series Intersections: Boundary Work in Science and Environmental Studies. Formerly the director of the Natural Resources and Rights Program at the Rainforest Alliance, an international nongovernmental organization, he is the contributing editor of *People, Plants, and Justice: The Politics of Nature Conservation* (2000) and *Culture and the Question of Rights: Forests, Coasts, and Seas in Southeast Asia* (2003), and coeditor of *Representing Communities: Politics and Histories of Community-Based Natural Resource Management* (in press). He has written on the cultural, legal, and political dimensions of environmental issues in Southeast Asia and has conducted field research in Sulawesi, the Maluku Islands, Sumatra, and Java (Indonesia). His recent work focuses on environmental rhetorics of risk, disease, and national security.